THE ADDICT
AND THE LAW

CHAPTER I

ADDICTION AND THE LAW

> *"With the language of this law we can trap addicts like animals."*
>
> —COMMENT BY AN OFFICIAL

THE present program of handling the drug problem in the United States is, from the legal viewpoint, a remarkable one in that it was not established by legislative enactment or by court interpretations of such enactments. Public opinion and medical opinion had next to nothing to do with it. It is a program which, to all intents and purposes, was established by the decisions of administrative officials of the Treasury Department of the United States. After the crucial decisions had been made, public and medical support was sought and in large measure obtained for what was already an accomplished fact.

Another unusual feature of the federal narcotic laws is that, while they are in legal theory revenue measures, they contain penalty provisions that are among the harshest and most inflexible in our legal code. This chapter is concerned mainly with the way in which the addict is affected by the law—primarily federal but also state and local.

The basic antinarcotic statute in the United States is the Harrison Act of 1914.[1] It was passed as a revenue measure and made absolutely no direct mention of addicts or addiction. Its ostensible purpose appeared to be simply to make the entire process of drug distribution within the country a matter of record. The nominal excise tax (one cent per ounce), the requirement that special forms be used when drugs were transferred, and the requirement that persons and firms handling drugs register and pay fees, all seemed designed to accomplish this purpose. There is no indication of a legislative intention to deny addicts access to legal drugs or to interfere in any way with medical practices in this area. Thus, the act provided that:

Nothing contained in this section shall apply: (a) to the dispensing or distribution of any of the aforesaid drugs to a patient by a physician, dentist, or veterinary surgeon registered under this Act in the course of his professional practice only.[2]

Other portions of the act which exempted persons who obtained drugs pursuant to a prescription from a registered physician from the penalties of the law qualified this exemption by noting that the prescription had to be "for legitimate medical purposes," and "prescribed in good faith." Nowhere in the statute was there a definition of what constituted legitimate medical practice or good faith in the doctor's dealings with drug users. Hence this exemption became a matter of controversy in the early years of enforcement of the Harrison Act.

There were two major influences which led to the enactment of federal narcotic legislation at that time. One of these was that American representatives to international conferences had, before 1914 (e.g., at The Hague Convention in 1912), urged other governments to establish systems for the internal control of narcotic drugs. It was therefore inconsistent that the United States itself did not have such a system. The other influence developed from a growing realization that there were relatively large numbers of addicts in the United States and an impression that the problems posed by this fact were not being effectively met by the various measures adopted by different states and localities.

EARLY INTERPRETATION OF THE ACT

The passing of the Harrison Act in 1914 left the status of the addict almost completely indeterminate. The Act did not make addiction illegal and it neither authorized nor forbade doctors to prescribe drugs regularly for addicts. All that it clearly and unequivocally did require was that whatever drugs addicts obtained were to be secured from physicians registered under the act and that the fact of securing drugs be made a matter of record. While some drug users had obtained supplies from physicians before 1914, it was not necessary for them to do so since drugs were available for purchase in pharmacies and even from mail-order houses.

In 1915 a Supreme Court decision in the *U.S.* v. *Jin Fuey Moy* case[3] took the first important step which ultimately led to the outlawing of the addict when it ruled that possession of smuggled drugs by an addict was a violation of the law. As regards the section of the Harrison Act which specifically stated that the possession of drugs by unregistered persons was to create a presumption of guilt the defense had contended that it referred only to persons required to register and not to all persons. It was argued that making possession of illegal drugs a crime for anyone had the effect of creating an entire class of criminals with a stroke of the pen. A similar doctrine during the prohibition era would have meant that any person with a glass or a bottle of liquor would have been subject to a prison sentence if he were unable to prove that it was not bootleg liquor. This decision had the effect of forcing the addict to go to the doctor as the only source of legal drugs left to him. This remaining source was shortly eliminated by further court decisions in the doctor cases.

The early Supreme Court rulings concerning the doctor's relationship to addicts were based upon cases involving physicians who had prescribed large quantities of drugs to many addicts in an indiscriminate manner. The Webb case[4] in 1919, the Jin Fuey Moy[5] and the Behrman[6] cases, in 1920 and 1922 respectively, were decisive ones of such a nature. In the Webb case the court ruled that a prescription of drugs for an addict "not in the course of professional treatment in the attempted cure of the habit, but being issued for the purpose of providing the user with morphine sufficient to keep him comfortable by maintaining his customary use" was not a prescription within the meaning of the law and was not included within the exemption for the doctor-patient situation. The Supreme Court, in reaching this decision, apparently did not bother to consult medical opinion on the matter, for it said that the contrary interpretation "would be so plain a perversion of meaning that no discussion is required." Later, in the Jin Fuey Moy case of 1920, the Court ruled that a doctor could not legitimately prescribe drugs "to cater to the appetite or satisfy the craving of one addicted to the use of the drug." Treasury Department regulations still use the Webb case language when they instruct the physician that he may not provide narcotics for a user "to keep him comfortable by maintaining his customary use. . . ."

The Behrman case in 1922 gave further support to the idea that it was not legitimate for a physician to prescribe drugs for an addict, for in it the court ruled that such prescriptions were illegal regardless of the purpose the doctor may have had. The decision in this case seemed to deprive physicians of the defense that they had acted in good faith, for Dr. Behrman was convicted despite the fact that the prosecution stipulated that he had prescribed drugs in order to treat and cure addicts.

After the Behrman case the legal position of the addict seemed quite clear. He was simply denied all access to legal drugs. The rulings by the Supreme Court seemed to be moving toward the idea that the physician could not legally prescribe drugs to relieve the addict's withdrawal distress or to maintain 'his habit, but could provide drugs only to an addict undergoing institutional withdrawal and then only in diminishing doses. However, criticism of the law from medical sources may have shaken the Court's confidence, for even before the Linder decision[7] in 1925, a note of doubt crept into some decisions. For example, in the Behrman case, in which vast quantities of drugs had been prescribed, the Court suggested that a single dose or even a number of doses might not bring a physician within the penalties of the law.

The Supreme Court decisions up to 1922 made it impossible for doctors to treat addicts in any way acceptable to law enforcement officials. The ambulatory method of treatment had been condemned, and since addicts were not accepted in hospitals, the doctor's right to administer diminishing doses during an institutional cure was mainly theoretical. The danger of arrest and prosecution was clearly recognized after 1919, when the first of the important doctor cases had been decided by the Supreme Court. Most doctors simply stopped having anything to do with addicts and the few who did not do this found themselves threatened with prosecution. The illicit traffic burgeoned during these years as addicts who had formerly obtained legal supplies turned to it in increasing numbers.

If the legal situation created by court decisions on the doctor cases had been left as it was in 1922, the addict's legal status and his relationship to the medical profession would at least have been relatively clear. A definite rule prohibiting medical prescriptions for users except under extremely restricted circumstances seemed to be in the process of emerging from a series of court decisions which were reasonably unambiguous and consistent with each other. The Treasury Department, entrusted with the enforcement of the law because it was a tax measure, had drawn up regulations which were based upon these early decisions. These regulations instructed doctors as to when they might give drugs to addicts and when they might not, and advised them to consult the police for advice in doubtful cases. The whole theory implicit in them was that addiction is not a disease at all but a willful indulgence meriting punishment rather than medical treatment. Regular administration of drugs to addicts was declared to be legal only in the case of aged and infirm addicts in whom withdrawal might cause death and in the case of persons afflicted with such diseases as incurable cancer. Current regulations of the Federal Bureau of Narcotics are still substantially the same with respect to these points.[8]

THE LINDER CASE (1925)

Unlike the doctors in the earlier cases, Dr. Charles O. Linder, a Seattle practitioner, provided only four tablets of drugs for one addict. The addict, a woman, came to his office in a state of partial withdrawal and he provided her with drugs to be used at her discretion. She was an informer who reported the incident to the police and Dr. Linder was prosecuted for criminal violation of the law. According to previous court decisions and the Treasury Department regulations in force at the time, Linder should have been convicted, and he was. The lower court could hardly have reached any other decision, for Dr. Linder had obviously given drugs to this user to relieve withdrawal distress and to maintain customary usage and there was no thought of cure.

Nevertheless, after prolonged litigation, which is said to have cost Dr. Linder $30,000 and caused him to be without a medical license for two years, he was finally exonerated by the Supreme Court. In its opinion, a unanimous one, the Court discussed the earlier doctor cases of Doremus, Jin Fuey Moy, Webb, Balint, and Behrman. While it did not specifically repudiate the doctrines drawn from these cases concerning the doctor's right to prescribe for addicts, it did explain that these cases had involved flagrant abuse and that the decisions had to be considered in this context.

Reiterating that the Harrison Law was a revenue measure, the Court added the following important statement:

It [the act] says nothing of "addicts" and does not undertake to prescribe methods for their medical treatment. They are diseased and proper subjects for such treatment, and we cannot possibly conclude that a physician acted improperly or unwisely or for other than medical purposes solely because he has dispensed to one of them, in the ordinary course and in good faith, four small tablets of morphine or cocaine for relief of conditions incident to addiction. What constitutes bona fide medical practice must be determined upon consideration of evidence and attending circumstances.[9]

Commenting upon the Webb case, the interpretation of which it did not accept, the Court commented that the rule therein formulated

must not be construed as forbidding every prescription for drugs, irrespective of quantity, when designed temporarily to alleviate an addict's pains, although it may have been issued in good faith and without design to defeat the revenues.[10]

Of the Behrman decision the Court similarly warned:

The opinion cannot be accepted as authority for holding that a physician who acts bona fide and according to fair medical standards may never give an addict moderate amounts of drugs for self-administration in order to relieve conditions incident to addiction. Enforcement of the tax demands no such drastic rule, and if the Act had such scope it would certainly encounter grave constitutional difficulties.[11]

The two new elements in this decision are (a) the Court's explicit espousal of the view that addiction is a disease and (b) the rule that a physician acting in good faith and according to fair medical standards may give an addict moderate amounts of drugs to relieve withdrawal distress without necessarily violating the law.

This opinion, which is still the controlling doctrine of the federal courts, seems to make nonsense of what had gone before, for it said that the addict who had been denied medical care by earlier decisions was a diseased person entitled to such care. More important still, it clearly implies that the question of what constitutes proper medical care is a medical issue and therefore, presumably, one to be settled, not by legislators, judges, juries, or policemen, but by the medical profession. Certainly the federal courts in particular cannot legally tell doctors what to do with addicts if addiction is viewed as a disease.

The logical consequences which seem to follow from the acceptance of the Linder opinion were spelled out by Federal Judge L. R. Yankwich in 1936:

> I am satisfied therefore, that the Linder case, and the cases which interpret it, lay down the rule definitely that the statute does not say what drugs a physician may prescribe to an addict. Nor does it say the quantity which a physician may or may not prescribe. Nor does it regulate the frequency of prescription. Any attempt to so interpret the statute, by an administrative interpretation, whether that administrative interpretation be oral, in writing, or by an officer or by a regulation of the department, would be not only contrary to the law, but would also make the law unconstitutional as being clearly a regulation of the practice of medicine.[12]

The references to administrative interpretation and regulation in this statement refer to Treasury Department regulations already referred to, which do in fact instruct physicians as to when they may and may not prescribe drugs for addicts. If this opinion is correct, the conclusion is inescapable that the present punitive system of dealing with addicts and the Treasury Department regulations on which it is based are in direct violation of federal law and based upon an unconstitutional interpretation of the Harrison Act.

If the Linder case dictum that addiction is a disease had been taken literally, a rational procedure which might have been adopted is suggested by what was done in Britain when the same disagreement arose between enforcement authorities and British physicians concerning the physician's right to prescribe regularly for addicts.

The Government was asked to set up a committee of medical men to investigate the question. The Rolleston Committee was the result. After extensive hearings in which this committee listened especially to the testimony of medical men with particular knowledge and experience of the subject, the committee reported that doctors might prescribe drugs regularly for addicts and specified the conditions under which this might be done and the precautions which should be observed. This report, published in 1926, then became the official interpretation of the Dangerous Drugs Laws of 1920, which were very much like the Harrison Act in all respects except that they were not called tax measures.

No similar appeal to the medical profession was made in the United States, where the courts themselves have tried to formulate the relevant rules. The only recourse to medical advice has been through the use of expert testimony in the usual pattern, with prosecution experts supporting the prosecution's view, defense experts opposing them, and the jury choosing between the conflicting views. This makes a jury of laymen the arbiters of a technical medical dispute and in practice means that the courts intervene in a medical controversy on the side of the faction which supports the government's enforcement program, by subjecting others to criminal trial.

OTHER INTERPRETATIONS OF THE LINDER CASE

As far as enforcement policies are concerned, the Linder case has had practically no effect and remains a ceremonial gesture of no practical significance for either addicts or physicians. Most assistant prosecutors acquiring trial experience in narcotics cases, and most police officers, probably do not know of its existence, for there is no reference to it in most of the literature issued by the Federal Bureau of Narcotics. The risk of arrest remains as before for physicians who attempt to treat addicts as diseased persons and addicts still find that the doors of the hospital and the doctor's office are closed to them.

There are a number of reasons for the impotence of the Linder doctrine and prominent among them is the legal confusion in the subsequent cases. Since the Linder decision appeared in 1925, the Supreme Court has not had the opportunity to expand and clarify it by ruling on other similar cases. Reasons for this lack of opportunity are probably that few reputable physicians care to play Russian roulette with their careers by challenging existing enforcement practices, and second, that the government has been careful about prosecuting certain types of cases so as not to give the Supreme Court a chance to expand and emphasize the precedent of the Linder case.

Nevertheless, in June 1962 the Supreme Court did again affirm its position in the *Robinson* v. *California* case.[13] This case involved a tèst of a California statute making it a crime to "be addicted to the use of narcotics" and providing that any person convicted under this provision be required to spend at least ninety days in confinement in a county jail. In ruling that the California statute was unconstitutional and in violation of the Eighth and Fourteenth Amendments because it prescribed cruel and unusual punishment, the majority opinion refers to the Linder case. There follows this remark: "To be sure, imprisonment for ninety days is not, in the abstract, a punishment which is either cruel or unusual. But the question cannot be considered in the abstract. Even one day in prison would be cruel and unusual punishment for the 'crime' of having a common cold."[14]

The lower federal courts were no doubt reluctant to follow the logical implications of the Linder case, for this would have meant upsetting an established enforcement policy vigorously supported by police propaganda and to some extent by popular opinion and by part of the medical profession. In 1925 this policy had been in operation for a decade. Apathy in the medical and legal professions, based in large part upon the addict's low social status, his lack of funds, and the fact that he is a difficult and troublesome person, contributed heavily to the reluctance to change the status quo.

A legal device favoring this conservative position was to interpret the rule of the Linder case as one which supplemented rather than replaced the older ones. Thus the Circuit Court of Appeals of the 10th Circuit, in *Strader* v. *United States*, reversed the conviction of a doctor and stated:

The Statute does not prescribe the diseases for which morphine may be supplied. Regulation 85 [of the Federal Bureau of Narcotics] issued under its provisions *forbids the giving of a prescription to an addict, or habitual user of narcotics, not in the course of professional treatment, but for the purpose of providing him with a sufficient quantity to keep him comfortable by maintaining his customary use. Neither the statute nor the regulations preclude a physician from giving an addict a moderate amount of drugs in order to relieve a condition incident to addiction* [withdrawal distress], if the physician acts in good faith and in accord with fair medical standards. [Italics added.][15]

The italicized statements formulate two mutually incompatible rules. The first is that of the Webb case; the second, that of Linder. A doctor who provides an addict with drugs to relieve withdrawal distress necessarily also keeps him comfortable by maintaining customary use. No medical person acquainted with addiction would ever have been guilty of making this absurd statement, which makes a distinction without a difference. Since both of these rules apply simultaneously to the reputable physician who treats an addict, there is no way of knowing whether he will be convicted under the first or exonerated under the second.

Without analyzing in detail other specific post-Linder cases, the following general points may be made concerning them and their implications: (1) the courts have not relinquished their right to rule on the good faith of the physician or to submit this question to the jury, and since no definite rules defining good faith have ever been formulated, the physician can only discover whether he acted legitimately *after* a criminal trial; (2) a physician's sincere conviction that the oath of his profession and his ethical duty to relieve human suffering and to give first importance to the welfare of his patient obligate him to provide addicts with drugs has not been an effective legal defense; (3) physicians of admitted integrity and sound professional reputation have continued to be arrested, indicted, and convicted; (4) medical experts of national reputation in the field of addiction, whose opinions of the proper treatment of addicts would ordinarily be regarded as of decisive significance in defining legitimate medical practice, have been indicted, tried, and convicted for acting in accordance with their beliefs; (5) the federal courts have done next to nothing to restrict their jurisdiction in narcotic cases in a manner consistent with their own doctrine that addiction is a disease.

In connection with point (4), two additional cases should be mentioned, those of *United States* v. *Anthony* and *Carey* v. *United States*.[16] These two cases involved three physicians, Carey, Williams, and Anthony, who were asked by the City of Los Angeles, at the behest of the Los Angeles Medical Association, to take over the treatment of addicts who were former patients in that city's narcotics clinic. All were convicted in federal court for violations of the narcotic laws. The conviction of Anthony was reversed in an appeals court, but the appeals of Carey and Williams were rejected on technical grounds and their convictions stand. Of the three, E. H. Williams was a prominent author included in *Who's Who*, a former associate editor of the *Encyclopaedia Britannica*, and a nationally known expert on narcotic addiction whose writings are still read with respect.

The irony involved in the conviction of E. H. Williams is emphasized by the fact that in his trial, the stool pigeon who testified in court against him admitted that he was under the influence of drugs being supplied to him regularly by government agents. In most of the other doctor cases, drug-using stool pigeons were also used, as the records indicate. The courts have deplored this practice but have tolerated it as a necessary expedient in law enforcement, thus sanctioning the provision of drugs to addicts by the police while denying the same right to physicians.

On June 14, 1938, Congressman John M. Coffee of the state of Washington, in an address to the House of Representatives on the narcotics question, made the following statements concerning the cases of the three Los Angeles physicians referred to above and some of the persons involved in it:

The extent to which unlawful activities in the distribution of narcotics have invaded official life is cogently suggested by several recent happenings:

HANSON AFFAIR IN NEVADA

First. The arrest, prosecution, and conviction of the chief Federal narcotics agent for the State of Nevada—Chris Hanson—and a confederate who was formerly a revenue officer, for direct dope peddling and connivance with a gang of Chinese racketeers in June 1937. Hanson was sentenced to 10 years in the Federal penitentiary at McNeil Island and a fine of $9,000. It is to be noted that Hanson was chief Federal narcotic agent at Los Angeles, California, at the time of the arrest and prosecution there of physicians, through which the closure of the beneficent narcotics clinic of the county medical association and board of health was effected—and the 75 rehabilitated patients thrust back into the hands of the dope peddlers. Incidentally, it should be noted that the U.S. attorney who cooperated with the narcotic agents in the prosecutions in question was ousted from his position for his action in this affair, along with the two assistants directly involved, one of whom was held for contempt of court because of his reprehensible actions. The character of the associates of the Federal narcotics agent is further evidenced by the arrest and imprisonment of another officer—investigator for the State medical board of examiners—who had an active share in the frame-up of clinic physicians.

It is perhaps not without significance to note that no Federal bureau or agency had any share in the initial investigations through which Chief Federal Agent Hanson and the former customs officer were entrapped at Reno. On the other hand, the Commissioner of Narcotics took an active hand in the questionable proceedings at Los Angeles which led to the arraignment of the assistant United States attorney for contempt of court. And he is on record as regarding that case as the most important in the history of the Narcotics Bureau, with its record of many thousand cases.[17]

That the Linder case is an embarrassment to the Federal Bureau of Narcotics is strongly suggested by the consistent failure of this Bureau to call attention to it. In one of its publications the Bureau disputes the usual interpretations and argues that the Linder decision is explained by a defect in the indictment, which did not allege that Dr. Linder acted in an unprofessional manner:

It seems, therefore, that the substance of the holding was that, in the absence of an averment in the indictment that the sale was not in the course of professional practice only, the Court could not find as a matter of law that the sale of the tablets by Dr. Linder "necessarily transcended" the limits of professional practice.

We submit that the Linder case did not lay down the rule that a doctor acting in good faith and guided by proper standards of medical practice may give an addict moderate amounts of drugs in order to relieve conditions incident to addiction. What the Court stated in the Linder case was that the opinion [in the Behrman case] "cannot be accepted as authority for holding that a physician, who acts bona fide and according to fair medical standards, may never give an addict moderate amounts of drugs for self-administration in order to relieve conditions incident to addiction." This is not an affirmative declaration that a physician may continue to dispense narcotic drugs to an addict to gratify addiction.[18]

The Bureau then goes on to call attention to the fact that many doctors have been convicted subsequent to the Linder case for supplying drugs to addicts and that in at least ten instances these convictions were upheld by United States Courts of Appeals.

The Bureau in this statement, which is one of the exceedingly rare occasions in which it takes any note whatever of the Linder case, makes no mention of the doctrine of the federal courts that addiction is a disease. Regardless of the merits of the Bureau's position from a legal or a logical point of view, it is this position upon which its regulations are based and it is these regulations, rather than the decisions of the courts or the statutes themselves, which directly guide enforcement policy. The Bureau's interpretation clearly leaves the determination of legitimate medical handling of addicts within the police domain and justifies, however shaky the reasoning may seem, the continued prosecution of reputable physicians.

OFFICIAL INCONSISTENCY

It is difficult to understand the concern of officials and courts to prevent doctors from keeping addicts "comfortable" as though there were something inherently reprehensible in this. The same officials and courts know that drug-using informers working for the government are kept "comfortable" and that addiction is used as leverage to compel addicts to act in the interests of the police. This use of addicts as informers is sometimes called a "dirty business," involving as it does the exploitation of disease, but it is nevertheless sanctioned or at least tolerated by the courts. When the police see to it that an informer is provided with drugs they are not concerned with effecting a cure nor with the addict's welfare. The doctor, on the other hand, finds that the operation of the law prevents him from acting in the interests of an addict patient. It is generally thought to be one of the noble functions of medicine to relieve unnecessary suffering and to keep patients in comfort, and yet the medical man who seeks to apply these principles to drug users is threatened with criminal prosecution.

The withdrawal distress that develops several hours after an addict is deprived of drugs is often a severe and prolonged ordeal that harms the addict's health and sometimes even results in death or in suicide. When the courts tacitly approve of present police practices which cause addicts repeatedly to undergo this experience without medical attention they in effect set up the narcotics detective as a judge and as an executioner, and invite the drug peddler to substitute for the doctor in ministering to the addict. The drug peddler is perhaps the most despised criminal in the United States today, but as the law is presently enforced, he is the only person to whom the addict can go to secure relief from his suffering. The courts appear to have been indifferent to this fact.

In addition to these practices of the police, it is of interest to note that Public Health Service officials at the Public Health Service Hospital at Lexington, Kentucky, which specializes in handling addicts, provide regular supplies of drugs to addicts over a period of time preliminary to complete withdrawal. This is recognized by experienced practitioners as a desirable practice because it permits the addict's health to be built up and it allows for a period of needed psychological preparation for the ordeal of withdrawal. Outside of an institution this practice has the added virtue of removing the user from the control of the underworld drug peddler. Nevertheless, current enforcement practices effectively deny the ordinary physician the right to do this.

Other Lexington practices have even more drastic implications. For example, in experimentation with human subjects in that institution nonusing, former-addict inmates have on frequent occasions been deliberately provided with drugs so as to reestablish active addiction. The Lexington officials are specifically authorized by law to experiment in this manner and the subjects they employ are always carefully selected volunteers who are withdrawn from the drug in ample time before release from the institution. Nevertheless, it seems very doubtful if such experimentation would be permitted if providing an addict with drugs were actually viewed as a crime. One may ask, if the physicians at Lexington have so much latitude, why should similar privileges not be extended to other doctors and researchers?

It is probably pointless to indicate that the theory that the narcotic laws are merely revenue measures rather than police measures strains the imagination and is not taken seriously. For example, on this theory the police officers who forcibly pumped out the contents of a drug peddler's stomach in the Rochin case[19] were interested only in the infinitesimal unpaid tax on the drugs found in his stomach. While the courts invalidated this technique, they have more recently approved of a similar forcible search of a drug peddler's rectum on the grounds that probable cause existed for believing that a quantity of drugs was there concealed.[20] The penalties provided for violators also clearly do not make sense as tax collection devices.

Apart from the many obvious absurdities of the tax law theory, this view may have contributed to the fact that the narcotic laws make no distinction in principle between the perpetrator of the crime and the victim of it. Under the tax theory it is possible to argue that the addict aids and abets the peddler in the evasion of the tax by buying and possessing illicit drugs. Under this theory the rational solution which would facilitate the collection of the tax would be to give the user access to legal drugs from registered physicians.

If the peddler's crime is regarded as something other than a tax matter, it must be conceded that the harm done by him is upon the addict. This would seem to imply that the function of the law is to protect addicts from peddlers—an obvious absurdity unless it is thought that addicts are protected from the peddler by being in jail while the peddlers largely remain outside.

From a moral point of view the chief wrong committed by the drug peddler seems to be that he makes money from addiction, but this interest in a "fast buck" is common in our society. Addiction itself cannot be attributed to the peddler except in the very general sense that it is the illicit traffic that now makes drugs available. The use of drugs is usually a voluntary matter, voluntarily begun and voluntarily continued. Whatever harm is involved in taking drugs is a harm which the individual does to himself; it is not one done to him by someone else. It is in this respect similar to the abuse of alcohol, tobacco, barbiturates, tranquilizers, sleeping tablets, and other substances the taking of which is not considered criminal.

The theory that the narcotic laws are tax measures has obscured and confused issues and prevented such questions as, "Who is the criminal?" "Who is the victim?" "What is the crime?" from being asked and rationally considered in shaping the statutes. The inclusion of the use of certain drugs within the scope of the criminal law may well be a mistake, an unwarranted extension of legal controls into the medical field and into the sphere of essentially personal behavior with which the criminal law ought not be concerned, and which it cannot in any case control.

The reason for the lack of distinction in the statutes between addict and peddler again represents a sacrifice of principle for expediency. The original formulation in 1915 of the theory that mere possession of illicit drugs by an addict was an offense may well have reflected pressure from enforcement sources, which have always complained of the difficulty involved in proving sale. The possession doctrine makes it easier to convict peddlers, and even easier to convict addicts. Placing the victim of the peddler under the same penalties as those provided for peddlers serves another extremely vital enforcement function by providing the leverage to force addicts to cooperate with the police in trapping higher sources of supply. All of this makes sense from the enforcement viewpoint, but it does not make sense if the addict is viewed as a diseased person, for it subjects him to exploitation not only by peddlers but also by the police, and it causes him to be sent to jail or prison solely because he is addicted or because he refuses to become an informer. In practice the injustice involved is enhanced by the relative ease with which addicts are apprehended and the great difficulty in apprehending important illicit traffickers.

To appreciate the consequences of the Harrison Act one needs to consult some of the opinions expressed at the time that it went into effect by intelligent and well-informed observers. As a single illuminating example, I shall reproduce some of the relevant comments of Dr. Charles E. Terry, who had been working with addicts in Jacksonville, Florida, from 1911 until the Harrison Act went into effect in 1915:

One of the most important discoveries we made at that time was that a very large proportion of the users of opiate drugs—not cocaine— were respectable hard-working individuals in all walks of life, and that the smaller part only, according to my figures about 18 per cent, could in any way be considered as belonging to the underworld. In this 18 per cent were included those who used cocaine, as well as the true opiate addict.

Of the total number of registered addicts, about one-half were personally known to me. Many of these came regularly for their prescriptions, while others who could well afford to pay for their prescriptions, but were aware of our interest in the subject, came to me for advice and help. One of the first questions that I was asked, and this practically invariably, when it was seen that I was not trying to persecute but merely to discover facts, was "Where can I get treatment? How can I get rid of this thing?" I have yet to see the first drug addict who does not honestly wish to be cured, and I have known them in all walks of life from the preacher to the prostitute.

When this law began to operate and large numbers of addicts, men and women, and even boys and girls, came to what rapidly developed into a clinic though it was not so intended at first, I had no fixed ideas as to the nature of drug addiction. I had never discussed its characteristics with medical men. I had never attempted to treat the condition, and I was as nearly as a physician may well be, unbiased. I had of course heard of gradual reduction, certain of the chain-store methods with chloride of gold, hyoscine, etc., and before our clinic had been running long, someone called my attention to the Towns-Lambert specific. I was even tempted to try by gradual reduction to get certain individuals who were particularly anxious to be cured, off their drugs. I early discovered that I at least could not do it, and that the condition to which I brought them was worse than that of which I attempted to relieve them.

In every case records were kept and efforts made to determine the causes or cause leading to the addiction. If any ideas lingered that inherent depravity was a common actuating cause, they were soon dispelled by the histories we recorded. We also discovered that it was not a problem for legislation or for police activity alone but that it was a real medical and health program, and lacking any accurate knowledge of a satisfactory method of treatment we found ourselves in a most difficult and equivocal position. The more we looked into different methods of treatment, the more we became convinced of their unsatisfactory nature.

In 1913 at the meeting of the American Public Health Association, held in Colorado Springs, I reported our findings and experiences, and urged the association to take the matter up as a public health problem of importance.

At this stage the truth of my opening sentence is apparent, for while I recognized the medical and public health angles of the problem, I still felt that rigid laws offered great promise. I felt with others that a national law which would control interstate traffic in these drugs would solve the greatest part of the difficulties confronting us. It must be borne in mind that at this period only a few states had restrictive laws that were not openly broken on every side and for the most part the formality of a physician's prescription was rarely observed by druggists in dispensing any of the addiction or habit-forming drugs. Effectual restrictive legislation had never been tried and it was perhaps not unnatural to suppose that with the well-known sources of supply curbed, the use of these drugs would be very materially if not entirely prevented. It is obvious, however, that we had counted without the peddler. We had not realized that the moment restrictive legislation made these drugs difficult to secure legitimately, the drugs would also be made profitable to illicit traffickers.

I had had practically no experience with this fraternity for a reason which I now understand well, namely because we furnished in the health office free prescriptions for those unable to pay for them, nor did we try to dictate to them the quantities they should take or for that matter humiliate or persecute them in any other way. As a consequence the peddler could not make a living in our town, though he had begun to flourish in Massachusetts and New York.

Feeling as I did about the need for further restrictive legislation, I looked forward to the passage of the Harrison Act, and during the months immediately preceding its beginning operation in May 1915 we tried to prepare our indigent cases for the drug deprivation which we believed was in store for them. They were urged to reduce their daily amount to the lowest possible limit, and they earnestly cooperated, and looked forward as did we to the time when they would be cured. Meanwhile, a fund was raised by private subscription and hospital and nursing facilities provided for about 20 beds. These beds were filled and refilled until between 65 and 75 patients had been treated. This is one of the experiences in my attempts to work out this problem which I do not like to recall. A local physician kindly volunteered to treat these cases. Although not practicing, I visited them daily, and the nursing attention they received was of the highest order. The method of treatment employed was that known as the Towns treatment [rapid withdrawal plus administration of a belladonna mixture]. We felt, as do most when contemplating drug addiction treatment, that a certain amount of suffering was necessary, but I was not prepared for the extreme suffering which I witnessed in these cases, nor was I prepared for one death which occurred in an apparently healthy woman. With the exception of 2 or 3, all of these cases relapsed within a very short time after their discharge as cured, and I realized more than ever that here was indeed a medical problem and I began to harbor my first doubts as to the wisdom of blind restrictive legislation. And by this I mean legislation based upon habit and vice theories of drug addiction and upon the assumption that satisfactory methods of treatment are generally available.

While my active health administrative work ended in January 1917, membership on the committee on habit-forming drugs of the American Public Health Association made it necessary to continue to keep in touch with the problem and situation, and it was not a far call to a determined effort to find all that medical literature offered.

Here again is recalled an unpleasant chapter when I found that for 4 years I had been attempting to administer this problem in an American city through the workings of what I believed to be a modern health department without having really made any earnest effort to inform myself as to the true nature of narcotic drug addiction.

In reviewing my own medical training I realized that I had never been shown a case of narcotic drug addiction, that I had never been given the opportunity to observe the symptoms of drug withdrawal, and that the only lectures to which I had listened in connection with opium and its derivatives dealt with its therapeutic properties, while its addiction-forming properties were mentioned in but the most casual manner. Was not my own ignorance directly attributable to this lack of medical instruction?

That my experience was not unique was determined by the committee on habit-forming drugs of the American Public Health Association, through a questionnaire submitted to the medical schools of the country.

It would seem unnecessary to state that the narcotic drug addict must be supplied with his drug in doses physically necessary until such time as he may receive treatment which will leave him in at least as good condition as that in which it found him. That to supply this drug is not only necessary, but is vital, that to deny it is to cause a physical and possibly a moral wreck, while to heap contumely upon narcotic drug addicts as a whole is to drive them to the underworld for their supply. It never must be lost sight of that among the sufferers from this disease are numbered many of the highest intellectual types of men and women in the business and professional worlds, and that individuals of this type may not contemplate the indignities which many administrators seek to heap upon them, through their ignorance of the true nature of this condition and their apparent misconception of the character of its victims.

The above statements must not be interpreted to mean favoring or recommending the indefinitely prolonged supplying of narcotic drugs to addicts. They mean only that such supply is at present a temporary necessity designed to tide over a period of medical education after which an enlightened profession will easily relieve their condition. There is no disease known to medicine that offers greater hope of cure than does narcotic drug addiction-disease, when once practitioners shall

have come to study the drug reactions and the symptom-complex of
the malady in the same spirit of scientific investigation that they accord
the other clinical entities.

Narcotic drug addiction-disease will never be solved by forcible measures only. There is a place and a great need for such measures and they
should be limited to this field alone, namely to the control of traffickers,
exploiters, charlatans and quacks.

Yet even here police measures to be successful must go hand in hand
with intelligent medical services. If anyone doubts this let him try to
extinguish the underground traffic in narcotic drugs by police measures
alone. Experience has shown this to be impossible during the 4 years'
enforcement of various restrictive legislative and administrative experiments.[21]

PENALTIES AND THEIR EFFECTS

The Harrison Act of 1914 provided only for a maximum prison
sentence of ten years, leaving the precise determination of the term
to be served in the hands of judges. While considerable federal
legislation has been enacted in this field since 1914, the basic pattern
and legal situation established by the 1914 act has not been changed.
In 1922 the Jones-Miller, or Narcotic Drugs Import and Export,
Act was passed. In 1924 the manufacture of heroin was prohibited,
and in 1937 marihuana became subject to federal control through
the Marihuana Tax Act. There were many other minor amendments and changes with which we shall not be concerned here.

After World War II there have been two important changes in
federal law which have greatly increased the penalties for narcotic
violators. The first of these was the 1951 act known as the Boggs
Bill or the Boggs Amendment; the second was the Narcotic Drug
Control Act of 1956. Apart from a variety of provisions designed
to make it easier to secure convictions, the changes in penalties
were the outstanding features of these statutes. The 1951 act substituted for the old ten-year maximum, the following schedule of
graduated sentences:

For a first offense	Not less than 2 years or more than 5 with probation permitted.
Second offense	Mandatory 5 to 10 years, probation and suspension of sentence excluded.
Third and subsequent offenses	Mandatory 10 to 20 years with probation and suspension of sentence excluded.

The 1956 measure extended this trend toward more severe and more inflexible penalties with the following schedule of punishments:

First possession offense	2 to 10 years with probation and parole permitted.
Second possession or first selling offense	Mandatory 5 to 20 years with probation and parole excluded.
Third possession or second selling and subsequent offenses	Mandatory 10 to 40 years with probation and parole excluded.
Sale of heroin to a person under 18 by one over 18	10 years to life with no probation or parole, or death if recommended by a jury.

It will be noted that the principal change made by this measure was to extend the maximum sentences of the 1951 act and to eliminate parole for all but first offenses for possession. The elimination of parole meant that these narcotic offenders could not become eligible for release under supervision after serving one-third of their sentences, as was true of most other federal prisoners, but were required to serve two-thirds of their sentences. The other one-third of the prison term consists of "good time," which is deducted for good behavior in prison.

Before the 1951 act, federal judges were able to and did impose very long prison sentences upon big-time narcotics dealers on the relatively rare occasions when such offenders were brought before them. For example, the 1936 annual report of the Federal Bureau of Narcotics (p. 30), fifteen years before the Boggs Act, notes that six principals in the Ginsberg-Moody case of that year received prison sentences of 50, 20, 20, 20, 17, and 10 years. Sentences of this length were obtained by imposing consecutive sentences on multiple counts or charges. The standard federal indictment for sale, for example, involves three counts for each separate sale so that a peddler who made two such sales prior to the Boggs Act might have been convicted on at least six separate counts, each of which was punishable by a prison term. Since it is at the discretion of the judge whether he wishes to have sentences on such multiple counts run concurrently or consecutively, it was a simple matter to sentence major offenders to very long prison terms despite the ten-year maximum.

Important peddlers are generally first offenders and the Boggs Act actually lowered the maximum penalty applicable to them by reducing the maximum for a first offense from ten years to five. The 1956 law corrected this oversight. Contentions that judges were to blame for the rise of addiction rates after the war because they were too lenient with peddlers are unsupported by any real evidence. The present mandatory minimum for big peddlers is only five years. What he is given beyond that figure rests upon the discretion of the judge, as it did before 1951. The effective limitation upon judges now applies mainly to the sentencing of small offenders and addicts, where the minimum sentences of 2, 5, and 10 years have real meaning. The greatly increased average sentence of today is largely the result of the increased mandatory minimum prison terms which must be imposed upon these minor violators, who constitute the bulk of those convicted.

The 1951 and 1956 narcotics statutes are characterized by harshness and inflexibility of penalties and by the extraordinary limitations placed upon judicial power to mitigate sentences in accordance with circumstances surrounding individual cases or to place certain persons on probation rather than sending them to prison. They have aroused opposition from judges and from many other sources. The power to mitigate punishment, which was taken out of the hands of the judges, was not simply eliminated by these laws as one might suppose from merely reading them; it was rather transferred to the police and prosecutors. The latter can now virtually fix sentences in most instances by manipulating the charge and recommending sentences to the court, and they can grant probation in the same way. Since the 1951 and 1956 laws were virtually written by police and prosecution interests, it is not surprising that this should be so, for laws of this sort give police and prosecutors greater freedom in making deals with offenders and permit them to punish defendants who refuse to cooperate with a minimum of judicial interference. The serious question which is raised, however, is whether the administration of justice ought to be placed so completely in the hands of prosecution interests.

When the Boggs Act was passed in 1951 many of the states passed "Little Boggs Laws" of their own, just as they later imitated the 1956 legislation. An illuminating illustration of this trend was provided by New Jersey in 1956, when the state legislature passed bills to increase penalties for narcotics violators to the following levels:

Sale of narcotics by one older than 21 to a person under 18	Mandatory minimum 20 years.
Ordinary sale—first offense	Mandatory minimum 10 years.
Second sale offense	Mandatory minimum 20 years.
Third and subsequent offenses	Mandatory minimum 30 years.
Use of child under 18 to handle narcotics	Mandatory minimum 20 years.

Suspension of sentence and probation were barred.

Governor Robert B. Meyner, in vetoing these bills, analyzed their effects in a statement which is applicable to the antinarcotic laws generally:

Illegal traffic in narcotics is dirty and tragic. All responsible citizens would welcome some magnificent measure which would blot it out. I deeply appreciate the high purpose which motivated these bills, but I cannot escape the conviction that they would defeat themselves and in the course of that failure would leave a path of injustice.

The simple truth is that narcotic violations do not follow a single, simple pattern which may thus be adjudged *en masse* in advance of their commission. I could not approve these measures unless I could in good conscience say that I reasonably believe that all who hereafter may fall within the sweep of these bills would merit the inexorable and inflexible punishment which the bills would require. I confess that such prescience is not mine.

Let us take a few examples culled, not from a fertile imagination, but from the hard experience of men charged with enforcement of narcotic laws.

Some university students, while at college, acquired marihuana from a peddler and distributed some of it to friends in New Jersey while home on vacation. The students were convicted but sentence was suspended and the defendants placed on probation. These young men have gone on to become useful and valuable citizens. But under Assembly Bill No. 488, they would have to be sentenced to 10 years at hard labor, and if one of the students was 21 years or over and the marihuana was given to one under 18, the mandatory minimum of 20 years would be imperatively imposed.

A druggist who answered an emergency call of a physician and delivered a narcotic without a written prescription would face a mandatory minimum of 10 years, beyond the power to suspend. An inexperienced drug clerk who sold more than 4 ounces of Brown's Mixture or Stokes Expectorant without a prescription would face a mandatory sentence of 10 years, and if the buyer was under 18 and the clerk was over 21, to a mandatory 20-year sentence. A druggist or physician who fails to maintain the detailed records required by chapter 18 or to retain them for the prescribed period would have to be incarcerated for a minimum of 2 to 10 years depending upon which of the many sections of the act he violated because these bills would forbid the suspension of sentence and probation. One who violates the provisions of the act relating to labeling would, without regard to varying circumstances, be subjected to the mandatory minimum of 10 years.

A drug user who, facing imminent arrest for possession, slips the narcotic to his son under 18 to conceal his offense, would fall within the mandatory minimum of 20 years provided in Assembly Bill No. 490.

A drug user, who pools his funds with other users and purchases drugs which he divides with them, may be deemed to be a seller depending upon the ages of the parties.

Such are the implications of these bills. They far exceed in severity and scope the bills now under consideration by the Congress.

Because of the importance of this matter, I held a public hearing to which were invited both advocates and opponents of the bills. The conflicting views were ably and forcefully presented.

The proponents of these bills seek to reach or frustrate the non-addicted supplier of drugs. If the bills reached only him, I would unhesitatingly give my approval. But they are not so confined and although the deterrent quality of punishment may be conceded in certain areas, the question remains whether deterrence may not also be achieved by severe sentences where the facts so warrant, without the inherent self-defeating weakness of laws which are excessively severe in cases involving individuals whose offenses do not merit the punishment commanded by the bills. . . . The bulk of the narcotic problem is centered in Essex County. Yet the Chief Probation Officer of that county advises that in the 5 years 1951 to 1955, there were only 282 drug cases in the County Court of Essex County, only 42 of which were for selling. In recent years the non-addict promoter, peddler, or pusher has constituted but a minute percentage of the defendants. For instance, among the 55 persons convicted in the County Court of Essex County in 1955, only one was a non-addict peddler. There is no reliable evidence of increase in the traffic in our State. In these circumstances, we should hesitate before embarking upon a new program of mandatory minimum sentences devoid of discretion to fit the punishment to the offense and the offender.

Public officials representing a tremendous number of years of practical experience in law enforcement in general and narcotics in particular joined in opposition to these features of the bills. On the State level, the Attorney General of New Jersey, the Commissioner of In-

stitutions and Agencies and the Principal Keeper of the New Jersey
State Prison oppose the measures. The Conference of County Judges
unanimously disapproves of them, and all of the county prosecutors
express the same opposition. The experienced Chief Probation Officer
of Essex County condemns the measures. This opposition springs not
from a desire to retain the power vested in county judges, or the opportunity which prosecutors or probation officers have to be heard in
connection with sentencing—a power and opportunity which less conscientious men would gladly forego—but rather from a conviction
born of long exposure to the problem, that the bills would neither serve
the public nor do justice to its members.

We have had some experience with mandatory legislation of such
severity. Under our fourth offender statute which required a mandatory life sentence, the diminishing returns and stark inequity of its provisions led to an amendment which vested discretion at the trial level.
California forbade probation in narcotic cases in 1951, but found it
necessary to repeal its legislation in 1953. The reasons are readily apparent.

Further, when the punishment is shockingly beyond the offense and
the offender, officials charged with the execution of the laws are driven
to devices to escape the legislative mandate. Prosecutors are reluctant
to prosecute; grand juries will not indict; judges join in refined con-
structions to avoid palpable injustice and thereby the law is weakened
in later applications to real culprits; petit juries, when the stakes become known, refuse to convict. A mandatory sentence which may not
be suspended means that the accused necessarily defends; he has nothing to lose. There is thus devoted to prosecutions valuable manpower
which would be more productive in additional investigations. The
weak link in a criminal chain, who would speak and inform in hope
of leniency, is silenced.

The self-defeating infirmity inheres not only in a severe mandatory
penalty which may not be suspended, but as well in an unduly severe
mandatory penalty for a first offense even though it may be suspended.
When the mandatory minimum is thus unrelated to a just result, the
sentencing judge is driven to suspend the sentence, although he believes
that the actual execution of a prison sentence less than the statutory
minimum would be more fitting.

Thus, the public interest would be disserved. And perhaps of greater importance would be the abandonment of our principles of justice. We are dedicated to justice not only to the public at large but also to the individual. Justice to the individual means treatment which accords with the offense and the offender. Equality of justice necessarily means equal treatment under like circumstances and rejects identical punishment for all who trespass, without regard to the facts of the particular case. We have developed an extensive program of presentence investigation and probation to this end. We salvage when we can.

The bills seem to embrace the tenet that injustice to individual defendants is a fair price to pay for the deterrent effect upon the addict as well as the non-addict sellers. We do not sacrifice individuals for the common good; rather we find the common good in doing justice to the individual. And justice to the individual, with adequate deterrence to others, can best be achieved at the hands of an alert, conscientious and competent trial judge who has before him all of the facts relating to the offense and the offender. His is the real and intelligent opportunity to reach a sound judgment.

For these reasons, I cannot approve of bills which would impose severe mandatory penalties upon first offenders without the safety valve of the probation program. Nor can I approve of excessive mandatory minimum sentences for first offenders which may drive trial judges to suspend sentence rather than to impose a jail sentence deemed to be oppressive. I am willing to approve increases in the authorized maximums, to the end that, in appropriate cases, sentences may be imposed which will both fit the situation and serve to deter others.[22]

The unusual feature of Governor Meyner's excellent analysis of the proposed narcotics legislation in his state is his stirring affirmation of the ideal of justice and his rejection of the tenet that "injustice to the individual is a fair price to pay for the deterrent effect upon the addict as well as the non-addict sellers. . . . We do not sacrifice individuals for the common good; rather we find the common good in doing justice to the individual." These considerations of justice have played little part in most recent antinarcotic legislation. The emphasis has been instead upon deterrence at any cost, and justice has been sacrificed in the interests of police expediency. Even in New Jersey the laws in effect when Governor Meyner

vetoed the proposed changes are not models of justice and contain
the same defects as those which the Governor condemned.

Before about 1930 drug offenses were generally regarded as a
matter of federal concern and very few of the states had adequate
laws or did a great deal in this field. When the Federal Narcotics
Bureau was created in 1930 it at once set about securing greater
cooperation from the states and tightening up the legal situation by
urging upon them the enactment of a Uniform Narcotics Law
which was prepared between 1927 and 1932.[23] This law, modeled
after the federal statutes, was designed to facilitate enforcement
by promoting cooperation between federal and nonfederal officers,
by creating uniform standards of record-keeping on state and federal levels, and by eliminating certain gaps in the provisions of the
federal laws occasioned by constitutional limitations upon the police powers of the national government.

The Uniform Narcotics Act has been adopted by most of the
states although the penalty provisions, left blank in the recommended Act, vary from state to state. As penalties were increased
by the 1951 and 1956 national legislation, the states have quickly
followed suit and in many instances enacted even harsher penalties.
In addition, many of them, as well as some municipalities, have
enacted special measures aimed particularly at addicts. Addiction,
for example, has been declared to be a crime in itself in some states
and in others it has been included in the definitions of vagrancy
and disorderly behavior. Addicts have sometimes been required to
register and carry cards identifying them as addicts and hundreds
of drug users in Chicago have been prosecuted for being "loitering
narcotic addicts." Some states also have "needle laws" which make
it a punishable offense for addicts to have in their possession the
paraphernalia required to make an injection.

Most of this type of legislation at the local level is designed to permit the arrest and incarceration on sight of known drug users and has the effect of making the drug addict a virtual outlaw. There is no pretense, in most of it, of any acceptance of the Supreme Court's dictum that addiction is a disease and should be handled medically. Many of these measures, if they were to be challenged in the higher courts, would probably be declared unconstitutional, but only rarely have they been so challenged. Similar measures against drug peddlers would be quickly taken to the higher courts because peddlers, unlike addicts, are fairly likely to have the necessary financial means.

The Indiana statutes present an interesting and fairly typical example of state legislation of the type discussed. A 1957 act specifies that "A person addicted to the unlawful use of narcotic drugs is hereby declared to be dangerous to the public peace and to the welfare and safety of the citizens of this state; and it shall be unlawful for any such person to go on, into or upon any street or public highway, alley or public place unless such person can present positive proof that he is under the care of a licensed physician for the treatment of such addiction."[24] Another part of the Indiana law makes it "unlawful for any duly registered physician, licensed veterinarian or licensed dentist to write, issue, deliver or dictate either directly or indirectly any prescription to or for any habitual user of any drugs enumerated in this section. . . ."[25] Under these provisions the ordinary active addict in Indiana cannot leave his room or his home without automatically being in violation of the law. The requirement that an addict present proof that he is under the care of a physician is tantamount to requiring him to prove that he is not using drugs, i.e., that he is not an addict.

The purpose of the laws cited above is stated to be that of furnishing "a legal means for the segregation and quarantine of narcotic drug addicts in the state of Indiana, and to promote the public peace and protect the safety and welfare of the citizens of the state."[26]

CHAPTER 2

THE STRATEGY OF ENFORCEMENT

In order to understand the full significance of the severe mandatory penalties now provided for narcotics law violators by federal law and the local legislation and police practices which frequently make the drug user a virtual outlaw, it is necessary to know something about the basic strategy used by the police in the attack upon the illicit traffic. Because narcotic offenses usually involve a transaction between a willing seller and a willing buyer, there is in a sense no "victim" involved—at any rate there is no one who will rush to the police to complain that he has been wronged. In order to make their way into the toils of the illicit traffic it is therefore necessary for the police to use artificial leverage of some sort to obtain information and evidence and to secure reluctant cooperation from participants in the traffic. This entrée into the illegal distribution system is usually provided initially by addicts acting as informers or "special employees." The effect of the heavy mandatory penalties is to give police and prosecutors enormous leverage in securing information and cooperation from addicts and in punishing those who do not cooperate.

To many persons it will seem that the uses to which addicts are put in the enforcement process involve a great deal of cruelty and even sadism on the part of police officers. Actually, this conclusion is unwarranted, for individual police officers often feel compassion for the addicts they arrest and treat them with as much considera-tion as they can. While there undoubtedly are occasional brutal and sadistic narcotics policemen, the crux of the matter is that it is the system that is cruel in its effects regardless of the disposition or inclinations of individual officers.

ARBITRARY ARREST OF ADDICTS

The police practice of using addicts as pawns in the effort to trap peddlers and as sources of information was frankly admitted by prosecutors and police officials before congressional subcommit-tees. In Chicago in particular Senator Price Daniel pressed officials for explanations of the extraordinarily large number of persons who were discharged after being arrested. The Chicago officials were thus compelled to explain that the high percentage of discharges was due to the fact that the arrests, usually of addicts, were illegal and were largely for the purpose of securing information and re-cruiting informers.

Lt. Joseph J. Healy, head of the narcotic bureau of the Chicago police department said, in a written statement:

19. In this same period the record shows 5,361 charges of chapter 193-1 subsection 13 of the municipal code of Chicago which is the disorderly conduct chapter amended in 1951 to include known narcotic addicts. It is only by the arresting and detention of addicts and the subsequent judicious interrogation of these persons that the police gain informa-tion relative to the movements and methods as well as the identities of certain narcotics peddlers and pushers. This number comprises 70.2 per cent of the gross arrests.[1]

He explained police practices with regard to addicts as follows:

Lt. Healy: . . . every time our men see these addicts on the street loitering around, they bring them in. That is how we get our informa-tion on the peddlers, from the addicts.

Mr. Speer: You mean when you see an addict on the street, whether or not you suspect that he may have narcotics on him or in his possession, you arrest him and bring him in for interrogation?

Lt. Healy: We do, unless he has a very good excuse for being at that certain point.[2]

Assistant State's Attorney Peter Grosso commented further on the police practice of arresting addicts on sight:

. . . it is true that it is probably contemplated they will be discharged, but they do serve a purpose in having to be processed through our department, because we operate on a premise in order to catch a dope peddler you must have an addict. Before you catch a big dope peddler, you have got to have a small one. . . .[3]

Mr. John Gutknecht, former professor of law, the State's Attorney, indicated that this police tactic was illegal and appeared mildly troubled by the violation of civil rights involved:

Mr. Gutknecht: In view of my background as a law professor, I am very jealous of civil rights, civil rights of individuals. One of the things I determined when I got in here was that I was going to be particularly careful about that. I must say this to you, that where narcotic addicts are concerned, I haven't many complaints, though I do know the police are a little prone to pick up these men. They have protection of an ordinance, and I must say that the problem is so serious that even if we must admit some of their civil laws or civil rights are being violated, you have to go along with a certain amount of the fringe violation, if you see what I mean.

Senator Daniel: Yes.

Mr. Gutknecht: So I think you will find that a lot of these arrests and subsequent discharges are in the form of a security measure that possibly we should not countenance, but I don't know how else you can function.

Senator Daniel: You completely answered my next question. My next question was going to be this: How do you reconcile the large number of arrests for Chicago for the period 1953 and 1954, 6,643 with convictions, 3,350, just barely over fifty per cent of the arrests, and I believe you have answered it already.

Mr. Gutknecht: I think you will also have to agree that neither Mr. Tieken in his capacity nor I in my capacity—and we both have civil rights laws to enforce—can, with our multiple jobs, get too excited if a known addict has been unlawfully arrested and then discharged, knowing that because he is a known addict the police have to take little extra measures.[4]

The policy of police harassment of drug users is extremely injurious and demoralizing in its effects upon the addicts. Indeed, it is probably more injurious to the addict's health than is the taking of drugs itself. The policy of repeated arrests with brief periods of detention means that the user suffers deprivation symptoms while he is held and questioned. He earns his release by giving the police information or is routinely released if he cannot be charged with an offense. Since the period of detention is not ordinarily long enough for withdrawal to be complete, there is no expectation that the released addict will abstain from immediate relapse. Repeated partial withdrawals of this sort in police lockups without medical attention are bound to have devastating effects upon the user's health and morale. The expression, "murder on the installment plan," might be more appropriately applied to this aspect of the present treatment of addicts than to any other.

THE STRUCTURE OF THE ILLICIT TRAFFIC

Virtually all of the drugs used by American addicts are imported into this country from abroad. They arrive in relatively pure form and as they pass from the hands of one dealer to the next in the long chain of distribution which reaches from the importer to the ultimate consumer they are progressively diluted and progressively broken up into smaller and smaller units. Dilution at the lowest level is probably usually in excess of 90 per cent and sometimes reaches 98 per cent or more. It has been estimated that smuggled drugs may pass through as many as fifty or a hundred hands before they reach the user. In this hierarchy only the lower reaches are relatively well known. The higher echelons are obscured by lack of

information and by the fact that operations on this level are conducted by organized mobs directed by persons who are not addicts,
who remain behind the scenes, and who employ others to act as
their agents. For example, an ignorant seaman may be approached
in a foreign country by a person unknown to him acting in behalf
of someone else and offered a sum of money to smuggle a package
with unrevealed contents into this country to be delivered at a
given address to an individual who is also acting as an agent for
persons unknown. If the persons directly involved in the transaction are apprehended they cannot help the police because they
usually do not know who the behind-the-scenes directors of the
operation are, and even if they do know they are not likely to talk
because of the threat of death which the underworld mob holds
over the informer. In these higher echelons there are ordinarily no
addicts involved, because the underworld mobster knows that they
are unreliable on account of the tremendous leverage which the
police have in dealing with them.

J. Lombard, United States Attorney for the Southern District
of New York, told the Price Daniel subcommittee about the higher
branches of the traffic and the difficulties encountered in trying to
get at the persons in the upper brackets:

I would like to suggest that we are dealing with a rather unusual
crime, a rather unusual situation in this sense. The narcotics traffic is
run by people who operate on an international scale, and in this country on an interstate scale. They are professional criminals. They have
lots of money. They have powerful allies. They have expert knowledge
as to how to evade the law and to escape detection. They are not themselves addicts. In fact, they seldom handle any drugs. They have no
bank accounts. They deal only in cash. Their errands are run by others.
Their messengers do the transporting and the selling. In short they operate behind a shield of henchmen.

Now, to get evidence sufficient to convict a big operator, as you can
see, is very difficult at best. As a rule, we get nowhere near the big operator when we simply arrest the pusher and the small dope peddler. We

are just at the bottom of the ladder. There may be 8 or 10 rungs of the ladder before we get to the big dealer who has been responsible for the importation of the drug.[5]

Numerous other witnesses provided similar descriptions. State's Attorney Gutknecht of Chicago graphically illustrated the difficulties in getting information on upper level peddlers with the following account:

Last month I had two defendants that I had in my own office, talking to them, trying to get some information, with nobody else there, unrelated cases, a week apart. The wording was a little different but each one of those defendants, when I tried to get him to help in connection with pushers, the sellers, the higher ups, said to me, "Well, Judge, what can you do? You can give me a couple of years. I have been there before. You can give me time. If I tell you and it gets out, I will be dead before the week is over."[6]

Lt. T. F. McDermott of the Philadelphia police had a similar complaint:

We have tried everything that we know of to get everyone that was involved in this racket, whether they be white or colored, it didn't make any difference. And it seems when we get to a certain level we arrest them, and if there is anybody above that level where we arrested Graves, they just stop, they refuse to tell us. Now, we believe there were some other people involved behind Graves, Miles, and DeLoach, but after we talked to them about that they just cut us off. We believe that they definitely had a white connection.
   Senator Daniel: Were they white men?
   Mr. McDermott: No, Negroes.[7]

It is a common observation in large northern cities that the persons in the top levels of the traffic are usually white mobsters, and that Negroes appear mainly in lower-level operations. In Chicago, and in other northern cities, the top peddlers are said to be mainly of Italian origin.

The following laconic item from a Chicago newspaper illustrates the hazards of the "stool pigeon's" life and one of the ways in which peddlers protect themselves from such persons:

> Virgel (Hound Dog) Wilber, 30, who had a record as a dope peddler and user, failed to appear before George B. Weiss in Felony Court yesterday on a narcotics charge. . . . Wilber's body had been found earlier in the day amidst overturned furniture in his third floor apartment at 1409 E. 66th St. He had been shot three times in the head with .45 caliber bullets. . . . Witnesses told police they heard shots just before a man fled from the building.
>
> The court case grew out of the finding of $5,000 worth of cocaine and heroin Oct. 31 in Wilber's apartment at 6443 Kenwood Ave. This raid was made after seizure of $500 worth of heroin in the apartment of James Miller, 31, of 4644 Prairie Ave., who identified Wilber to police as his supplier.[8]

The killing in this case was undoubtedly carried out by the peddler next in line above "Hound Dog" Wilber, who either knew, or feared, that Wilber would betray him to the police. Such a killing makes a great deal of sense when one considers that had he been detected as a narcotics peddler, the unknown drug peddler who murdered Wilber would undoubtedly have received an extremely severe sentence. On the other hand, it could be taken for granted that the Chicago police would not be too concerned over the death of "Hound Dog." Even had the murderer been apprehended and convicted, the sentence might well have been little more severe, or even less severe, than for the narcotics offense.

The huge spread between the legal and the black market prices for drugs, or between the cost of illicit drugs abroad and their ultimate price in this country, is the source of the profits which sustain the entire structure of the illicit traffic. While these profits accrue to peddlers and dealers at all levels, they are greatest at the upper levels, where operations are on a larger scale and are more stable because police intervention is difficult and rare. At the lowest level the addict-pusher turns his profits back into the traffic to keep himself supplied. Nonaddicted peddlers who sell to addict consumers are readily apprehended and, because of the heavy penalties attached to drug law violations, this highly dangerous occupation is likely to attract mainly the ignorant, unsophisticated, or otherwise incompetent members of the criminal world. The large profits which some of these persons may obtain therefore usually turn out to be very transitory or they are eaten up by expenses involved in trying to stay out of jail or prison.

The consequence which follows from this, which is of concern in evaluating the effects of enforcement, is that the major profits of the illegal drug trade are made by one set of persons while the major risks are taken by other persons. In the aggregate, for example, addict-pushers and even addicts who are not pushers serve proportionately more time in prison than do the nonaddicted big dealers and smugglers. If this were not true the trade could not continue to exist. The addict performs an essential role in the drug traffic just as he does in the enforcement of the drug laws. The power of the habit, which makes it easy for the police to extract information from the user, also makes it easy for addicts to be used to distribute drugs to fellow addicts, a task in which the risks of detection are at a maximum. With statistical information as bad as it is, the arrest and incarceration of addicts makes it possible for police officials to create the public illusion that the drug traffic is being severely dealt with, whereas, as a matter of fact, it is primarily the victims of the traffic and the small fry who suffer the major punishment.

This point is widely recognized and admitted even by the police and hardly needs documentation. If proof were needed one might note that it is generally conceded that it is the function of federal narcotic agents to handle the big dealer and smuggler cases, while the "retail" trade is dealt with by the local police. The number of cases handled by federal agents is very small compared to those dealt with at lower levels, but even most of the federal cases involve only minor peddlers. This is conclusively demonstrated by the fact that around fifty per cent of federal drug law offenders are each year reported by the Federal Bureau of Prisons to be addicts. Wardens of penitentiaries are fully aware and often state that very few big operators in the illegal drug trade are entrusted to their care.

The illicit drug traffic has adapted itself so well to the measures taken against it by the police that despite the continuous flow of newspaper accounts of "dope rings" being broken up, it is very difficult to find addicts who have had to go without drugs for more than a day or two because no supplies were available. The user usually knows of more than one possible source and, when the peddler he is dealing with goes to jail, simply switches to another. It seems, therefore, that the illegal drug trade at the lower levels, and probably the upper also, is not in the hands of a monopoly but is decentralized with many networks of distribution functioning independently of each other within the same area. The destruction of one of these networks merely diverts customers to those that remain.

MAKING A BUY

Only rarely are the police able to break into the traffic at higher levels where there are no addicts. This usually occurs in one of these ways: (1) an undercover agent (a policeman) may work his way into the confidence of the underworld by posing as a criminal; (2) a smuggling or distributing mob may tip off the police concerning a competing mob, especially if the competition is deemed to be unfair; and (3) a criminal facing serious charges may use his knowledge of the narcotic traffic to bargain for a lighter sentence for himself. None of these alternatives presents a dependable technique for getting at big dealers. The undercover agent, for example, must have considerable ability in order to deceive criminals and he must assume the risk of being killed, especially if he is not known to be a police officer and is suspected of being simply an informer.

There are relatively few good undercover detectives. Moreover, an undercover man cannot long remain unknown. An appearance in court, for example, is sufficient to reveal his identity and end his usefulness. The other two alternatives are of relatively little use because of the strong underworld taboo on informers and the merciless punishment that is meted out to them by the organized gangs.

Some of the police informers may be used only once while others may be used repeatedly for long periods of time and be moved about from one city to another. The police ordinarily try to keep the identity of their informants secret even from other informants and other policemen. They try to avoid the necessity of having them testify in court if they hope to make use of them in the future.

When the drug addict is used in "making a buy," he is ordinarily first supposed to be searched by the police to make sure that he has no drugs in his possession. He is then supplied with marked money; i.e., bills of which the serial numbers are recorded (or which have been dusted with invisible powder) and he is then taken into the vicinity in which the peddler who is being sought is operating. Remaining in the background, the police send the addict "stool pigeon" to the peddler with whom he is already acquainted. When the sale is completed, the addict informs the officers, who seek to arrest the peddler before he has disposed of the marked money. The drugs which the addict purchases are supposed to be turned over to police to be used, along with the marked money, as evidence in court. In practice, the "stool pigeon" often, perhaps usually, appropriates some of the evidence for his own use before he turns the remainder over to the police. He is expected to do this because this is part of his reward and a vital element in his motivation to engage in this unpopular and dangerous business.

In practice, the above account of making a buy is much oversimplified. The peddler is usually well aware of the standard practices of the police and seeks to thwart them by a wide variety of stratagems. Automobiles are frequently used, the collection of the money and the delivery of the drug may be handled as separate operations in different places by different persons, and precautions may be taken to dispose of the marked money before it can be recovered by the police. When complications of this kind occur, the police may have to depend upon the word of the "stool pigeon" as to what actually happened and they may have difficulty in proving the case in court. This is especially true because the word of an addict is highly suspect since his testimony is tainted by the fact that it is secured by means of threats of punishment and promises of reward. In order to keep track of what the informer does and to provide independent corroboration of his testimony, the police try to observe the transaction if at all possible. Sometimes the informer is equipped with a wireless transmitter so that the police may listen in on his conversation with the peddler. Peddlers have learned of this practice and counteract it by requiring customers to disrobe to prove that they are not so equipped. To eliminate the possibility of selling drugs directly to a narcotic agent, many pushers refuse to have any business dealings with anyone who is not an addict and they may require proof of addiction from a new customer.

The expression "buy and bust" is used to describe the police practice of obtaining evidence against a peddler and then arresting him, often waiting to make the arrest when he has returned to his place of residence or perhaps to his automobile. In theory the police officer seeking entry is supposed to knock, identify himself as a police officer, and ask admittance. In practice this procedure would give the culprit time to dispose of his drugs by flushing them down the toilet, for example. What the police therefore do is simply to batter down the door and rush into the room or apartment as quickly as possible to forestall actions of this kind. Search without warrant is legally permissible when a legitimate arrest is made. Hence, if a peddler is arrested in his home or in his automobile, a search of the automobile or of the premises may be made legally. From these practices one can readily understand why the police sometimes jocularly describe the sledge hammer which is used to smash the door of the suspect's residence as their "master key."

It can readily be understood that it is important to the narcotics police to have a fund of money available with which to make buys and to pay stool pigeons. Some of the money used in the purchase of evidence is never recovered and if this fund is limited police tactics may be adapted to the idea of maximizing the probabilities of recovery. Also, should a large peddler be spotted, the police may be unable to raise enough money to make a buy from him. A police technique based on the assumption that most of the public money spent to purchase heroin as evidence will be lost is that of the so-called "mass raid."[9] New narcotic agents who are unknown in a given locality are provided with money to make purchases from peddlers over a period of time—perhaps several months. During this time the agents gain the confidence of underworld persons and quietly accumulate evidence and knowledge of the higher reaches of the local traffic. Then, on a prearranged date, the accumulated evidence is used at one time to arrest and convict a large number of persons, some of them perhaps being relatively important traffickers. The effect of this is said to be salutary since the roof seems to cave in suddenly for the peddlers and dealers. The disadvantages of the technique are the expense involved in diverting substantial funds into the traffic without hope of recovery, and the fact that undercover narcotic agents soon come to be known.

HANDLING THE "STOOL PIGEON"

The narcotic "stool pigeon" differs from the ordinary informer in two important ways; namely, that he himself violates the law almost constantly while he works for the police by reason of the fact that he is an active addict, and that he not merely gives information but actively assists the police in trapping fellow addicts and peddlers. He is thus, in reality, an enforcement officer of sorts, and is ordinarily referred to officially as a "special employee."

The "stool pigeon" is usually inducted into this activity by pressure of various sorts depending upon circumstances and the resistance offered. An inexperienced addict may give way at once when threatened with arrest, or in the face of a prison sentence and the promise that if he cooperates he will receive a short sentence, be placed on probation, or perhaps released. The police sometimes offer an addict leniency if he agrees to turn in one or more peddlers. The most effective reward of all is that the informer may be allowed to continue his habit, at least temporarily. Persons who show unusual ability may make informing a career and use it to maintain their habits over a period of years. Usually, however, the active career of the "stooly" is brief because he soon comes to be known.

When the utility of the addicted informer is at an end the police commonly get rid of him by sending him to jail or prison. It is often believed that under these circumstances the fear of underworld vengeance and a bad reputation in the underworld may provide the informer addict with incentives to avoid relapse. Addicts who have difficulty making a living and supporting their habits in the usual ways sometimes make nuisances of themselves with the police by insisting on trying to be informers when they do not have the needed skills and connections. These may be gotten rid of by "burning"—i.e., by permitting them to be seen in the company of a police officer in such a way as to expose them to the peddlers.

The most effective punishment used to induce addicts to talk and to cooperate is, of course, the withdrawal distress. This is frequently supplemented, depending upon the inclinations of the police officer, by all of the usual third-degree tactics. The low social status of the addict and his characteristic lack of means make the use of rough tactics relatively attractive and safe. Even if the user should appear in court with injuries and bruises no one is likely to take his word for it that he was beaten by the police. The ordinary

victim of third-degree practices is helpless enough in seeking remedies; the addict is even more so. The police characteristically deny
that the suspect has been mistreated or assert that the obvious injuries and bruises were sustained as a consequence of resisting arrest or trying to escape. In view of the addict's unusual vulnerability to police pressure it is small wonder that the narcotics police
in some areas have estimated that fifty per cent or more of those
arrested break down under pressure and agree to cooperate.

The manner in which charges are manipulated by prosecutors
and police to reward informers was frequently indicated before
congressional investigating committees. Mr. Anslinger, head of the
Federal Narcotics Bureau, speaking to the Daniel subcommittee,
noted with approval that Michigan had enacted a law requiring the
imposition of a twenty-year sentence as a minimum for a first selling offense, and commented on the utility of this law in recruiting
"stool pigeons":

> Now, if a man is arrested for trafficking, and he wants to avoid that
> 20-year penalty, there have been some 20-year penalties meted out
> there, he will find it to his credit to go to the enforcement officers
> and assist those officers in finding sources of supply, which is being
> done in a lot of cases in Detroit, and in some cases the charge then is
> changed from sale to possession.[10]

This was a recurring theme of law enforcement officers who testified before the Senate subcommittee. W. Wilson White, a Pennsylvania district attorney, commented that the narcotic laws were sufficiently flexible to permit informers to be rewarded:

> The act is yet flexible enough that in the face of first offenders, as
> you know, there may be probation; in the case of informers, who are
> necessarily involved, probation can be quietly granted, and we do not
> run into difficulties there.[11]

It is of interest that while the Narcotics Control Act of 1956 was
deliberately framed so as to restrict the discretion of judges it was
thought necessary to maintain and even enlarge the discretion of

the police and prosecution. The latter, as noted above, under the system of mandatory penalties now in effect, can reduce charges, place on probation or simply not prosecute at all, thus taking over from the judges the effective power to fix sentences.

The subcommittee noted that big illicit operators use as their representatives persons who have not been previously convicted of a narcotic charge. It was illogically suggested that this practice could be remedied by increasing penalties for first offenders; in other words, to deter Mr. X, whom we cannot catch, let us punish Mr. A, whom we can catch. The real purpose, or at least a more important and more logical one, is indicated by the comment of Illinois State's Attorney John Gutknecht:

> That is an additional help we will gain from this because if every one of these first offenders knows they are going to jail unless they can buy immunity—I will put it that crudely; we never promise immunity— in other words, we get a lot of people, weak ones, that offer to put somebody else on the spot, knowing that if they do it they may get some help from us. That is a racket they indulge in.
> But any time we can get a real first offender to turn up somebody good higher up in this nefarious practice, I will take the responsibility, once we get the other fellow, of going before the court and saying, "This man put his finger on and helped us get a real conviction here. In the interest of justice I think we should have a nolle prosse."[12]

The use of addict "stool pigeons" is so common that it is sometimes an embarrassment to the police. It tends to create a class of law violator who is to a degree and for varying periods of time exempt from the penalties of the law. Because of the secrecy shrouding the informer, the police sometimes arrest each other's stool pigeons and the latter sometimes try to make buys from each other. Arrested addicts sometimes indignantly ask to be released on the grounds that they are working for the police.

Professional informers are hated and mistrusted persons and are often of the lowest and must untrustworthy character. They do not trust each other, the police for whom they work, or anyone else, and in turn are trusted by no one, least of all perhaps by the police who use them. They are primarily interested, directly or indirectly, in the drugs which support their habit and which are their reward, and in avoiding punishment. The desperate informer who is being paid for the cases he makes is not likely to hesitate to commit perjury, to "frame" another addict, or to make a false identification if that is required of him. The police in turn often commit perjury to corroborate the informer's testimony, to conceal the fact that they are or have been providing him with drugs, and in general to cover up the many unpleasant and illegal aspects of this type of law enforcement.

The minor offender who is compelled to give information is fully aware of the personal danger that this may entail, and he is caught in a very painful dilemma. If he refuses to cooperate he is denied drugs, and may be handled roughly and have "the book thrown at him" in court. If he agrees to act as informer he has the underworld vengeance to consider. A way out of this dilemma is to betray those who have the least power to retaliate. Thus an addict may turn in other addicts, or he may reveal the identity of minor individual peddlers and conceal the names of those whom he fears. Instead of turning in higher sources of supply, a peddler may turn over his customers to the police. Since the narcotics detective is usually interested in getting the big offenders, the informer will try to convince him of the importance of the persons he betrays, and will often portray as pushers persons who he knows are merely users. If the detective does not know too much about who is who in the traffic, and if he is having a hard time making cases, he may be easily convinced. Once the arrests are made it is in the detective's interest also to exaggerate the culprit's importance, and to overstate the amount and value of whatever drugs are seized. As a consequence, newspaper accounts regularly exaggerate the significance of the countless "dope rings" that are broken up by the police.

In earlier years narcotics agents openly doled out daily rations of drugs to informers, thus operating what might be called a kind of "clinic system" of their own. Reducing or withholding the rations was a stimulus to keep the informer busy. In those early days the penalties for violators and for informers were milder than at present and drug peddlers were less wary. It was considered reasonably smart, for example, for peddlers to plant a spy to note who was getting rations at the police clinic. All of this would be considered extremely elementary today; narcotics agents and detectives no longer dole out drugs as openly and directly, nor are informers dealt with as crudely.

Drugs are still being handed to addict-informers by individual detectives who do not tell their superiors about it. The latter undoubtedly often know that this is done, but they officially disapprove of it, deny its occurrence, and refrain from seeking information about it. Drugs are provided to the informer by discreet and indirect methods such as allowing him to appropriate some of the evidence or authorizing a doctor to write prescriptions for him. In some instances informers peddle the drugs so obtained to supplement the pay they receive from the government. It is said that some peddlers just across the border in Mexico sell drugs to customers from the United States, betray them to the American authorities, and then collect rewards when the American peddlers or addicts are arrested upon recrossing the border—thus obtaining a double income from the same transaction.

DOPE DRIVES

When there is little public excitement or newspaper publicity about the "dope menace" the police do not exert themselves to arrest and imprison all of the addicts and small peddlers known to them. Instead, they use these persons as sources of information to lead them to the higher sources of supply. Dope drives are ordinarily public-relations enterprises designed to appease an aroused public or to impress legislatures. They are to a considerable extent self-defeating when viewed from the standpoint of law enforcement, because they usually result in the rounding up of many addicts and minor offenders most of whom are held briefly and released while a few are sent to jail. This has the effect of disrupting police lines of attack upon the higher bracket peddlers, who are untouched by the drive, are probably safer from arrest than before, and whose profits are increased by the higher prices which drives produce.

Conscientious police officers in the narcotics field know that arresting numerous street addicts does not significantly touch the traffic, and they are inclined to be contemptuous of it. They are interested, not simply in making arrests, but in making important ones, that is, of relatively big dealers. As a practical matter of police administration, however, a compromise of some sort must be made between a policy of arresting many unimportant offenders and one of arresting fewer but more important law violators. The "few but important" argument may obviously be used as a cover-up by an incompetent or lazy officer. Since officers often appear in court on their own time or for minimum pay, it is understandable that they may be reluctant to make too many arrests. A "quota system" is sometimes used to deal with this problem and is said to have been used by the more than two-hundred-man narcotics squad of New York City. This system requires a certain minimum number of arrests per month per detective—allegedly six—for a time in New York.

In 1959 this system came under attack in New York. The following article by Barbara Yuncker in the *New York Post* of July 7, 1959, gives revealing information concerning it:

The policy of setting quotas for narcotics arrests came under new attack today by the former head of the Federal Bureau of Narcotics for the New York area.

James C. Ryan, district Supervisor until last year, told The Post that a main reason for his having retired at the age of 50 was that he and his 65-man office were being "crowded to produce more arrests," without proper regard to the importance of those arrested.

DENIES FEDERAL QUOTA

This alleged pressure is similar to that of the quota system which The Post recently disclosed was causing grave morale problems in the Police Dept's 200-man Narcotics Squad.

Samuel Levine, acting district supervisor for the Federal Bureau of Narcotics, denied his agency had a quota system.

"Our directive," he said, "is to concentrate on the major traffickers."

Ryan laid the pressure he experienced to "officials in Washington" and indicated he feared such a policy could result in the arrest mainly of users and pushers instead of suppliers.

"We were arresting top violators and developing as many cases as we could," he said. "They wanted more arrests. You can figure out from that what kind of arrests they would be."

This attitude, he said, was bound to hamper slow-developing under-cover work leading to significant arrests. It is his belief that all top racketeers are involved in narcotics.

PRESSURE STILL ON

To the best of his knowledge high-arrest pressure is still on, he said.

Ryan emphasized that he had no quarrel with longtime Narcotics Commissioner Anslinger. He attributed the high-arrest philosophy to the second or third echelon of the bureau.

Arrest totals, Ryan said, are no standard of effective control.

"If you get one important case a year, you're doing a good job," he added.

CITY COPS AGREE

City Narcotics Squad detectives have privately expressed the same attitude. However, under department pressure, none of them is willing to be quoted. They were given the alternative of living with the quota system of six arrests a month or being sent back to the uniformed force.

Perhaps the opinions expressed by Mr. Ryan in the *New York Post* article were based upon incidents of the type in which he was involved in 1952 when the Federal Narcotic Bureau staged a national crackdown during which about five hundred persons were seized. Since this national drive provides an extraordinarily good illustration of the real nature and purposes of such police enterprises it is worthwhile to notice how it was staged and what the bag actually amounted to.

At 5:15 P.M. on January 4, 1952, Harry J. Anslinger, U.S. Commissioner of Narcotics, announced a series of dawn-to-dusk narcotics raids in cities throughout the nation, at a Washington news conference.[13] The raids were aimed primarily, he said, at second and third offenders among peddlers in the teen-age trade and would result in "a sharp reduction in drug addiction particularly among teen-agers." He said, further, that these raids would take hardened narcotics dealers out of the trade for a long time and that the groundwork for indictments against some outstandingly "large-scale racketeers" was being laid. Important underworld characters were allegedly seized. He would not estimate how much public money had been spent to buy narcotics as evidence but said, "It was mighty high. That heroin is getting to be worth one hundred times its weight in gold and that's what we have to pay for it." Mr. Anslinger went on: "Most of those arrested are dangerous fellows. The fact they're facing from five to twenty years in jail makes them the most dangerous we've gone against yet. We knew that all along and if there was any shooting to be done our men were the ones who were going to do it."

The largest number of arrests (58) in any city occurred in New York under Mr. James C. Ryan. The same issue of the *New York Times* which carried Mr. Anslinger's version of the drive also carried a detailed story of the catch in New York, a city which is generally conceded to be a bastion of the illicit traffic and the home town of many of the most important racketeers in the trade. Nevertheless the New York catch evidently did not include a single even moderately important peddler and consisted in part merely of users, as the following quotes from the *Times* article indicate:

> Some of those arrested, it was stated, were "important," but prisoners did not include members of an organized ring. Those seized were said rather to have been "loosely interlocked". . . .
>
> There were some seizures of narcotics, but no large ones. . . .
>
> United States Marshal William A. Carroll said that a number of prisoners, including some of the twelve women arrested, fell to the floor in their cells and gave other evidence of suffering from deprivation of drugs. . . .
>
> In comment on the raids Mr. Ryan observed: "Perhaps we didn't get any international peddlers, but that's because the big shots are much too smart to contact teen-agers."
>
> Forty-eight of the prisoners . . . were arraigned late yesterday afternoon. . . . The women were held in $1,000 bail each, the men in $3,000 bail each, with the exception of one whose bail was set at $1,500.

Concerning the fixing of bail it should be noted that for an important peddler bail is never fixed as low as $3,000 and would rarely be as low as $15,000. This item alone indicates that the New York raids netted, not a collection of sharks as the screaming headlines and the Washington handout suggested, but only a haul of minnows. In making this haul, Mr. Ryan stated that more than $10,000 had been spent in making buys.

From the standpoint of law enforcement arrests ought to be made when sufficient evidence to convict is at hand, and not on a specific prearranged date. To schedule arrests for a specific time, as was done, is itself an indication that the whole affair was motivated by political and publicity considerations. In 1951 the Congress enacted the Boggs Bill, which sharply increased penalties for narcotics offenders. It also greatly enlarged the budget of the Federal Narcotics Bureau, authorized the employment of more agents, and provided more money to be used to purchase illicit drugs as evidence. Public concern over juvenile addiction was at a fever pitch at that time and the police were being blamed for it by some. Federal narcotics officials had generally discounted this problem, arguing that the extent of such addiction was being greatly exaggerated. Nevertheless, the drive was said to have been aimed at this teen-age problem. It thus served, not only to justify the Narcotics Bureau in the eyes of Congress, but also to appease and quiet a worried public.

To exemplify the important type of narcotics case which is usually absent during drives, as well as to demonstrate the level at which bail is set in such cases, a news item out of Indianapolis on April 16, 1960, may be considered:

Federal and City narcotics agents broke down the door of an Indianapolis apartment Friday and arrested a man and a woman described as top figures in international dope peddling.

Jeremiah Hope Pullings, 41, and Delores Keeby, 28, who posed as his wife, were held for bonds of $65,000 each. . . .

Edward Cass, federal narcotics agent, said the two were among the more important of 18 persons, including three Chicago narcotics detectives, who were indicted last September on charges of illegal drug sales, importation, and conspiracy. . . .

Pullings has been linked with the Chicago police scandal, agents said, and was thought to have used two policemen as narcotics couriers.[14]

Doubt is cast upon the alleged importance of these persons by the fact that evidence seized in their apartment indicated that they had personally handled drugs. It is generally said that big shots have others do this for them.

Apart from the high bail, the case has other interesting features, such as the allegation that three narcotics detectives from Chicago were involved in the ring. The "buy and bust" technique which it illustrates is standard, although it evidently failed in this case because Pullings locked himself in the bathroom and appeared to have disposed of his drug supply before the second door could be battered down. The police assertion that the door to the apartment was smashed because they were refused entry is also standard.

Public demand for dope drives often develops from newspaper publicity or from merchants who complain of the losses which addicts cause them. The drive which is supposed to appease the merchants and quiet the public does so primarily through the publicity which it is given. In actuality the police of large cities like Chicago and New York cannot round up a sufficient proportion of the users to make much difference, and if all users could be apprehended and convicted there would be no place to send them. Dope drives, from an economic viewpoint, might be expected to reduce the demand for drugs if significant numbers of users were sent to jail. Under these circumstances illicit prices would be expected to drop. In practice the effect is the opposite; illicit prices rise during drives and the predatory activities of addicts who remain at large are stepped up proportionately.

The police ordinarily interpret a rising arrest rate as evidence of increased police efficiency and a determination to stamp out the problem. A declining arrest rate, on the other hand, is cited as evidence that addiction is declining and that the police have things under control. Another index used to demonstrate police effectiveness is the price of the drug and the degree of dilution, a high price and heavy dilution being regarded as evidence of a scarcity of drugs. Prices are always said to be rising and dilution increasing, but the same claim is made year after year, decade after decade. It is true that illicit prices have risen, but it is not clear how much of this rise reflects inflation. The figures published by the Federal Narcotics Bureau in its annual reports do not justify the perennial claims that are made concerning dilution.

The incarceration of drug addicts is usually justified on the ground that it prevents them from stealing and from spreading the habit. While it is true that an addict cannot steal while he is in jail, it is erroneous to suppose that the drug habit is not spread within prisons and jails. In greater or smaller quantity, drugs are probably smuggled into virtually all of our penal institutions, and there the intimate association of addicts and nonaddicts encourages the spread of addiction.

Among the more bizarre reasons sometimes given for locking up drug users are that they are thus protected from peddlers, and the suggestion, submitted by the former United States Commissioner of Narcotics, that locking up addicts is an effective way of undermining the peddler's business by depriving him of his customers:

> From the practical standpoint it is fundamental that a business, legal or illegal, would be bound to fail if deprived of customers, and the peddler of narcotic drugs is no exception. If the peddler were deprived of a market for his illegal wares, he would cease to exist. As long as the addict is at liberty to come and go, the peddler has a steady customer. When the addict is institutionalized he not only loses his value to the peddler but he is also prevented from contaminating others.[15]

POLICE CORRUPTION

Because of the drug user's low social standing, vulnerability to arrest, and reputation for unreliability he would be an excellent source of graft for dishonest policemen if he had money. Since he ordinarily has no funds and few possessions, his usefulness in this respect is confined to helping the police to trap peddlers, who often do have funds and possessions which may be acquired with relative impunity. It is often reported that peddlers offer bribes to arresting officers and one can only guess that there are other unreported bribes which are offered and accepted. When the door of the drug seller's room or apartment has been battered down and he has been taken away, the police state that the premises are frequently looted by unknown persons. Actually, these "unknown persons" are sometimes the police themselves. If the peddler accepts goods in exchange for drugs, his quarters may contain articles stolen by addicts and bartered for heroin. These articles, as well as the personal possessions of the arrested peddler, offer substantial attractions for policemen who are not above the temptations of easy money.

The greatest potential source of illicit monetary gain is, of course, from seized supplies of drugs if they can be turned back into illicit channels. Because of the policeman's contacts with addicts and peddlers who act as stool pigeons for him, it is comparatively simple for such matters to be arranged. In view of the poor pay, low standards, and low morale which characterize many of the municipal police forces in this country, it is unreasonable to suppose that all of the drugs seized from peddlers are simply destroyed. Besides their monetary value, they provide the logical and most economical means of rewarding informers. The Chicago newspapers have reported that members of the narcotics squad in that city frequently have had to use their own personal funds to make buys from peddlers. It would be naïve to suppose that money so spent is not recovered.

Some of the more direct techniques used to make law enforcement profitable may be illustrated by a hypothetical instance which will be described as though it actually occurred.

A police informer made a purchase from a Spanish-speaking heroin peddler who was also an addict. Following the "buy and bust" method four members of the narcotics squad suddenly burst into the seller's apartment by battering down the back door. In the apartment were found the peddler and his wife, their three children, and some other adults. All of the adults were shackled together and forced to sit on the floor. The peddler was slapped, and one of the adults was struck with a pistol for speaking in Spanish.

The noise and confusion frightened the children and aroused the neighbors who came to see what was going on. Some of the neighbors were allowed to take the children away. The apartment was searched for drugs and a quantity of heroin was found. There were also various articles such as wrist watches, portable radios, jewelry, and other items which had apparently been accepted in payment for drugs. These articles, and other items which were the personal possessions of the peddler and his wife such as clothes and two dish cloths worth about ten cents each, were sorted into piles by the officers. Two officers took the suspects to the police lockup, while the other two stayed behind and carried off all the goods that had been sorted out. No receipt was given. The police said that the articles appeared to have been stolen and would have to be checked. It was later denied that any goods had been removed and suggested that looters may have entered the apartment. None of the goods was recovered or heard of again.

When the peddler was arrested he had about one hundred dollars on his person, including ten dollars of marked money which had been given him by the informer. This ten dollars was taken by the police and a receipt was given for the remaining ninety. In the police lockup he was approached by a bailiff, asked if he had any money, and advised to get a lawyer. The bailiff put the defendant in touch with a lawyer and the latter stated that from $500 to $600 would be required for a defense. The defendant thereupon turned over the ninety dollars as a preliminary payment. The lawyer later visited the peddler's wife and informed her that the defense would cost about $1,500. She sold the family automobile, almost the only remaining property of any value, gave the lawyer the $100 that she obtained for it, and then went on relief with her three children.

When complaints were made and the case attracted outside attention, various witnesses were offered threats and inducements to retract their charges or to keep quiet. It was pointed out that even if the charges were true the person involved was, after all, only a dark-skinned, Spanish-speaking heroin peddler who deserved nothing better, suggesting that the unusual feature of this case was not what was done but that it attracted attention. The peddler was offered an opportunity to "cop a plea" and receive a light sentence if he would agree to induce his wife to drop her charges against the police. When the case appeared in court and it was proposed to dismiss the lawyer originally recommended to the suspect by the bailiff at the police station, the arresting officers sought to exert pressure to prevent this. This suggests that part of the lawyer's fee, for which he did next to nothing, was turned back to the police.

THE FAILURE OF ENFORCEMENT STRATEGY

The basic reason for the evident ineffectiveness of police tactics is that they do not ordinarily reach the real culprits—those who make the big money from the traffic. The stool-pigeon technique is ideally adapted to catching expendable addicts and small peddlers; in the nature of the case it is relatively ineffective in trapping the kingpins. The alleged leniency of judges and the present severity of penalties are both irrelevant, for the offender cannot be punished until he has been apprehended. The central unsolved problem is that of identifying and preparing a case against the important offenders. Increased penalties, limited judicial discretion, and the denial of probation and parole do not contribute to this end; indeed, they probably make it more difficult to get at the key figures by causing them to be more cautious. While present police tactics are filling jails and prisons with relatively minor narcotic offenders, the illicit traffic shows no signs of drying up and is, in fact, probably more profitable than ever for the higher-ups.

Cops-and-robbers stories pertaining to the dope traffic with which the public is regaled distract attention from a fundamental economic dilemma which nullifies enforcement efforts. The illicit narcotics traffic is a business activity in which the customary economic factors, such as those of supply, demand, cost, risk, and so on, operate as they do in other businesses. Enforcement operations directed at illicit dealers in narcotics tend to reduce available supplies, increase risks, and increase the prices paid by consumers. In-

creased prices mean increased profits for the operators who know
the ropes and are able to avoid police detection. Clearly if police
activities were to frighten prospective criminal entrepreneurs from
entering this racket the effect would be to produce a relative scarcity of drugs and increased profits, which, in turn, would tend to
counterbalance the increased risk. Under these circumstances it
is inconceivable that the illicit traffic in narcotics could be wiped
out by police action unless something were done to eliminate or
greatly reduce the demand for illicit drugs.

The effective demand for illicit narcotics obviously comes from
the addict. To reduce the demand it is necessary to take the addict
out of the market (a) by curing him of his craving, (b) by locking
him up in establishments to which peddlers do not have access, or
(c) by providing him with access to legal drugs. It is fair to say
on the basis of presently available evidence that the only one of
these three alternatives that has been successful anywhere in minimizing illicit operations has been the third, but from all indications,
if there is to be a new program in this country in the near future,
it will be based upon the first two of the above alternatives and will
reject the third.

CHAPTER 3

NARCOTICS OFFENDERS IN COURTS AND PRISONS

In the earlier chapters it has been pointed out that the most widely heard explanation of the gravity of our drug problem is the one offered by the Federal Bureau of Narcotics and by the police generally. According to this viewpoint the reasons for the disturbing narcotics situation are to be found primarily in the leniency with which offenders were handled in the courts. In addition to the emphasis on the desirability of heavy penalties, police spokesmen also characteristically complain of judicial leniency and lack of uniformity in sentencing, and of restrictions imposed upon enforcement officials by court decisions interpreting the Bill of Rights and often unduly limiting the freedom of action of the police.

While undoubtedly the police often have legitimate grounds for complaining about what judges do, it should be remembered that the police view of the narcotics problem and of what happens in the courts is inevitably biased. Police are generally disposed to be critical of judges in all areas of criminal law enforcement, and judges in their turn, like defense lawyers and prosecutors, tend to see things from their own particular occupational perspective. A balanced view requires that none of these particular perspectives be accepted on faith as the correct one, as the police interpretation in the area of narcotics has usually been.

THE ATTACK ON THE JUDICIARY

A representative criticism of judges was made by the *Los Angeles Times* in connection with proposals in California to stiffen penalties and limit judicial discretion in narcotics prosecution according to the pattern which is now the rule in virtually all the states as well as on the federal level. In an editorial entitled "Frustrated Narcotics Fighters," this newspaper presented views which correspond closely to those so often set forth by the police to congressional subcommittees:

State judges and law-enforcement officials are like deck hands working the pumps of a leaking ship. They must bend their backs and sweat —and their pumps had better be functioning efficiently—but they cure nothing; the ship's carpenters have got to go below on the double to plug the hole in the ship's side.

Some suggested changes in state narcotic laws—on improvements in pumps and their management—have been sent to Sacramento. The proposed amendments to the statutes have two aims—harder penalties for narcotics violators and easier rules for the police who must catch them. . . .

But proclaimed penalties do not stop the narcotics traffic; they must be imposed on the violators. The present penalties, which may be too mild, have never been tested for their full effect. Some of the recent records tend to show that offenders are treated too leniently in the courts. The statistics suggest that judicial discretion is almost boundless.

Several undercover men of the Los Angeles Police Department were assigned last year to make narcotics purchases from pushers. They submitted their evidence to the Los Angeles County Grand Jury, which returned 90 indictments. Then the police rounded up 79 indicted persons. This is what happened to them:

9 without prior convictions turned over to the Youth Authority.
5 without priors sentenced to prison.
14 without priors sentenced to county jail (less than a year).
1 without a prior given probation.
9 with priors sent to prison as first offenders (priors ignored).
1 with a prior sentenced to jail (less than a year).
8 with priors sent to prison (priors recognized).
47 cases disposed of with some kind of sentence.

7 acquitted.
3 dismissed.
9 identified but not apprehended.
10 not identified and not apprehended.
3 still pending.
32 cases, making a grand total of 79.

Here is justice holding not a balance but a sieve. Note that 10 defendants with prior narcotics convictions were sentenced as first offenders. Also note that while the police department made 90 cases, all with sales to police officers, only 47 resulted in prosecution (by February). The indictments were returned last August. The tabulation suggests that harsher penalties, particularly for those with prior narcotics convictions, might not make much difference in the dope trade—unless judicial discretion were circumscribed by the legislature. Perhaps it should be mandatory upon judges to recognize prior narcotics convictions in sentencing a defendant in a present narcotics case.

The record embitters zealous law-enforcement officials naturally, and they have other complaints against the courts, which cut them very fine on search and seizure in narcotics cases under the so-called exclusionary rule. Police have a hard time digging into narcotics cases because violations differ from other crimes; there are no "victims" to turn in reports. . . .[1]

An examination of the figures presented in this editorial indicates that the results which the *Los Angeles Times* complains of cannot be attributed to the judges but that the blame falls upon the police and the prosecutors. Thus of the 90 persons indicted, 30 were evidently never brought to court at all. This is a police responsibility. Ten cases were acquitted or dismissed, probably either because the evidence was inadequate or because the prosecutor chose not to prosecute. This, again, is a police or prosecution responsibility and not a judicial one. The fact that in ten instances prior narcotics convictions were ignored does not tell us why they were ignored. It is the duty of the prosecutor to certify prior convictions to the court and judges cannot take them into account unless this is done. State and federal law generally imposes heavy mandatory penalties upon second and third offenders and judges cannot legally ignore prior convictions under these circumstances if the prosecutor has called the court's attention to them properly.

Considering that 30 of the 90 original cases were not brought to court, and taking account of the three that were pending, it appears that the courts convicted 47 of the 57 defendants who were brought before them. This is not a bad record. Clearly the judges cannot be blamed for the 30 who were not apprehended.

The editorial writer implies that the sentences imposed were too light in some of the cases. Since no information was presented concerning the persons involved or the circumstances surrounding the offenses, it is impossible to judge. The writer of the editorial seems to assume that all narcotics offenders should automatically be given the maximum sentence and no doubt objected to the fact that one was granted probation.

What the editorial fails to take into account is that it is common in state courts for prosecutors to recommend to judges the sentences to be imposed and for the judges to follow these recommendations in a large proportion of the cases. The prosecutor frequently determines what penalty he will ask for after consultation with the police. Both police and prosecutor bargain with the defendant, offering him reduced punishment for information, for assisting in trapping other offenders and for pleading guilty rather than demanding trial. Police in some metropolitan areas have stated that fully fifty per cent or more of the apprehended narcotics offenders agree to act as informers or to provide other forms of help to the police. It therefore seems certain that some of the lighter sentences were agreed upon as rewards for informers upon recommendation of the prosecutor and the police. It is also possible that some of the 30 who were not brought into court were being used as informers. Prior narcotics convictions may well have been ignored for the same reason.

The figures presented by the *Los Angeles Times* were probably part of a police handout; it is ironic that they point, not to judicial inefficiency, but to that of the police and prosecution. It is the prosecutor, not the judge, who is usually described as the nearly absolute ruler of the whole judicial process; responsibility for the results must be allocated accordingly. It is the discretion and arbitrary power of prosecutors and policemen, rather than of judges, that needs to be curtailed in the interests of a more efficient administration of justice.

Since prosecutors and police place such great emphasis upon the necessity for recruiting informers, and since recent antinarcotics legislation has been designed to facilitate such recruitment, it is to be expected that informers will continue to be rewarded, by lighter sentences, by substituting probation for imprisonment, by overlooking prior convictions, by charging them with lesser crimes than they in fact commit, by not prosecuting them, and by other similar devices. It is further to be expected that blame for the resultant "sieve-like" characteristics of justice will continue to be placed upon judges whenever possible. It is axiomatic that officials enjoy the exercise of power and will not easily give it up or jeopardize it by accepting the responsibilities which it entails.

The criticism of judges in the *Los Angeles Times* editorial is not an isolated or unusual one. The arguments it presents are almost exactly the same as those which were presented before the various congressional subcommittees which have investigated the narcotics problem by innumerable prosecuting attorneys, chiefs of police, and narcotics agents. The main difference is that this editorial attempts to present statistical evidence to support its charges; most attacks upon the judiciary have been made without such evidence.

The *Los Angeles Times* editorial was a part of a vigorous anti-narcotics campaign waged in California which resulted in new legislation and a new and severe program for the handling of addicts either under criminal charges or under what is called "compulsory civil commitment." This campaign included not only attacks upon judges, but there were also the usual contemptuous references to "bleeding hearts" and "sob sisters."[2] The California program adopted in 1961 has been highly touted by California politicians, especially by the governor of that state, as a solution to the drug problem.

Judges make excellent scapegoats in matters of this kind because they are handicapped in answering their critics. While many of them are not well informed on the narcotics question, and while many are influenced by police propaganda and material in the mass media, they still do not relish the fact that recent legislation is aimed directly at limiting their discretionary powers as though they could not be trusted to handle narcotics offenders in a responsible manner, whereas the police and prosecutors can.

It is easy to understand that the Federal Bureau of Narcotics and the police in general should criticize judges and even that attempts should be made to blame the judiciary for the narcotics problem. It is not so easy to understand why Congress and the public have been so willing to accept these charges without supporting evidence and without giving the judges an opportunity to be heard in their own defense. Despite the fact that a significant proportion of our national legislature is made up of persons with legal experience and training, they have appeared, in this instance, to be extremely willing to accept a common police concept of the judge as an official who hampers efficient law enforcement by restricting the freedom of action of the police and by putting obstacles in the way of public-spirited prosecutors.

At the hearings before the Hale Boggs' subcommittee in 1955 and 1956, criticism of federal judges was especially prominent. Senator Burr P. Harrison of Virginia, for example, commented as follows:

The need for this legislation grows out of the fact that the federal judges are not doing their duty. Is that not about the sum and substance of it?[3]

Mr. Harrison followed up his question by asking whether prosecutors, police, and juries were doing their duties, and by a process of elimination placed the blame upon the judges. He noted that he would support the new legislation (the 1956 act) but expressed the following reservations concerning it:

I just do not know how you can, by legislation, supply some of these federal judges with the spine that they do not have. There are a great many fine men on the federal bench today, but there are just too many political touts and parlor pinks utterly incapable of understanding the danger of organized crime and organized subversion.[4]

The Boggs Subcommittee Hearings of 1955-1956 include reports from district supervisors of the Federal Bureau of Narcotics on the attitudes of judges in the various districts. This congressional subcommittee, like other congressional bodies that have investigated the narcotics problem, took it for granted that police reports upon judges alone provided sufficient evidence for the evaluation of a judge's competence. The police conception of what a judge should do is especially well indicated by the many letters of federal narcotics agents published in the Subcommittee Hearings of 1955-1956. The following comment in a letter from narcotics agent Albert D. Cook of Columbus, Ohio, is an illuminating example:

The United States district judge, Mell G. Underwood, Columbus, Ohio, has always taken a dim view of any offender of the narcotics laws. He has complied with the Boggs Act (1951) in every respect. He has never granted probation to any offender of the narcotic laws for a first offense unless such a recommendation has been made by the United States attorney and concurred by the narcotic agent.[5]

In subsequent years various members of Congress have taken the opportunity, when it was offered them by Bureau spokesmen, to join the attack upon judges. For example, in hearings before House subcommittees in 1961 and 1962 on the matter of budget appropriations for the Bureau, there was reiteration of the Bureau's claim, by Henry L. Giordano and by Harry J. Anslinger, that judicial leniency was primarily responsible for ineffective narcotic law enforcement.[6] Representatives John R. Pillion, J. Vaughn Gary, and Otto E. Passman strongly supported this stand, expressing vehement hostility to federal judges and evidently elaborating and extending their points in "off the record" discussions with the Bureau spokesmen. Pillion, for example, remarked:

> Where you find agents who risk their lives and perform intensive investigations and dig up and produce evidence sufficient to convict, then you find a "blockhead" on the bench who practically destroys the worthwhileness of this work, and I sat on the bench for many years. The leniency and the overindulgence for some of our criminals on the part of judges is a disgrace.[7]

POLICE COMPLAINTS CONCERNING THE COURTS

To illustrate some of the other typical criticisms which policemen make of courts and judges we will turn to remarks offered by Lt. T. T. Brown of the Oakland, California, Police Department in a recent book.[8] In some respects Brown's views are untypical, for he disapproves of long mandatory sentences and is willing to allow judges to exercise their discretion in fixing sentences. He also observes that the "light" sentences sometimes imposed upon narcotics offenders are frequently recommended by the police as rewards for underworld informers, who, he concedes, supply the information on which about 90 per cent of the prosecutions are based.[9] Nevertheless, Lt. Brown in other respects shares many views commonly expressed by police officials. Like federal narcotics officials, he is disposed to refer to nonpolicemen with views different from his as "self-styled experts" or "do-gooders."

Lt. Brown grudgingly concedes that the Supreme Court of the United States and the Bill of Rights of the Constitution have their legitimate places and functions in the American way of life.[10] However, he complains of a too liberal interpretation of the constitutional guarantees by the present Supreme Court, which, he says, has "taken vigorous steps to suppress any freedom of action of law enforcement officers. . . . The precious protection promised by the Bill of Rights has practically licensed the seller of dope," he adds.[11] He remarks in summary:

In countless other ways the decisions of the courts have gladdened the hearts of the criminals, hampered law enforcement in making arrests, placed unreasonable limitations on the police in the interrogation of suspects, and the introduction into evidence of voluntary and truthful confessions of criminals: All because the courts put "the freedoms" above common sense, justice, and fear of minority segments whose underlying motives are subversive and not the advocacy of democracy.[12]

Lt. Brown concedes that drug addicts should be handled medically and that they cannot be properly treated in prison. Nevertheless, he sees nothing amiss in using them as informers. The narcotics racket, he suggests, is a dirty one which must be handled with dirty methods. Known informers, he observes, are frequently murdered, beaten, stabbed, and otherwise manhandled by those whom they betray. Lt. Brown does not provide his readers with any exact or detailed account of how addict informers are dealt with by the police or how they are used in making cases. He complains that narcotics violations differ from other criminal activity in that the police do not have the help of a "victim" in preparing the case. The general public is rarely aware of drug law violations and even when an ordinary citizen knows of one he ordinarily prefers not to become involved. Narcotics offenses, it is strongly suggested, should be given special consideration and the usual rules pertaining to police actions should be relaxed.[13]

Concern over the protection of the police stool pigeon causes Lt. Brown to list as "disastrous decisions" a number of cases in which the courts ruled that the informer's identity had to be revealed in court when such disclosure is "relevant and helpful to the defense of the accused or essential to a fair determination of a case."[14] Brown wants to preserve the anonymity of the "faceless informer" in narcotics cases, and if this is done what will prevent an expansion of the practice? It will be recalled that during the McCarthy era federal employees sometimes lost their jobs on the basis of information from unidentified sources and that public reaction against this has been strong. As the penalties for narcotics offenses have been increased it is inevitable and quite understandable that the courts should become a little more fussy than before about unidentified informers, especially when they are known and conceded to be among the lowest types found in the underworld.

Another complaint made by Lt. Brown has to do with the so-called federal "exclusionary rule" which prevents the use in court of evidence obtained by illegal means. Brown notes that the California Supreme Court adopted this rule in 1955 in the Cahan case, and, like many other California police officers, he deplores this fact.[15] Instead of stressing the notion that the police ought to obtain evidence by legal means, emphasis is placed upon the notion that the courts should overlook police violations of the rules in the prosecution of the accused. Brown offers the wholly futile suggestion that police officers should be discouraged from violating the laws of arrest, search and seizure etc., not by freeing the accused but by prosecuting the individual policeman. He repeatedly suggests that courts ought to trust the police more than they do.

The general impression created by Brown's discussion is that almost the only obstacles that stand in the way of locking up the key figures of the dope traffic are the courts and the Bill of Rights. He notes that in California, as elsewhere, a large proportion of arrests are not followed by convictions but fails to explain that most of these arrests are of addicts and insignificant street peddlers and that some of them are probably so flagrantly illegal that convictions would be impossible except in a "kangaroo court." California legislators, he notes, were told that very few important illicit drug distributors are to be found in the California prisons.[16] Brown suggests that this is because such offenders are sent to federal prisons, but the inquiring student who looks for these bigshots in federal prisons will find that they are not there either. The facts are that big dealers are not often in prison simply because the police do not often apprehend them and do not know who they are. This is a point which Lt. Brown did not make.

A PROSECUTOR'S VERSION OF NARCOTICS LAW ENFORCEMENT

A sounder and more logical evaluation of narcotics law administration than that of the *Los Angeles Times* was presented in 1955 to the Senate subcommittee under Price Daniel by Warren Olney III, who was Assistant Attorney General in charge of the Criminal Division of the Department of Justice which prosecuted federal narcotics cases. Mr. Olney's comments apply to the federal courts only and they pertain to the 1951 legislation known as the "Boggs amendment." Since that time, the 1956 Narcotic Control Act has increased penalties even further and imposed additional restrictions on judges.

The difficulties in narcotics law enforcement stressed by Mr. Olney bear no resemblance to those emphasized in the *Los Angeles Times* editorial:

Because of the various presumptions of guilt arising from the possession of narcotics in several of the narcotics statutes, the prosecution of narcotic violators, once they have been apprehended, actually presents no great problem.

As a matter of fact, it is our opinion that narcotics violators are frequently convicted on evidence that would not suffice in most other types of cases. . . .

The problems we do encounter seem to stem directly or indirectly from the fact that the present penalties are heavy and that the courts have little or no discretion in imposing sentences.

One problem we have noted more frequently in recent months is the reluctance of some courts to convict or affirm convictions where the mandatory sentence appears to be out of line with the circumstances in a particular case. The same penalties are applicable to the vicious, despicable, bigtime racketeering violator as to the pitiful victim of the sordid business who has become ensnared by it and has found it necessary to become a small-time pusher or peddler of the drug to satisfy his own addiction, or to the ill-fated physician who becomes involved and resorts to various illegal stratagems to obtain drugs for himself.[17]

Mr. Olney took note of the problems created by the use of addict stool pigeons and hinted of illegal police practices:

Another problem inherent in many cases is the nature of the witnesses frequently necessary to the Government's case; that is, the informer or so-called special employee who is used to make the buy and who is also often a narcotic-law violator or addict himself.

Of course, enforcement necessarily requires the use of witnesses of that type. However, it has been pretty generally recognized by the courts and apparently by the juries that the Government must rely on this type of person rather than the good citizen who has no dealing with narcotics. . . . The real difficulty, if any, lies in enforcement and in apprehending the more important violator who is most elusive.

When he is caught, he rarely escapes punishment, even though the evidence is not always as strong as might be desirable.

I think perhaps that last sentence would be more accurate if I said, "When he is brought into court he rarely escapes punishment." There are a very considerable number—in my judgment, too many—who are caught but are never brought into court, for the reason that it is apparent on the face of things that there is something irregular about the manner of arrest or the manner of obtaining evidence which would make bringing them into court useless.[18]

Mr. Olney, in the last part of the above statement, takes note of the difficulty of apprehending important violators and hints of police tendencies to use illegal methods to secure evidence and to make illegal arrests. The police have consistently blamed judges for the failure to convict, but Mr. Olney's statement indicates that the real blame is probably more often that of the police and the prosecutor. If the evidence presented in court is insufficient, or if illegal methods have been used by the police, the defendant cannot be convicted without debasing the law. It is the sworn duty of a judge to see that trials are fairly conducted, that police and prosecutors themselves do not violate the law, and that defendants are convicted according to due process of law and on the basis of evidence. They cannot be convicted simply on beliefs and suppositions or because of evil reputation.

Mr. Olney also commented on some of the undesirable consequences of the high mandatory penalties:

Not strictly a prosecution problem, but nevertheless one which is frequently presented to the Criminal Division for explanation and resolution, is a difficulty stemming from the minimum and the mandatory penalty provisions of the Boggs Act. . . .

One judge, in a letter to the Department, sought advice as to whether there might be some legal way of reducing a sentence of 5 years which he had imposed upon a second offender. In that case, the defendant had been found guilty of purchasing two quarter grains of morphine sulphate. There was no evidence that he had ever engaged in the sale of narcotics; he had simply been an addict for several years. He had previously pled guilty to a charge of purchasing morphine in the same way for which he had served 18 months. The court was extremely reluctant to impose the minimum term of 5 years required in the case of second offenders under the act. It was necessary in that case to advise the court that there was absolutely no way in which a legal sentence other than a minimum jail term of 5 years could be imposed.

Furthermore, the minimum mandatory provisions of the Boggs Act may, at times, even thwart the rehabilitative process. This possibility was demonstrated not too long ago in the southern district of New York where the court desired to impose consecutive sentences upon the defendant, who had been convicted under several counts of an indictment. The court desired to grant probation on the subsequent term for the purpose of keeping control of the defendant after service of his jail sentence, and thus insure his reincarceration in the event he committed any offense during the 5-year period after his release.

Such a sentence, however, would have been illegal inasmuch as the defendant, being a subsequent offender, was subject to no other sentence upon conviction than a jail term. Although the court had the right to make that term run concurrently with the terms imposed on the other counts, it did not have the authority to impose a consecutive term and order probation thereon to commence at the expiration of the other jail sentence.

Thus the action of the court was so restricted that the rehabilitation of the defendant was somewhat less assured than had the court been authorized to proceed as it desired.

Furthermore, under the present provisions of the act, a first offender must be imprisoned for a term of at least 2 years unless he is granted probation. This results quite frequently in the courts granting probation to first offenders, although were it not for the mandatory provisions of the act, the courts would probably be inclined to impose a jail sentence of something less than the 2-year minimum. . . .

We have run into, as I have mentioned here, practical resistance on the part of certain judges in certain areas to following the provisions of the Boggs Act. We have had the experience of the United States Attorney pointing out to the judge what the law requires in the way of minimum sentence at the time of sentence, only to have the court impose a jail sentence for a far less term, maybe a half of what the law says it should be, but doing that knowing full well that the defendant will never object and is not going to appeal, and that the Government can't appeal; there is nothing we can do about it.

It isn't a healthy situation at all to have a law that is so rigid in its provisions that judges feel that they have got to disregard its plain language in order to come out with what they think is a just result.[19]

In cases of the sort described, in which the minimum penalty prescribed by the law is obviously unjust and excessively severe, the question naturally arises as to why the defendant was tried under this penalty provision. Prosecutors and police can, at their discretion, turn a defendant over to nonfederal courts where the penalties are lower, charge him with a lesser offense and overlook prior convictions. The fact that they do not do so in certain instances may be explained by the desire to punish the defendant for not "cooperating" with the enforcement officials.

Federal cases may be transferred to lower courts for a variety of reasons. In some instances it may be done to secure a lighter sentence to reward an informer; in others to secure a heavier one when state laws are more severe than the federal. In other instances, the consequences of illegal and irregular practices by federal agents may be avoided by transferring the case to a state court. Cases may also be transferred from state to federal courts for this reason. State and federal agents frequently cooperate in handling of important cases so that prosecution may be handled in either the state or federal courts depending upon the advantages to be obtained.

INCREASED PENALTIES, GUILTY PLEAS, AND APPEALS

The criminal who knows that he faces extremely severe penalties upon apprehension and conviction tends to take unusual precautions to avoid arrest and is more likely to resort to violence either against the police or against the informer who has betrayed him. When apprehended, he exerts greater effort to avoid conviction and appeals his case whenever he has a chance and possesses the necessary means. Under the system of mandatory penalties, offenders are aware of the tendency of judges to impose the minimum sentence in a large percentage of the cases. This causes them to feel that there is no point in a plea of guilty, and that they have everything to gain and nothing to lose by fighting the case to the limit and carrying it to the higher courts whenever possible. Mr. Olney made the following observations concerning this tendency:

Another problem, if it can be so designated, is the more frequent and vigorous defenses waged, especially by second and third offenders facing long prison terms if convicted. While less than 13 per cent of the offenders disposed of in the fiscal year 1950 elected to face trial, approximately 22 per cent did so in 1953 and 1954.

There appears to have been a corresponding increase in the number of appeals and the number of motions to vacate sentence by persons convicted and those who have pleaded guilty. These contests raise all possible legal defenses, particularly entrapment and illegal search.[20]

Statistical data presented by Mr. Olney seem to indicate a clear trend in this direction after the 1951 Boggs Act.[21]

Year	Number of Defendants	Those Acquitted	Those Dismissed	Guilty Pleas	Tried and Convicted
1950	2,400	80	184	1,907	229
1951	2,332	70	234	1,745	283
1952	2,121	68	184	1,523	346
1953	2,336	96	237	1,589	414
1954	2,220	71	239	1,491	419

The last two columns indicate that, while the total number of defendants on federal narcotics charges remained fairly constant there was a steady tendency for guilty pleas to diminish and for the number demanding trial to increase. This trend, of course, makes more work for the courts. It has probably been intensified by the 1956 law.

It is obvious that if all persons charged with crime were to exercise their constitutional rights to the full by pleading not guilty and demanding a jury trial, this would create an impossible logjam in the courts. In order to induce defendants to plead guilty in a substantial portion of the cases it is ordinarily regarded as necessary that they be rewarded with shorter sentences for doing so. This implies, on the other hand, that an accused person who elects to demand jury trial, thus putting the state to a great deal of inconvenience and expense, should receive little consideration when he is sentenced after a jury has found him guilty. If a relatively minor narcotics offender is convicted for the first time in a federal court for a selling offense he is very likely to be sentenced to the minimum of five years without parole regardless of whether he pleads guilty or not. Hence, there is no incentive in this situation for "copping a plea." It is better for the defendant, if he can afford it, to fight the case and to hire a sharp criminal lawyer who will drag it out over a long period of time hoping that the prosecution will make mistakes which will benefit his client. Even if the latter is ultimately convicted the sentence may still be for the same five years. If the prosecution has made serious mistakes or if there is a question of illegal police practices the case may be successfully appealed. In any case the defendant has little to lose except money and he may gain his freedom.

To carry out the legal strategy that offers the highest probability of beating the rap calls for the expenditure of money. The addict invariably has no money and is rarely able to hire a competent attorney to defend him in court. A lawyer who had to depend solely upon addicts as clients would, if he did not actually starve to death, certainly make a meager living.

This is probably a basic reason for the lack of attention given the problems of addiction by the appellate courts, by the legal profession, and by legal scholars. The latter are primarily concerned with opinions of the higher appellate courts, to which cases involving addicts rarely come. Competent defense lawyers would much rather represent drug peddlers than drug users because the former can afford to pay substantial fees and the latter cannot. This is also no doubt the reason for the fact that the higher courts devote a disproportionately large part of their time to cases involving the defenses of entrapment and illegal search and seizure in prosecutions of narcotics peddlers and very little time to issues pertaining to the legal rights of addicts.

UPGRADING OF NARCOTICS OFFENSES:
MISDEMEANOR TO FELONY

Part of the trend toward heavier punishment for narcotics offenders on the state level is represented by upgrading misdemeanors to the felony level.[22] A misdemeanor is ordinarily subject to a maximum sentence of twelve months in jail and legislatures consequently assume that if they, for example, change possession of narcotics from a misdemeanor to a felony, the offense of illegal possession will be more severely punished. The argument for increasing the penalty is often that it is easier to prove possession than sale and that when possession is merely a misdemeanor actual peddlers who can be convicted only of possession escape with light sentences. By upgrading possession it thus becomes possible to punish a defendant as a peddler without having to demonstrate in court that he actually is one. State legislatures are extremely impressed by this arrangement because they generally believe that, regardless of the evidence available in court, the police know in advance who the peddlers are.

Changing possession from a misdemeanor to a felony, however, has effects of a self-defeating nature which legislatures usually ignore. Felony prosecutions, for example, take much more time and require the police to spend a great deal more time in court. Misdemeanor cases are usually disposed of within a day or two of arrest with a minimum of legal ceremony and without the necessity of providing attorneys for indigent defendants. A felony prosecution may require a preliminary hearing, a grand jury hearing, an arraignment and a trial at which the indigent defendant may have to be provided with an attorney at public expense.[23] While the policeman appears in court only once in the misdemeanor proceedings, he may have to appear several times in the course of a felony prosecution. Policemen are usually poorly paid for this time spent in court. A felony court (usually a county or district court) pays much more attention to legal formalities and rules than does the misdemeanor court (usually a municipal or police court). The net effect of increased severity of punishment is thus, that its certainty is diminished as the probabilities of acquittal because of "technicalities" are increased. It is a recognized legal principle that the more punitive a law the greater will be the emphasis upon a literal interpretation of the law and strict adherence to the procedural rules and the greater will be the tendency to resolve all doubtful matters in favor of the accused.

More important, perhaps, than the above considerations is the fact that the extra effort and time which felony proceedings cost the police will inevitably lead them to make fewer arrests for possession than would be the case if it were a misdemeanor. Because the number of police officers and the time at their disposal is limited, they of necessity adapt themselves to such changes in the law so that actual police routine and total arrests remain fairly constant. With possession defined as a felony, fewer possession charges will be filed and a larger proportion of actual possession cases will be prosecuted on lesser charges, such as loitering, addiction, vagrancy, and any others which continue to be classified as misdemeanors. The net effect is that approximately the same numbers of offenders are arrested and sent to jail or prison with about the same sentences as before, the only difference being that the labels have been changed. The addict who last year was sent to jail for six months for possession may now be sent to jail for six months as a "disorderly person."

Extremely high minimum penalties for sale of illicit drugs produce similar effects upon the machinery of law enforcement. Michigan, for example, has found that the effect of a 20-year minimum penalty for sale in that state has been to make it difficult to convict.[24] By common consent, judges, prosecutors, and others col-

laborate in avoiding the imposition of this severe penalty by allowing defendants to plead guilty to lesser charges. Over a period of a
number of years in Detroit it is reported that of more than 400
arrests for sale less than 4 per cent were convicted for that offense—
most of the others being permitted to plead guilty to the lesser
charge of possession. It has been reported that unsophisticated defendants who offer to plead guilty to charges of peddling drugs in
Michigan courts sometimes find that the judge will refuse to accept the pleas and, instead, have someone explain prevailing practices to the naïve offender.

Upgrading narcotics offenses from the misdemeanor to the felony level, and increasing penalties generally, thus may have the
effect of drastically changing arrest and conviction rates for certain types of offenses without in actuality changing the total narcotics situation in any material way. Regardless of whether the
number of addicts in a community is increasing or decreasing,
sharp upgrading of offenses and heavy increases in penalties are
virtually certain to reduce convictions and arrests, thus creating
a pleasant statistical mirage. The police are not likely to complain
in this situation because public criticism of them is quieted and
because the heavy penalties give them increased leverage in bargaining with narcotic offenders.

The tendency for customary police practices to continue regardless of changes in the law is illustrated in the opposite direction by
the effects in California of the U.S. Supreme Court's nullification
in 1962 of a California statute defining addiction as a punishable
offense (*Robinson* v. *California*). The Court in this case reaffirmed
its view that addiction is a disease, not a crime. Statistical reports
from the California State Department of Justice suggest that the
main effect of the decision has been that addicts who were formerly arrested as users are now arrested on other charges.[25] The
effect of the decision, be it noted, was definitely *not* that of com-
pelling California to handle addiction as a disease.

THE PROSECUTOR

It has been indicated that recent narcotics legislation has increased the powers of prosecutors at the expense of judges. The reader may inquire if this is not perfectly appropriate and desirable. Can't prosecutors be trusted to use these powers wisely and in the public interest? The answer to this question is an emphatic and unqualified "No, they cannot." It is wrong in principle and vicious in practice to give the prosecutor the power of a judge, for the prosecutor in our system of justice is one of the two contending parties. To give him control of the trial and the power to determine the penalty is the equivalent, on the personal level, of permitting a person who accuses you of doing him wrong to decide whether or not you are guilty and to determine the appropriate punishment.

It is generally recognized by students of the American system of criminal justice that the prosecutor almost completely dominates the nonfederal judicial system. A noted criminologist has made the following observations:

The prosecutor determines whether a particular case shall be prosecuted. He determines whether a compromise shall be accepted, which generally means a plea of guilty to a lesser offense in return for a recommendation for mitigation of penalty. He is responsible for the organization and presentation of evidence before the court, and upon his efficiency in doing this the decision of the court depends. He is generally very influential in regard to the disposition of cases, suggesting to the judge or jury the appropriate penalty. In fact, he is almost the absolute ruler of the whole judicial process.

At the same time this prosecutor is generally elected and, as is true of other elected officers, he secures his position primarily as a favor of the political machine. Explicitly or implicitly this means subservience to the wishes of politicians, and it means also distraction of attention from his official business for the sake of political activities; he must be careful not to antagonize any large organized group. Also, his record must show a large proportion of convictions in cases which go to trial. It is customary in elections for the prosecutor to present statistics on this point. . . .

The assistant prosecutors, also, secure their positions in many cases because they have been active in political organizations, although in some communities the bar association urges and assists the voters to make selections on the basis of efficiency. The assistant prosecutors are generally inexperienced in this work at the time they are appointed and are dismissed when the administration changes. Responsibility for their work is generally not definitely located and their work is usually not well organized. In the inferior courts the assistant prosecutors generally make little preparation and even when the case comes into court they pay little attention, except in spectacular cases.[26]

The Wickersham Report makes the following statement concerning the prosecutor:

The system of prosecutors elected for short terms, with assistants chosen on the basis of political patronage, with no assured tenure, yet charged with wide undefined power, is ideally adapted to misgovernment.[27]

The power of the prosecutor in narcotics cases is even more absolute than it is in ordinary criminal prosecutions because of high minimum mandatory penalties, which, as we have seen, transfer powers from judges to prosecutors. In the large metropolitan centers where narcotics cases are numerous they are handled as a rule by inexperienced prosecuting attorneys of the type described above. These assistants view their service in the prosecutor's office as an opportunity to acquire trial experience and to move on to other and better jobs. They do not ordinarily have any special information or training pertaining to the drug problem and because of the temporary nature of their jobs they are not interested in acquiring it. With prosecutors in general they share the "batting average" theory that they should seek the highest possible proportion of convictions and the longest possible sentences. In theory, the prosecutor, as an agent of the state, is interested in ascertaining the facts and doing justice; in practice, he is often most concerned with winning cases, getting publicity, making money, and acquiring trial experience.

Under these circumstances it is easy to understand that the prosecutor handling narcotics cases in the big cities works closely with the police and, to a large extent, shares the police viewpoint. The inexperienced assistant assigned to narcotics cases for the first time learns the routine procedures from the police, who know them better than he does. It is to his advantage, both politically and personally, to cooperate closely with them.

Under existing circumstances the main limitation upon the prosecutor's enormous powers in narcotics cases is represented by a competent defense counsel who is prepared to appeal the case if necessary. Since it is only the bigger peddlers who ordinarily have sufficient funds to engage such lawyers, these offenders are in a position to take advantage of the assistant prosecutor's inexperience and lack of preparation. The ordinary addict-defendant is either not represented by counsel at all or is represented by the shyster type who more than matches the assistant prosecutor in inefficiency and lack of preparation. Representation by counsel of this type often does the defendant more harm than good by irritating the judge. Defense lawyers of this type cannot afford, because of the small fees, to make a protracted defense or to carry the case to an appellate court and are usually not interested in doing so. As a result, addicts are routinely and easily convicted and the prosecutor has only to worry about the relatively infrequent cases involving important peddlers who are represented in court by well-paid, competent, and often unscrupulous counsel. Illegal police practices and mistakes and inefficiency of prosecutors fairly frequently prevent the successful prosecution of such cases but they make little difference with addict defendants and minor peddlers, who make up the bulk of the cases which fatten the prosecution's batting average.

While there are, no doubt, some prosecutors who recognize the inequities involved in the present system, they seem to be few in number and they rarely express themselves forcibly in public on this matter. Those who have done so have usually been federal prosecutors, who are appointed rather than elected, and who represent a higher level of responsibility and competence than that of the average state or local prosecutor. It is unreasonable to expect prosecutors to object to a system which gives them the enormous power and virtually unlimited discretion which they now enjoy. In the hearings before congressional subcommittees, many prosecuting attorneys testified. With very few exceptions they joined with the police in attacking the judiciary branch, and in supporting measures designed to increase their already enormous powers.

We are concerned here with the system rather than with individuals, for there are individual prosecutors in this country, especially perhaps outside the large cities, to whom the usual generalizations do not apply. However, as the prevalence of the expression "the prosecutor's complex" suggests, it is difficult for a person who specializes in sending people to jail and prison not to be influenced by his occupation, just as it is difficult not to enjoy the exercise of power. It is interesting that in the last few years, reacting to the demand for a medical approach to addiction, programs of compulsory civil commitment have been devised in New York and California largely by prosecutors, and that these plans shift some responsibility but no real power to physicians.

A MISCARRIAGE OF JUSTICE

The case involving Max Kaplan and Nathan Kaplan originated in New York in 1937.[28] Max was a heroin salesman and Nathan a shirt salesman. The two became confused with each other because of a possibly perjured identification of Nathan by a prostitute who was a drug addict. The two men closely resembled each other in appearance. Max was originally indicted for the crime; later the theory was developed that Nathan was also involved, and he was arrested. Nathan protested his innocence and fought the charge against him as vigorously as he could. He was nevertheless convicted in a jury trial and sentenced to twelve years in the federal prison at Milan, Michigan.

Shortly after the sentencing, Max, who was being sought by the police and was also thought to have been involved, consulted his lawyer, gave himself up, and, no doubt as a result of a bargaining process in which he agreed to "cop a plea," was sentenced to prison for 18 months for the same crime for which Nathan was already doing time. Max was sent to the same prison as Nathan, but the latter became aware of his presence there too late to establish contact with him before Max was released. When Nathan completed his twelve-year sentence he returned to New York to look for Max in order to clear himself. Max had indicated at the time he was sentenced that he alone had committed the crime and that Nathan had not been involved.

After several years of search, during which Nathan had difficulty finding regular work because of his prison record, he did finally find Max. The latter, after consulting his lawyer, gave Nathan the affidavit he asked for, proving, along with other evidence, that he was innocent of the crime. When Nathan took this evidence to court, the judge who heard it agreed that he was innocent, but after a long delay concluded that no legal remedy existed and suggested that Nathan apply for a pardon. After a delay of a year or more the request for pardon was denied. The case, which originated in 1937, was terminated eighteen years later in 1955 by the refusal of a pardon.

There are a number of interesting features of this case which deserve consideration. (1) Nathan's sentence was ten and one-half years longer than that of Max because he, being innocent, demanded his constitutional right to jury trial and fought against conviction, whereas Max, being guilty, pleaded guilty and thus saved the state the necessity of trying him. The question raised is that of judging what constitutes a reasonable reward for "copping a plea" and what is a reasonable punishment for not doing so. (2) There were at Nathan's trial three persons who might have identified him. Two of these said they had never seen him before, while the third, an addicted prostitute, identified him as the person who had handled the illicit heroin involved in the transaction. While the two Kaplans did resemble each other it seems probable that the informer may have insisted on her identification for the sake of the reward offered her by her police employers, who, it may be assumed, were sincerely convinced of Nathan's guilt. (3) No explanation is offered for the refusal of a pardon and one may only speculate concerning the reasons. Nathan Kaplan had, twelve years earlier, in 1925, been convicted of a narcotics offense for which he had been placed on probation. This incident allegedly frightened him enough to cause him to turn away from the narcotics racket and from criminal activity in general. If the pardoning authority consulted the Federal Bureau of Narcotics that agency would probably have advised against a pardon in line with its policy of no leniency for dope peddlers. (4) The prosecutor who sent Nathan to prison admitted *eleven years later* that he had suspected, when Max confessed to the crime and said that Nathan was not involved, that the latter should not have been prosecuted. However, he did nothing about it.

UNEQUAL ENFORCEMENT

Judges of lower courts have sometimes commented upon the singular absence in their courts of well-to-do addicts, such as those from the medical profession. Such persons are sometimes prosecuted, it is true, but often they are not. Sometimes they may be given a chance, or several chances, to cure themselves of their habits before they are prosecuted, or the addict's doctor may be privately assured by an agent that no action will be taken against him if he provides the addict with drugs. This form of what in effect is legalized addiction in the upper social strata has probably increased in prevalence as the legally prescribed penalties have become increasingly severe.

G. H. Stevenson, a Canadian physician and student of the drug problem, commented as follows upon this tendency:

> . . . we have one law for the slum-born or underprivileged addict, the socially handicapped addict, and another for the professional addict . . . there are physicians, nurses, druggists and dentists and veterinarians who are drug addicts who never get into jail, the excuse offered being that the doctor has a license to be in possession of narcotic drugs, but he's an addict for exactly the same reason that the socially handicapped person is an addict. . . . But the physician addict is treated by the law and the narcotics division and the police with the greatest consideration and gentleness, in marked contrast to the way the socially handicapped addict is used by the law and the police. . . . But, as a physician, I resent the fact that we physicians and other professional people are given preferred treatment as compared with the socially handicapped people, even though we have had many advantages in our homes and training and education in the narcotic habit. . . . If compulsory treatment is to be applied it should be applied to both groups equally. If punishment in prison is to be applied it should be applied to both groups equally, modifying the law if need be to see that both groups are treated equally, in contrast to the extreme leniency now shown the professional group and the extreme severity now shown to the socially handicapped.[29]

The Canadian expert did not, however, seem to be able to make up his mind as to whether the socially handicapped should be treated more leniently or the professionals more severely.

The tendency to be easy on addicts from the middle and upper classes and the medical profession is probably even more pronounced in the United States than it is in Canada, because penalties for narcotics offenses are more severe and inflexible in the United States. Many enforcement officials regard addicts essen-

tially as sick persons rather than criminals. When the addict is a
well-to-do professional man, such as a physician or lawyer, and is
well spoken and well educated, prosecutors, policemen, and judges
alike are especially strongly inclined to regard him as an "unfortunate" or as a "victim" of something like a disease. The harsh penalties of the law, it is felt, were surely not intended for a person like
this, and, by an unspoken agreement, arrangements are quietly
made to exempt him from such penalties.

Outstanding examples of such favored treatment of users from
the upper classes are provided by Mr. Anslinger, former head of
the Bureau of Narcotics, who, according to his own account, arranged to keep an addicted member of Congress, as well as a prominent Washington society lady who was addicted to demerol, out
of the hands of the police.[30] At lower levels, it is common for narcotics agents not to arrest doctors or nurses who are addicted, but
to turn them over to the medical profession. A narcotics agent in
the Toledo area frankly reported to his superiors that 18 physicians,
druggists, and nurses in his care were not prosecuted but "were
treated for addiction in lieu of prosecution."[31] Common justifica-
tions offered for this practice are that these addicted nurses and
doctors do not resort to serious crime to obtain drugs and that they
are valuable and productive members of the community. The only
reason that users in the medical profession do not commit the
crimes against property which other addicts do, is, of course, that
drugs are available to them from medical sources.

THE CHICAGO NARCOTICS COURT

The Chicago Narcotics Court may be considered as an example
of the way in which drug offenders of the ordinary sort are currently dealt with in many of our larger cities. We have already referred to the common police practice of arresting addicts on sight.
In Chicago there were, at the time I observed the court in action,

in addition to the usual statutes concerning possession and sale of illicit drugs, other state laws or city ordinances which provided punishment for addicts who loitered, who were found in possession of a hypodermic needle, who had failed to register as addicts, and who had registered but did not have their identification cards.

The Narcotics Court served both as a summary trial court and as a court of preliminary hearing for cases to be prosecuted later in the county criminal court. Cases of this latter type usually involved selling offenses and the defendants either engaged their own lawyers or had lawyers provided for them, if need be, in the county court. Most of the cases in the Narcotics Court, however, involved addicts—about nine of every ten of whom were Negroes—who were tried summarily and either acquitted, fined, or sent to jail by the judge. By special dispensation of the Illinois legislature, this court, although a misdemeanor court, was permitted to impose a jail sentence of as much as five years plus a maximum fine of $5,000.

The addicts processed in this court were as a rule not represented by counsel and were not entitled to court-appointed counsel if they were indigent. This fact alone tended to eliminate the right to appeal, since errors at a trial must ordinarily be objected to at the time if an appeal is to be made. Some addicts secured the services of a number of fly-by-night courthouse lawyers who circulated about the building and accepted cases for small fees, depending upon volume of business rather than quality to make their living.

As many as from 8,000 to 9,000 cases have been handled in this court in a single year, and sometimes there were more than 100 cases on a single day's docket. Nevertheless, the court was ordinarily cleared and all cases disposed of before one o'clock in the afternoon. Defendants, witnesses, lawyers, and prosecutors huddled before the judge's bench during a trial so that scarcely a word was audible to anyone not directly involved in the case. Defendants were disposed of rapidly, often convicted on the basis of scant evidence or with no evidence at all or simply on the word of a policeman. In some instances groups of young Negro males who had been picked up for "loitering" were found guilty as a group even though evidence to prove that they were addicts was not produced. Little attention was paid to the niceties of legal procedure, or to the rules of evidence, and no attention at all to illegal police practices such as illegal arrest and search and third-degree practices. The judge and the prosecutor stated that some of the statutes on which they were convicting defendants were unconstitutional, although they had never been tested, probably because if a defendant charged under one of these laws had a competent lawyer it was simpler to discharge him. As pointed out earlier, State's Attorney Gutknecht told the congressional committee that most of the addicts brought into the Narcotics Court had been arrested illegally.[32]

The officials of the court were low-level political appointees, none of whom was acquainted with the literature on addiction and very few of whom had more than a routine knowledge of the relevant law. The prosecutor stated his philosophy quite simply and briefly, namely, to send every defendant to jail for as long as possible. Visitors in the court markedly influenced the sentences handed out. When reporters and photographers from the Chicago newspapers were present, for example, more defendants were found guilty on less evidence than usual.

Writing from his experience with addicts of the type who are hustled through the Chicago Narcotics Court in record numbers, Nelson Algren has aptly summarized the legal status of the drug addict in most of our large cities:

The known addict lives in a totally lawless world, a man or woman with no rights at all, and an all-day dread of being locked up all night. You can turn out his pockets on the open street, walk into his home without a warrant, lock him up without bothering to book him, change the charge against him without informing him, send him to trial without a lawyer, and convict him on another addict's word.[33]

The Narcotics Court of Chicago was the first court of this type to be established in this country, and was hailed by some who did not know how it operated as a significant forward step in dealing with the drug problem. It was actually a kind of legal travesty in which all of the shortcomings of the present system of handling the drug problem and the injustice of current laws were illustrated in concentrated form. Respectable members of the legal profession usually knew nothing of it and never visited it.

The handling of drug addicts in city courts resembles reasonably closely the manner in which "vagrants" and "disorderly persons" are dealt with. Police, prosecutors, and judges know that any active addict brought before them must ordinarily be guilty of property crimes as well as of offenses against the narcotics laws. They are therefore inclined to assume guilt regardless of the quality of the evidence if addiction is admitted or known or if the defendant has been in court on prior occasions. Under these circumstances it is easy to understand the desire of these officials to send addicts to jail, since little else can be done with them under present conditions. Even in these courts there are many judges and other officials who regard addiction as a kind of disease akin to alcoholism, and who would be happy to be able to send the user to a hospital rather than a jail. Since medical facilities for the treatment of ordinary addicts are virtually nonexistent, the practical alternatives are to send the addict to jail or to let him go free to resume his habit. Hence, legal "technicalities" are sacrificed in order to get the addict off the streets. If the law is debased in the process this is commonly regarded as a fair price to pay for a desirable practical result.

NARCOTICS OFFENDERS IN PRISONS

In the following chapter it is indicated that the number of federal prosecutions for narcotics offenses declined between 1950 and 1960. During the same period, because of lengthened sentences and the denial of probation and parole, the number of prisoners confined for narcotics violations has increased sharply. The Federal Bureau of Prisons reports the number of prisoners serving sentences for these offenses as follows from 1950 to 1960:[34]

1950	2,017	1956	3,181
1951	2,264	1957	3,306
1952	2,713	1958	3,500
1953	3,114	1959	3,672
1954	3,184	1960	4,187
1955	3,241		

The Bureau of Prisons has repeatedly warned that this increase in the number of narcotics offenders in federal prisons has undesirable consequences because a large proportion of these prisoners are not eligible for parole and create custodial problems. In 1957 the Bureau commented as follows upon this problem:

. . . the 1956 law bars most persons convicted under it not only from the possibility of being placed on probation, but also from eligibility to parole consideration. Now for the first time since 1910, when the Federal parole law was originally enacted, a group of prisoners in federal institutions face no prospects of parole—no prospect of advancing their release dates except through statutory good time or executive clemency. This no-parole group in federal prisons numbered 479 at the year end, of whom a considerable number were serving extremely long sentences including one serving a life sentence. [At the close of the next year, 1958, this total of 479 had increased to 1,394.] This latter offender will be denied the privilege accorded other prisoners under life sentences of being considered for parole after 15 years. He and others who may receive comparable sentences can look forward only to remaining in prison for as long as they live.

This law has serious implications for the future of the Federal prison system. We look forward to an ever-increasing population of drug offenders in our already crowded penitentiaries. Sentences of 10, 15 and 20 years are already becoming common in certain districts, with some as long as 30, 50, and 80 years. There can be no question but that in the future the steady accumulation of long-sentence drug offenders will tax to a maximum the resources of our penitentiaries, particularly those at Atlanta, Leavenworth, and McNeil Island. The changes in prison population which will stem from the enforcement of this law will necessitate modifications of institution programs in which sound correctional practices may have to be subordinated to the needs of long-term custody.[35]

Obviously, similar problems exist in many state, county, and municipal penal establishments in areas where drug offenses are numerous. Lt. Joseph J. Healy of the Chicago Police Force boasted to the Price Daniel subcommittee that many of the Illinois institutions were "loaded" with addicts:

Now we have the house of correction loaded. I was talking to the warden today, and he said the place is loaded with addicts. The county jail is pretty well loaded. And last week at this hearing, there was a State Senator from the State of Illinois who testified as to the prisoners in Joliet; there is pretty close to a thousand addicts down there.[36]

It is noteworthy that some of the officials who must live on a day-to-day basis with the consequences of the present penalty provisions of our narcotics laws, i.e., prison wardens, seem to be strongly opposed to those provisions. From his survey, Senator Thomas J. Dodd, for example, found 92 per cent of the federal wardens opposed to the mandatory minimum penalties and 97 per cent to the denial of probation and parole.[37]

The bare statistics on the number of narcotics offenders in penal institutions, state and federal, do not do justice to the human problems involved. The prisoner serving a long sentence without the possibility of parole feels deprived of hope. He compares himself with rapists, murderers, and other types of criminals who are eligible for parole. Narcotics offenses, even those of peddling drugs, are never exactly alike and often there are mitigating circumstances which ought to be taken into account but cannot be because of the inflexible, mandatory nature of the penalties. The consequence is that unequal crimes are treated equally and there is, among these prisoners, an enormous fund of resentment and bitterness.

Unquestionably the legislators who enacted the 1951 and 1956 statutes had the idea in mind that the harsh punishment prescribed would fall primarily on the professional peddler of drugs. As written, the statutes do not, however, distinguish the professional peddler from one who temporarily succumbs to the temptation of easy money or from the person who is only peripherally and somewhat accidentally involved. Thus a twenty-five-year-old woman in Chicago who was in love with a heroin distributor was asked by him to transport a grip full of heroin. This woman had no prior criminal record and had worked regularly at the same place for a number of years. Being in love, she was willing to do whatever her lover asked her to. One would think that in a case of this kind the wisest social policy would have been to put this girl on probation. Under the law she had to be sentenced to five years in federal prison without the possibility of parole.

At the White House Conference a federal judge told of a Marine lieutenant with an honorable civilian and military record who crossed the border into Mexico, where he became drunk. When he crossed the border a marihuana cigarette was found in his pocket. Despite his blameless record, and despite the fact that he was a married man with a wife and children, he was prosecuted and convicted for transporting marihuana and had to be sentenced to five years in prison with no parole possible, by a reluctant judge.[38]

It is unnecessary to multiply examples of this sort. The laws are tailor-made to produce such results. They are based upon stereotyped thinking about drug peddlers and on the implicit assumption that all drug-selling offenses are essentially the same and that there are no mitigating circumstances.

Many persons who criticize the effects of current laws upon addicts are totally indifferent to what is done with so-called "peddlers" and frequently feel that no punishment is too severe for them.

Despite this common attitude, the question remains whether there exists any kind of criminal offense which is so severe as to justify abandoning the concept of justice in dealing with it.

In view of the large and growing numbers of prisoners serving long sentences in state and federal prisons without the possibility of parole, considering that some of these persons were sentenced with manifest injustice because of the extraordinary character of the laws, and since some of the sentences imposed undoubtedly reflected a kind of temporary mass hysteria generated by sensational and misleading propaganda, it is pertinent to suggest the need to provide relief for some of these prisoners. Certainly the wardens of our prisons would welcome such action.

THE COURTS AND THE PUBLIC

What happens to addicts and other drug offenders in court is a matter of considerable importance in enlisting cooperation and support for the agencies of justice. In general, one would expect that a public which has confidence in its police, its courts, and its laws, and which has learned to expect justice and fair play from these agencies, would cooperate with them in the enforcement process. For example, if the parents of adolescent drug users in our cities felt that it would be in the interests of their addicted sons to report them to the police, they would no doubt do so. The same holds for the members of the medical profession when they become aware of addiction on the part of a nurse or a doctor. The present attitude is largely one of noncooperation because it is felt that arrest and prosecution aggravate the plight of the individual user rather than helping him. The addict is not generally viewed as a criminal person, but as a sick person, and there is general agreement that he is more appropriately handled in hospitals than in jails or prisons. As a consequence, in all strata of our society the friends and relatives of drug users try to keep them from falling into the hands of the police. To be apprehended and processed by the legal system is justifiably regarded as a disaster second only to that of addiction itself.

As we have pointed out in earlier chapters, victims are not distinguished from criminals in this area of enforcement, where there are no natural complaining witnesses who will spontaneously seek the help of the police. The addict, it is felt, needs medical care, but this the police are not in a position to give. Hence the public, or that portion of it which is closest to the addict, withholds cooperation, and the police are forced to get along without what is ordinarily regarded as the indispensable basis of sound enforcement. The demand from the police that they be given special freedom of action in narcotics cases, that constitutional guarantees and the laws of arrest, search, and seizure be relaxed, and that the recruiting and protection of informers be given special legislative and court attention—all of these, no doubt, represent a search for substitutes for the popular support and cooperation which is lacking. The attacks on judges are part of the persistent human tendency to look for scapegoats and to pass the buck. This chapter is intended to suggest that the blame ought to be placed, not on judges or on police or prosecutors, and not on the Bill of Rights, but rather on the control system itself and on the assumptions upon which it is based.

CHAPTER 4

THE NUMBER OF ADDICTS
AND RECRUITMENT PATTERNS

THE number of drug addicts in the United States
has always been an essentially unknown quantity. Before 1914,
when addiction was not a criminal matter, a number of enumerations within states or local communities were made and the results
applied to the United States as a whole. The estimates derived by
these and other methods covered a very wide range, from one hundred thousand or so to more than a million. All of them were admittedly highly unreliable and they do not justify the confident
assertions now being made concerning the extent of addiction in
this country in earlier periods. Bad as they were, the pre-1914 estimates were not as unreliable as those made after that date and those
that are currently circulated.

After 1914, when addiction became a criminal act, counting addicts posed much the same difficulties that would be encountered
in a census of racketeers. The only relevant figures available on a
national basis are those pertaining to arrests, prosecutions, convictions, and commitments, and these are far from being complete or
reliable. The number of addicts arrested annually is not reported,

arrests for narcotics law violations are fully reported only on the federal level, and the number of addicts serving time in penal establishments is unknown. Since the range of estimates of the addicted population at present is at least as great as it was before 1914, one can make out a case for any trend one chooses by judiciously selecting the estimates.

Federal narcotics officials have vigorously promoted the view that the number of addicts has declined drastically over the years in this country. From a total of about 200,000 in 1914 the number of addicts allegedly diminished to about 48,000 or 60,000 during the time of World War II. The former figure of 48,000 was described as an irreducible minimum. In the Bureau's well-known and well-publicized ski-jump curve, discussed later in this chapter, the World War II minimum number of addicts is indicated as about 20,000 although the usual estimates given are 48,000 or 60,000. After the Bureau began its count of addicts (to be discussed later), it abandoned its former estimates and began to utilize numbers generated by its survey as an indication, not of the total addicted population, but of "active addicts"—i.e., persons actually using drugs illegally and reported as such to the Bureau. However, the word "active" is sometimes left out when this total is given, thus enhancing the tendency to view the number, not as a partial count, but as a comprehensive estimate. Thus the United States report to the United Nations Commission on Narcotic Drugs for 1960 states: "There were 44,906 addicts in the United States on the 31 December 1960. . . ."[1]

During the hearings held in 1955 in various sections of the country by the Senate subcommittee chaired by Price Daniel and the House subcommittee under Hale Boggs, the members of the subcommittees were given the 60,000 estimate, which they seemed to accept. As they moved from one part of the country to another they were given estimates by various local officials concerning

numbers of addicts in given counties, states, or cities. These estimates also appear to have been accepted. New York authorities
estimated 20,000, California 20,000, Illinois 10,000, and Ohio 15,000,
making a total of 65,000 drugs users in only four states. These local
estimates were based upon local surveys or upon police files. The
Ohio estimate was the result of a survey conducted in that state
with the assistance of the Federal Bureau of Narcotics. The California estimate was contained in the report of a Citizen's Advisory
Committee to the Attorney General in 1953. It stated:

It is known that we have in our State medical files some 32,000 persons
who are legally using narcotics medicinally, although a certain percentage of them may be using it illegally because they are going to several doctors concurrently. The State criminal files reflect that there
are approximately 10,000 additional traffickers or users of narcotics in
California. It is believed that 10,000 represents approximately one-half
of the total illegal addicts in this State. Our estimated total, therefore,
would be 32,000 medical or legal users and probably 20,000 illegal, a
total of 52,000 persons.[2]

California officials and police officers generally agreed that addiction in that state was probably increasing about as fast as the population. Disregarding the alleged 32,000 legal users, most of whom
were probably not addicts (if the figure itself is not in error), it is
impossible to take the 60,000 estimate for the nation as a whole
seriously in view of reports from individual states and cities. It is
of interest to observe that some twenty years earlier in 1931 a State
Narcotic Committee estimated that there were about 3,000 addicts
in California.[3]

Figures on narcotics from the state of California are of unusual
importance because the state has an exemplary centralized system
of collecting and processing the relevant data.[4] A Division of Narcotic Enforcement within the State Department of Justice provides

narcotic prescription order forms in triplicate to physicians. It is required that one of the three copies of all narcotic prescriptions be forwarded to the state office, where they are processed. Since these order forms are serially numbered this procedure enables state enforcement authorities to keep a close check on all prescriptions for narcotics and on the persons who receive them.

In addition, the Bureau of Criminal Statistics of the California Department of Justice has recently begun to issue comprehensive reports on arrests and prosecutions for narcotics violations within the state.[5] Both misdemeanors and felonies are covered. This Bureau reported that in 1960 some 16,000 persons were arrested in that state for narcotic offenses and that arrest rates for such offenses had increased about 12 per cent in each of the preceding two years. After 1960 arrest rates for offenses involving heroin or equivalent drugs showed a tendency to decline, as did arrests for marihuana violations. This decline was counterbalanced by very substantial increases in arrests for dangerous drugs other than opiates and marihuana, such as the barbiturates and amphetamines. It is impossible to know, from presently available figures, how to account for the decline in heroin-type arrests. It is possible that the decline may be due to an increase in the number of addicts in prison or that addicts are leaving the state. It is assuredly much too soon to say that the problem in California is on the wane.

There are obviously very large gaps in the estimates of the extent of the narcotics problem provided by the Bureau. A comprehensive view ought to allow for the following: (1) illegal addicts known to the police by reason of violation of narcotics laws; (2) illegal addicts known to the police through violation of other criminal laws; (3) illegal addicts not known to the police; (4) addicts securing legal drugs from doctors; and (5) incarcerated users. As we will indicate later in this chapter, the Bureau's estimates seem to consider primarily only the first of these categories and possibly some of the second. The others are almost entirely disregarded. Earlier estimates used as the basis of comparison invariably tried to take all categories into account.

A source upon which considerable reliance has been placed in determining the trend of addiction in this country has been the Army rejection rate of draftees on the grounds of addiction. During World War I, 3,284 persons from a total of 3,500,000 draftees were rejected because of addiction, or approximately one out of 1,000. During World War II the rejection rate for addiction has been given as one in 10,000 by Mr. Anslinger on the authority of a letter to him from Major Harold F. Dorn, Director, Medical Statistics Division, Army Service Forces, dated September 28, 1945.[6]

Mr. Anslinger applies these rates to the general population to obtain his estimates and to establish trends, but this is not correct procedure. It is known that the incidence of addiction is highest among young men of approximately military age and that it drops off rapidly among older groups. Also there are many more male than female users and there are almost no addicts below the age of fifteen years. According to Lawrence Kolb and A. G. Du Mez of the Public Health Service, if allowance is made for these facts in applying the Army findings to the general population the result is an estimated total of from 10,000 to 15,000 addicts during the first World War.[7] For the period of World War II the number would be considerably smaller. Obviously there is something drastically wrong with this method of estimation, and it was rejected as worthless by Kolb and Du Mez.

Even if the Army figures were to yield reasonable totals when applied to the general population, there are other considerations which would make them suspect. For example, during the second World War, punitive antinarcotic legislation had been enforced for more than thirty years; at the time of the first World War it had just been enacted and had hardly begun to be enforced. During the second World War it was Army policy to reject (classify as 4-F) persons who had been convicted of narcotic and other offenses, on the grounds of criminal record rather than addiction per se. Furthermore, the general climate of opinion concerning addiction was much harsher in 1941 than it was in 1916 and the motives for concealment and covering up were enormously increased. In order to know exactly how factors of this kind may have operated during the two war periods it would be necessary to know much more than is now known about the rejection of draftees during both wars. It is clear, however, that (a) neither of the rates is of any value as an indication of the number of addicts in the general population, and (b) the two rates are not comparable with each other.

THE SKI-JUMP CURVE

In an appearance before the Price Daniel Senate subcommittee, in 1955, Mr. Anslinger submitted a prepared statement in which he said:

Before the passage of national control legislation [in 1914] there was one addict in every 400 persons in the United States. By World War I this incidence had been reduced to about 1 in every 1,500 persons, and by World War II the incidence was found to be roughly 1 in 10,000 rejected for military service because of addiction. At this time the narcotic traffic in the United States was probably at the lowest ebb since the enactment of Federal legislation to control narcotics. Following World War II and the resumption of shipping there has been an influx of heroin from the Middle East and European countries. . . . The total number of addicts in the United States today is estimated at between 50,000 and 60,000 or an incidence of about 1 in 3,000 of the population.[8]

This version of the history of the drug problem has been embodied in what has been called the "ski-jump curve," which is reproduced here:

History of Narcotic Addiction in the United States

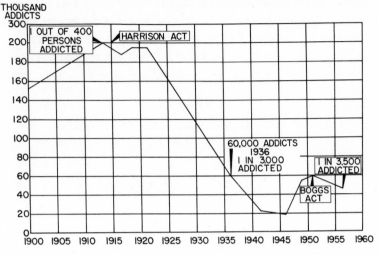

On the face of it this is a highly improbable curve. It suggests, for example, without making any allowance for the appearance of new addicts, that about 42,000 addicts vanished between 1914 and 1925, about 96,000 between 1925 and 1935, and approximately 42,000 between 1935 and 1945. When new and younger addicts are not being recruited in sufficient numbers to replace older addicts who die or quit the habit, it necessarily follows that the average age of the addicted population must increase. However, it is well known that between 1915 and 1945 the average age of known addicts declined considerably, and this demonstrates that we must assume a constant stream of new addicts being added each year. Bureau spokesmen have repeatedly said that each addict creates four new addicts during his career, but if this were true the addicted population would have had to increase geometrically. Additional difficulties arise with the curve if one tries to take into account the fact that in 1915 women addicts outnumbered men about three to two and whites outnumbered Negroes around nine to one, whereas in 1945 male addicts outnumbered females about 5 or 6 to one and whites outnumbered Negroes only about 3 to 1. From considerations of this sort alone, it is evident that the Bureau's ski-jump curve is mainly a fantasy and has little relation to reality.

Tables 1 and 2 and the chart based upon them indicate that the statistical data available in the United States do not support the

TABLE 1

Federal Narcotics Prosecutions (Marihuana excluded)
1915–1962

Year	Number	Year	Number	Year	Number
1915	498	1931	5116	1947	2340
1916	1540	1932	5323	1948	2814
1917	974	1933	4560	1949	3779
1918	1136	1934	5856	1950	4494
1919	1673	1935	6190	1951	3442
1920	2880	1936	5736	1952	2618
1921	2993	1937	4559	1953	2350
1922	5218	1938	4812	1954	1998
1923	5663	1939	4296	1955	2048
1924	5774	1940	3646	1956	1600
1925	7294	1941	3119	1957	1516
1926	6686	1942	2943	1958	1577
1927	6148	1943	3274	1959	1672
1928	6154	1944	2169	1960	1542
1929	6761	1945	1774	1961	1389
1930	7533	1946	2339	1962	1436

Sources: *Annual Reports of the Commissioner of Internal Revenue,* 1915-1926; *Annual Reports of the Commissioner of Prohibition,* 1927-1930; *Annual Reports of the Federal Bureau of Narcotics,* "Traffic in Opium and Other Dangerous Drugs," 1931-1962. The description of these totals has varied but they are believed to represent approximately the number of persons charged with criminal violations. Had marihuana cases been included in these figures after 1937, when the marihuana Tax Stamp Act was passed, there would have been no appreciable alteration of the trend, for the number of such cases is small.

TABLE 2

Nonfederal Narcotics Prosecutions (Marihuana included)
1932–1962

Year	Number	Rate per 100,000 pop.	Per cent of U.S. Covered
1932	2648	5.9	
1933	3370	7.9	
1934	3918	7.6	
1935	3679	7.9	
1936	3896	7.7	
1937	3996	7.2	
1938	4164	6.7	
1939	4599	6.3	
1940	5014	4.7	31%
1941	2593	3.8	
1942	1123	4.1	
1943	1361	4.6	
1944	1731	4.5	
1945	1935	4.0	33%
1946	2807	4.7	
1947	3388	5.3	
1948	4846	6.3	
1949	6546	9.5	
1950	8539	10.2	36%
1951	7119	12.8	
1952	10218	16.6	
1953	11974	19.2	
1954	14226	22.0	
1955	15937	24.1	40%
1956	16621	25.5	
1960	27735	25.4	60%
1961	29122	25.2	
1962	32956	26.7	65%

Source: *Uniform Crime Reports*, Federal Bureau of Investigation, Washington, D.C. Comparable figures are not available for 1957–59. The totals represent "persons held for prosecution." Various changes in the reporting system and methods of calculation make it extremely hazardous to regard these data as anything more than crude approximations. Reports issued by the F.B.N. indicate that approximately 10 to 15 per cent of these totals are marihuana cases. See *Daniel Subcommittee Hearings*, Exhibit 8, pp. 272-275.

Federal and Nonfederal Narcotics Prosecutions in the U.S., 1915–1962
(Gross Annual Totals)

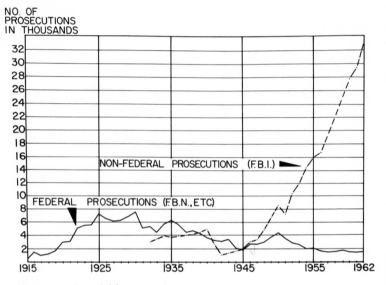

Sources: See Tables 1, 2.

Bureau's interpretation of the history of the problem and raise the question whether there are in existence such supporting figures.

In interpreting the trends indicated by the figures it must be remembered that while the reports on federal prosecutions are complete and cover the entire nation, those on nonfederal prosecutions are very incomplete and cover less than one-half of the country except in the years beginning with 1960. Neither the federal nor the nonfederal figures include addicts prosecuted for other than violations of narcotic laws. The sharp rise in the nonfederal totals after 1945 was no doubt influenced to an indeterminate extent by such factors as: (1) improved reporting, (2) increased numbers of police assigned to narcotics enforcement, and (3) intensified police activity resulting from public concern over the problem. The inclusion of marihuana cases in the nonfederal totals exaggerates them by approximately 10-15 per cent, but in view of opposing tendencies created by incomplete coverage and the noninclusion of addicts prosecuted for other than narcotics offenses, it is certain that the number of relevant prosecutions at the nonfederal level is considerably underreported. If these totals were to be increased to represent the total population of the United States an even more gloomy trend would be portrayed.

The Federal Narcotics Bureau has noted that before 1930 narcotic offenses had come to be regarded as of exclusively federal concern—a situation which it sought to correct after 1930. If this is correct, one may reasonably infer that there were proportionately fewer nonfederal prosecutions before 1932 than there were immediately after. If this is true it would appear that the total number of prosecutions (federal and nonfederal) probably did not decline between 1925 and 1939 and may have risen. The low totals for the period before 1925 resulted from the fact that the machinery of enforcement was being organized and that the Harrison Act of 1914 was being interpreted by the courts during this period.

In general, these statistical data provide no evidence of a declining narcotics problem in the United States at any time except during the period of World War II from 1940 to 1945. It appears, indeed, that the Narcotic Bureau's ski-jump curve faces in the wrong direction. The tables presented here suggest that the Bureau's estimates probably ignored nonfederal cases and relied unduly on the declining federal trend. (While the number of cases handled by the Bureau has been declining, its legislative appropriations have been increasing sharply; e.g., from $2,500,000 for the fiscal year ending June 1952 to $4,767,150 [1956, 1962 annual reports] for the year ending June 1963.) After having been considered as almost exclusively federal offenses before 1930, narcotics violations are now being handled overwhelmingly by nonfederal police. Local police officers probably handle from 20 to 40 narcotics cases for every one that is dealt with by a federal agent.

The ski-jump curve suffers further indignities if one examines closely the estimate of 200,000 addicts in this country in 1914. This estimate is admittedly derived from a very limited survey made in Michigan and reported in 1878 by O. Marshall. The results of this survey, when extended to the entire United States, yielded one of the larger estimates of the number of addicts at that time and this is no doubt why it was adopted by the Bureau. However, an estimate made in 1878 can scarcely be applied to the country 36 years later under greatly changed conditions. Moreover, Marshall's estimates, like other early estimates, included all drug users. As has been indicated, current estimates of the Bureau of Narcotics are concerned only with a portion of the addicted population.

It is more reasonable, in estimating the number of addicts in this country in 1914, to turn to the study of this matter made in 1924 by two U.S. Public Health Service officials, Lawrence Kolb and A. G. Du Mez.[9] These writers base their investigation upon the plausible assumption that before 1914 the needs of addicts were met by legitimately imported drugs, since there was little illicit traffic and addiction was not illegal. From the amount of legal drugs available, they subtracted the quantity estimated to be needed for medical uses and calculated how many addicts could have been supplied with a daily dosage of 6 grains of morphine from the remainder. Their conclusion was that the quantities of drugs available between 1910 and 1919 were sufficient to supply only about 100,000 addicts. This figure does not include an estimated 10,000 to 30,000 old and incurable addicts receiving drugs from physicians. It is therefore more nearly comparable with the Bureau's current estimate than others, such as Marshall's, which include all types of users.

For the period after 1914 the ski-jump curve evidently relies on the conclusions of the Kolb-Du Mez study. These authors estimated that addiction reached a peak in this country in 1900 and declined thereafter. While their conclusions may have some validity for the period before 1914, they are worthless for the post-1914 period because of their assumption that the trend of addiction in the country was not influenced by illegally imported drugs. This assumption is stated as follows:

It is realized that some of the addicts who were deprived of narcotics as a result of the decrease in the quantities of the drugs imported legally turned to the use of smuggled material after 1915, but in our opinion the number that obtained their supplies from this source was at no time large enough to affect the direction of the trend of addiction.[10]

On this assumption it was inevitable that these authors should find the decline in addiction which they reported after 1914. Since almost no supplies are presently being diverted from legitimate sources to the illicit market, the same assumption today would lead one to conclude that addiction has virtually disappeared. What these authors failed to recognize in 1924 was that smuggled supplies had already become virtually the sole source of the addict's supply and that the quantities of legally imported drugs had become totally irrelevant.

Gross annual totals representing enforcement activity between 1915 and 1960 have already been presented to indicate rough trends and to show how narcotics law enforcement has become, since 1930, a largely nonfederal police problem. The following two tables indicate how the problem is distributed by geographic regions and by size of communities and provide arrest rates rather than gross totals. They are based upon analyses made by F.B.I. statisticians and reported in the *Uniform Crime Reports*.

TABLE 3

Persons Charged with Nonfederal Narcotic Law Violations
1932–1962

(By Size of Community: per 100,000 Inhabitants)

Year	Total Rate	Over 250,000	100,000-250,000	50,000-100,000	25,000-50,000	10,000-25,000	Under 10,000
1932	5.9	8.5	8.2	3.1	2.3	2.5	3.6
1933	7.9	9.7	21.1	3.2	2.7	1.8	1.9
1934	7.6	11.4	9.0	4.0	3.0	2.3	1.0
1935	7.9	12.0	10.5	3.9	3.4	1.6	2.0
1936	7.7	11.9	6.8	4.4	3.2	1.1	1.7
1937	7.2	11.4	6.0	5.2	2.0	1.4	2.0
1938	6.7	10.0	7.6	4.0	2.4	1.8	2.6
1939	6.3	10.7	4.8	2.7	1.8	2.3	2.3
1940	4.7	7.7	3.7	4.9	1.2	1.0	1.1
1941	3.8	5.8	2.9	4.9	1.5	0.9	1.7
1942	4.1	7.7	3.5	3.7	1.1	1.6	2.2
1943	4.6	7.5	3.0	4.9	2.1	0.9	1.0
1944	4.5	7.4	3.5	4.5	1.8	1.3	1.2
1945	4.0	5.7	4.3	4.2	1.8	1.7	1.7
1946	4.7	7.1	4.7	4.7	2.2	1.8	1.5
1947	5.3	7.5	4.2	5.2	4.9	2.1	2.4
1948	6.3	9.9	6.2	5.9	2.9	2.0	2.6
1949	9.5	16.8	6.8	7.2	4.0	3.0	2.6
1950	10.2	18.8	8.5	5.7	2.7	3.0	1.5
1951	12.8	23.1	12.5	6.5	4.2	3.4	1.0
1952	16.6	28.8	12.1	9.2	4.5	3.0	2.7
1953	19.2	31.9	13.8	13.4	5.0	4.8	3.3
1954	22.0	37.5	12.9	12.8	4.3	5.4	3.3
1955	24.1	43.1	13.0	9.4	5.0	4.6	2.6
1956	25.5	46.6	12.6	9.4	6.2	5.5	2.3
1961	25.2	57.8	15.0	12.9	9.3	6.4	2.8
1962	26.7	61.7	15.0	13.5	8.3	5.1	2.8

Source: *Uniform Crime Reports*, F.B.I. Comparable figures for 1957 to 1960 are not available.

TABLE 4

Persons Charged with Violation of Nonfederal Narcotic
Laws by Geographic Divisions
1936–1956

(per 100,000 inhabitants)

Year	New Eng.	Mid. Atl.	E. No. Central	W. No. Central	So. Atl.	E. So. Central	W. So. Central	Mtn.	Pac.
1936	5.1	1.6	4.9	6.4	4.6	6.1	21.4	15.3	29.5
1937	3.4	2.3	4.5	5.0	5.4	5.0	22.5	13.5	26.7
1938	5.3	2.7	4.3	6.4	2.5	3.8	26.6	11.0	16.2
1939	5.5	3.0	4.5	12.0	2.3	2.6	24.8	7.0	5.9
1940	5.5	1.5	3.2	6.7	1.5	0.4	16.4	4.2	10.4
1941	1.6	1.2	2.5	1.6	1.8	1.8	18.5	6.1	11.5
1942	1.4	2.5	0.6	1.9	2.6	0.8	18.7	3.9	11.8
1943	1.3	1.9	3.1	1.4	5.9	4.7	16.4	3.4	14.2
1944	0.9	2.3	2.8	2.2	6.7	3.0	14.5	4.0	13.3
1945	1.6	1.8	2.7	1.7	1.7	1.8	19.1	4.4	10.7
1946	3.5	2.5	3.7	1.5	2.0	3.1	20.4	9.3	9.1
1947	3.0	2.5	3.3	1.2	4.5	8.5	15.3	9.4	16.5
1948	2.4	3.6	4.2	1.8	6.0	1.8	21.9	9.6	19.6
1949	4.2	4.3	6.9	2.2	10.1	2.9	33.3	12.1	28.2
1950	3.5	10.3	8.6	1.4	8.0	2.7	20.1	12.8	24.4
1951	4.6	9.5	12.1	1.4	15.6	2.6	22.8	13.0	30.6
1952	5.5	21.1	11.6	2.2	23.3	18.6	22.5	13.9	31.8
1953	7.6	25.6	12.8	2.4	24.1	20.9	25.1	16.7	36.9
1954	9.2	33.6	14.4	1.7	24.7	27.3	25.2	14.1	32.7
1955	9.5	38.0	17.6	3.7	24.9	9.4	32.6	15.2	31.2
1956	10.8	41.7	18.9	3.4	19.7	8.2	31.1	17.9	36.6

New England: Connecticut, Maine, Massachusetts, Rhode Island, Vermont, and New Hampshire
Middle Atlantic: New Jersey, New York, Pennsylvania
East North Central: Illinois, Indiana, Michigan, Ohio, Wisconsin
West North Central: Iowa, Kansas, Minnesota, Missouri, Nebraska, North Dakota, South Dakota
South Atlantic: Delaware, Florida, Georgia, Maryland, North Carolina, South Carolina, Virginia, West Virginia, District of Columbia
East South Central: Alabama, Kentucky, Mississippi, Tennessee

West South Central: Arkansas, Louisiana, Oklahoma, Texas
Mountain: Arizona, Colorado, Idaho, Montana, Nevada, New Mexico,
Utah, Wyoming
Pacific: California, Oregon, Washington

Source: *Uniform Crime Reports*, F.B.I. Comparable figures are not available after 1956.

It is especially interesting to observe, in connection with the alleged effectiveness of the 1951 legislation, that the overall arrest rate doubled from 1951 to 1956 and that arrest rates increased during this period in communities of all sizes and in all geographic divisions without a single exception. The concentration in large cities is especially marked and it will be noted that arrest rates are lowest in the West North Central states of Iowa, Kansas, Minnesota, Missouri, Nebraska, North and South Dakota. In only one region is there a definite tendency for the rates to decline after 1954 and this is the one which comprises Alabama, Kentucky, Mississippi, and Tennessee. It is possible that this reduction may be associated with change in policy at the Public Health Service Hospital for addicts in Lexington.

The Census Bureau's survey of prisoners and of commitments to penal institutions in 1923 permits us to supplement Table 4 by providing data concerning commitment rates by geographical divisions for drug offenses in 1923. These were given as follows in the 1923 survey:[11]

Commitments for Drug Offenses—Per 100,000 Population

North East	0.7	East So. Central	0.1
Middle Atl.	5.2	West So. Central	1.3
East No. Central	0.7	Mountain	3.2
West No. Central	0.9	Pacific	11.1
So. Atlantic	0.5		

THE FEDERAL NARCOTICS BUREAU'S SURVEY OF ADDICTS

In 1953 the Federal Bureau of Narcotics began to make a count of drug addicts in the United States on the basis of reports sent in by enforcement officials throughout the nation. It is impossible to form a very precise notion of how the survey is being conducted because the Bureau has never described the project in sufficient detail. Prepared addict-identification cards are evidently sent out to enforcement officials throughout the country and these officials are urged to fill out a card on every addict who comes to their attention and to mail the card to Washington for processing. In Washington the Federal Bureau of Narcotics checks the names on the cards that it receives against those it already has in order to eliminate duplication.

From 1953 to 1962 the Bureau has given the number of newly reported addicts each year:[12]

Year	Number	Cumulative totals	Total "active addicts" at year-end according to the Bureau
1953	8,911		
1954	8,542	17,453	
1955	9,387	26,840	
1956	9,296	36,136	
1957	8,047	44,183	
1958	7,453	51,636	46,266
1959	5,690	57,326	
1960	7,479	64,805	44,906
1961	7,041	71,846	46,798
1962	6,363	78,209	47,489

It will be noted from the above that while 78,000 addicts were counted during these ten years, 30,000 of these names were eliminated from the list by 1962. This discrepancy between the reported number of "active addicts" and the actual count began in 1958, when the Bureau added a footnote to its tabulations explaining that "3,541 of the addicts reported in 1953 have remained active throughout the five years 1954-58." Names of addicts are eliminated from the active list, apparently, when new reports are not sent in on them over a five-year period. An assumption underlying this procedure is that if an addict is using drugs he will be apprehended within five years. Hence, if the addict is not reported it is assumed that he is in prison, that he is dead, or that he has quit his habit—hence, that he is no longer an "active addict."

The names received by the Bureau are sorted into two general categories which are labeled "recidivists" and "new addicts." Both of these terms are misleading and ambiguous. One does not know, for example, whether an addict counted in 1953, and sent to prison for eight years, would be counted as a "new addict" or a "recidivist" if his name turned up again in 1961 long after it had been removed from the active list. Also, when the survey began in 1953 certainly there were many old-time addicts who must have appeared on the Bureau's list as "new addicts" and there must surely be persons of this sort showing up each year. The fact that an individual is listed as a "new addict" in the survey therefore has no necessary relationship whatever to the duration of his addiction or to his age, and the Bureau's annual totals of new addicts tell us nothing whatever about the rate at which people are becoming addicted.

Since the Bureau does not count incarcerated addicts as "active addicts" it would be important to know how many drug users are serving time in jails and prisons. No direct information on this point is available, but the Federal Bureau of Prisons does report that the number of drug law violators serving time in federal penal institutions in 1960 was 4,794.[13] A substantial proportion of these prisoners are known to be addicts. In addition there are addicts serving sentences in federal institutions for nonnarcotics offenses. Some indication of the number of addicts in state penal institutions may be derived from local figures such as those from New York, where the State Department of Correction had 3,249 former drug users in its institutions in 1956, comprising 20 per cent of the prison population. In 1956 23 per cent of the new admissions were drug addicts.

In the same year an additional 4,886 addicts were reportedly newly admitted to the correctional institutions of New York City alone.[14] In 1923, by way of comparison, a complete census of prisoners in all types of penal institutions in the United States indicated only 3,847 serving time for violations of drug laws.[15] Obviously, the number of addicts in our penal institutions is very substantial and ought to be taken into consideration in any realistic estimate.

It would be expected on a purely mathematical basis as the Federal Narcotics Bureau's enumeration goes on year after year that the number of newly reported addicts would decline as the enumeration became more complete. For example, in 1958, 14,899 names of addicts were actually reported to the Bureau.[16] Of these 7,446 had been previously reported, leaving only 7,453 so-called "new addicts." The 1953 total could not have been reduced in this manner because this was the first year of the survey and presumably most of those reported had to be "new" since they could have been reported previously only during the same year.

The point may be illustrated by a hypothetical example. Let us assume that a given community has exactly 10,000 addicts over a period of fifteen years and that a survey like the Bureau's is made in that community over this fifteen-year period. Let us suppose that after nine years 9,500 of these addicts had been counted, and the remaining 500 were enumerated during the tenth year. Obviously one could not conclude from the reduced number of "new addicts" during the tenth year that addiction in this community had been reduced by fifty per cent any more than one could conclude that the absence of any new addicts in the eleventh and subsequent years meant that addiction had been eliminated. This, however, is the way in which the Bureau interprets its findings![17]

For example, as evidence of the effectiveness of the Narcotic Control Act of 1956, the Bureau refers to the following reductions in the number of newly reported addicts during eleven months of 1958 as compared with the whole year of 1956:[18]

Area	New Addicts: 1956	New Addicts: 1958
District of Columbia	200	60
Ohio	92	37
Texas	523	175
Louisiana	142	50
Michigan	543	264
New York	4138	2836
Illinois	908	631
California	1568	1276
Missouri	210	136

Apart from the fact that if the Bureau's survey is worth anything at all the number of newly reported addicts should automatically decline, it is also obvious that the above illustrations presented by Mr. Anslinger were selected because they happened to show a decline and that contrary instances were ignored. Using the Bureau's own figures and selecting states in the same biased manner to present an opposite impression, the following instances may be cited to suggest a great increase in addiction from 1959 to 1960:[19]

State	New Addicts: 1959	New Addicts: 1960	Percentage Increase
Arizona	26	49	88
California	914	1,606	75
Delaware	1	12	1200
District of Columbia	125	159	27
Hawaii	5	10	100
Illinois	493	912	85
Indiana	54	95	75
Maryland	47	91	93
New Jersey	113	141	24
New York	2,875	3,372	17
Ohio	31	59	90
Rhode Island	75	94	25
Washington	9	51	466
Wisconsin	10	34	340

Henry L. Giordano, the new head of the Federal Bureau of Narcotics appointed in 1962, has continued the Bureau's practice of comparing incomplete current *enumerations* with comprehensive *estimates* of the past in order to maintain the fiction that the problem is declining. In a news release from Washington on November 10, 1963, for example, he is reported as saying that the number of addicts had declined from a recent high of 60,000 to a total of about 47,000 at the end of 1962. Special significance was attached to a decline in the number of new addicts from 9,337 in 1956 to 6,363 in 1962. Giordano makes the same points in an interview reported in January 1964.[20] Although the figures cited by Giordano are worthless for the purpose for which he uses them, and although this is recognized by all competent students who have examined them, they are nevertheless popularly accepted because the Bureau is in a position to repeat them endlessly in the mass media.

A comparison of the Bureau's survey as it applies to California with the results of a survey being made by the state of California is illuminating. Thus the Bureau gives the total of California addicts as 7,412 at the end of ten years of counting. The state of California, on the other hand, after only three and one-half years of its survey, has a list of 13,520 in December 1962 and estimates the total at about 20,000 (illegal addicts).[21] During the last four years the Bureau reported the following new addicts from California: in 1959—914; 1960—1,606; 1961—1,220; 1962—902. The state's survey reported about 7,400 new addicts in a year and a half ending in December 1960, about 3,500 in 1961, and about 2,500 in 1962. At the end of 1960 there were, according to the Bureau of Narcotics, 7,411 active addicts in California. During the next two years 2,122 new addicts were discovered but the total was increased by only a single addict!

There are many other unexplained inconsistencies and discrepancies in the figures which the Bureau of Narcotics publishes. For example, between 1953 and 1959 three new addicts were reported from Utah and the number of "active addicts" at the end of 1959 was given as one. Nevertheless, during the same years the Bureau's figures show 117 arrests and 101 convictions for narcotics offenses in that state.[22] If the 101 convictions involved nonaddicted peddlers, one wonders how they were managing to dispose of their wares.

The Bureau's survey is necessarily conducted on a voluntary basis, but no information has been published to indicate exactly how much cooperation has been elicited. There is no way of knowing how many agencies do not report or of evaluating the reporting that is done. W. B. Eldridge worked relatively closely with the Bureau in an attempt to discover the information that is absolutely necessary for a statistical evaluation of the project. He was unable to obtain it. He reports that no uniform standards or instructions appear to have been given to reporting agencies and that there is a great deal of confusion about what is supposed to be done.[23] When one remembers that the Federal Bureau of Investigation, after more than thirty years of effort, still has formidable unsolved problems in producing reliable and complete crime statistics, it would be surprising indeed if the Narcotics Bureau's survey were anything but extremely incomplete and unreliable.

If the Bureau had complete cooperation from all possible reporting agencies so that data would be sent to Washington on every addict coming to official attention, and if the names of addicts were dropped from the list only when they were known to be dead, then, after a period of years, the total count would have some real significance in estimating the extent of the problem. Under such circumstances of full reporting, one would expect that the annual totals of newly reported addicts might become relatively stabilized and that it might be possible to make some inferences concerning the number of new addicts being created each year. In 1958 the Bureau of Narcotics published data on the total number of addicts reported during the year which indicated that very close to 50 per cent were "new addicts." In a relatively complete survey one would expect that most addicts coming to officials' attention would already have been counted and that the proportion of new addicts would be considerably less than fifty per cent. In 1958 the proportion of new addicts was under fifty per cent in only four states and in the District of Columbia.

If one takes seriously the Bureau's assumption that the number of new addicts it reports represents the rate at which addicts are being created, one has other problems. Thus during the decade beginning in 1953 there were reported 78,209 "new addicts." Since the Bureau says there were about 60,000 addicts in the United States at the end of 1952 we would have a total of 138,000 addicts to account for. If there were only 47,000 left in December 1962, what happened to the other 91,000 during these ten years?

An analysis of the Narcotics Bureau's survey of addiction suggests that this enterprise may well be a public relations effort rather than a serious attempt at enumeration. Detailed descriptions of the methods employed have probably not been published because it is realized that they would not stand inspection. The indicated remedy is that the business of counting addicts should be turned over to the more expert, reliable, and experienced statistical services of the Federal Bureau of Investigation. It would be a relatively simple matter for this agency to extend its present reporting functions to include an annual count of addicts arrested for all offenses.

An article published in December 1948 by three Public Health Service officials at Lexington provides an illustration of the manner in which Bureau figures have misled experts as well as laymen. The article opens with the following statement:

When the Harrison Narcotic Act was passed in 1914 there were perhaps 150,000 to 200,000 narcotic addicts, mostly women, in the United States. Now, according to a recent estimate by Mr. H. J. Anslinger, Commissioner of Narcotics, there is about 1 addict per 3,000 of population, or a total of approximately 48,000, mostly men. This reduction has been largely due to the vigorous enforcement of the Harrison Narcotic Act and to Federal facilities for the treatment of addicts. Compared with the problems arising from the abuse of drugs such as barbiturates and alcohol, narcotic addiction is not a great public health hazard.[24]

This article was hailed by the press throughout the nation as an authoritative indication that the problem of drug addiction had been laid to rest. A Chicago newspaper headlined it: "Find Narcotics Beaten as U.S. Health Menace." Within less than two years the authors of this article were being besieged by an aroused public to explain the increased prevalence of youthful addicts. A glance at the tables presented in this chapter will indicate that the postwar increase in addiction was already well under way in 1948 when this article appeared. The 1948 total of nonfederal prosecutions, for example, was about 400 per cent higher than the 1942 total and the proportion of offenders under 25 years of age had increased from 17 per cent to 40 per cent.

The conclusions which emerge from this discussion are: that the number of addicts in the United States in 1914 is unknown and cannot be reliably estimated; that it is even more hazardous to estimate the extent of the problem today; and that federal narcotics officials have, over a long period of years, underreported and underestimated the problem.

THE AVERAGE AGE OF ADDICTS

It is worth noting that in the only national statistical reports on narcotics offenders in which age is given, those in the Uniform Crime Reports, the percentage of young persons increased progressively for two decades after 1932, when this data first began to be published. Thus in 1932, 15 per cent of the offenders were under twenty-five and 3.3 per cent under twenty-one years of age, whereas in 1961 41.7 per cent were under twenty-five and 19.5 per cent under twenty-one. It is practically impossible in view of what is known of addicts that their average age should decline while their numbers diminish. Since the decline in the average age of narcotics offenders, most of whom are addicts, appears in the figures between 1932 and our entry into the war in 1941, it seems possible that the number of addicts in the country may also have been increasing then. During this period the percentage under twenty-five increased from 15 per cent to 27 per cent and the percentage under twenty-one from 3.3 per cent to 10.1 per cent. Recent slight declines in the proportion of young persons have tended to increase the average age, but this effect has been produced more by an increased number of older addicts than by a decline in the number of young ones—in short, by the fact that the relatively large numbers of addicts in their late teens and early twenties during the 1945-55 period are now usually past the age of twenty-five years.

In 1923, when, according to the Narcotics Bureau's chart, there were about 180,000 drug addicts in this country, the Census Bureau made a virtually complete survey of all prisoners in penal establishments of all types in the United States and of all commitments to these establishments for the first half of the year. The survey covered state and federal prisons and reformatories, state farms, municipal and county jails, and workhouses and chain gangs. The average age at that time of the persons committed for violation of the drug laws was approximately thirty-one years.[25] The average age of known drug law offenders today is probably about twenty-six or twenty-seven.

Because the rate at which addicts quit the habit is low, and because the abstaining addict is always subject to relapse, it makes a great deal of sense to think of the addict population as one which is effectively reduced only, or at least mainly, by death. It is possible for the number of addicts to increase rapidly, as it seems to have done after the late war, but it can scarcely decline rapidly, since we may reasonably assume that the mortality rates of drug users do not change abruptly. This means that any claim of an unusually drastic decline in the number of addicts is highly suspect. It also means that the relatively sudden appearance of many new drug users among young persons will be noticed for many years to come.

Since addiction in the United States is usually acquired relatively early in life, an effective control program would have the long-run effect of gradually increasing the average age of known addicts. Actually no such trend is observable in the statistics of the drug problem in this country and has never been, as has been pointed out, except possibly for brief periods. Only if at some future time it should be noted that over a period of twenty years, for example, the average age of known addicts had increased, say from 25 years to 30 or more would it be justifiable to conclude that the problem was being effectively dealt with and that the stream of new recruits had been checked.

Studies made before 1915 indicate that addicts were considerably older than they now are and that the habit was acquired later in life. For example, C. H. Earle in 1880 reported the average age of a sample group as 39.7 and described the habit as a "vice of middle life." J. M. Hull, in 1885 found the average age of a series of 235 cases to be 46.5. A more extensive study was made by L. P. Brown of addicts who were registered and rationed for a brief period immediately preceding the enactment of the Harrison Act in the state of Tennessee. The average age on January 1, 1915, of the 2,370 registered addicts was 50 years and average age on acquiring the habit was given as 37.[26]

CRIME AND ADDICTION IN THE U.S. AND ABROAD

With a population as large as that of the United States, even if one assumes that there are 150,000 to 200,000 addicts, these are not large numbers; but if we compare ourselves with other nations they are enormous. The Senate subcommittee under Price Daniel, which accepted the 60,000 estimate from Mr. Anslinger, nevertheless noted that there were evidently more drug users in this country than in all the rest of the Western world combined. Most European countries, for example, estimate between 300 and 500 addicts.[27] Germany, with the most severe problem of any European country before the war, placed her total considerably under 10,000. Britain, with a population roughly one-third that of the United States, estimates fewer than 1,000 medical and nonmedical addicts. In the four years from 1946 to 1949 inclusive the French police reported the detection of 687 addicts, only one of whom was under the age of 20 years, with a median age between 35 and 40. In Canada, where the problem is relatively severe and handled about the same as in the United States, the number of addicts is unreliably estimated at between 3,000 and 4,000. One must go to Asia to find countries which have drug problems comparable in size to our own.

The number of addicts in a community or a nation is not the only or the most important measure of the problem. For example, if in two communities of equal size each with a thousand drug addicts, the addicts in one community are noncriminals medically supplied, while those in the second community are criminals purchasing illicit drugs on an illicit market and committing crimes to get money to buy expensive illicit drugs, the second community has a serious problem and the other a relatively minor one. In most of the countries of the West, except Canada and the United States, addicts are supplied from medical sources, so that, besides being fewer in number they are also less criminal than our own. In these countries the illicit traffic does not constitute a significant source of income for racketeering criminals nor does it make drugs of addiction sufficiently available and attractive to spread the habit among young persons, for almost all addicts in these countries are adults. The United States not only has more addicts than the rest of the Western world, but considered man for man American addicts constitute much more serious social liabilities than do those of Europe.

Let us consider for a moment that it is commonly thought that there are at least 10,000 addicts in the city of Chicago maintaining their habits with illicit supplies. If we assume that each of these addicts commits one property offense per day this would mean a total of 3,650,000 crimes per year. Such an army of 10,000 active criminals at large in a city of 4,000,000 is a factor of some importance and may have something to do with the wariness with which the inhabitants of that city walk the streets at night. Again, if we assume that each of Chicago's addicts spends $10 per day on drugs, this amounts to $36,500,000 per year paid into the hands of criminals, largely as tax-exempt income. This facet of the narcotics problem alone, though not as visible as others, is certainly one of its greatest evils.

Some brief numerical comparisons between the United States and some other countries that handle addiction as a medical problem will make the point we are concerned with. From official reports of the governments of Austria, Australia, Argentina, Belgium, Britain, Denmark, France, West Germany, Italy, New Zealand, and Switzerland the estimated total number of addicts in these eleven countries, with a combined population of about 250,000,000, is in the vicinity of 10,000; i.e., nearly the same total as that commonly given for Chicago with a 4,000,000 population.[28] In the eleven countries listed above about 700 persons were prosecuted in 1956 for violations of narcotic laws. In 1954 the Chicago Police Department reported that it processed through its narcotics bureau 7,639 narcotic offenders. Thus, *in proportion to population* Chicago seems to have, on the basis of these figures, about 60 times as many addicts as the above eleven foreign countries and about 600 times as many narcotics prosecutions. The penalties imposed upon narcotics violators in the eleven foreign countries almost always involved maximum fines of less than $400 and jail sentences of less than one year, with most offenders being fined. The number of addicts below the age of 20 or 21 years among the known addicts of these nations was reported as less than twenty-five.

In all probability the above numerical comparisons understate the difference between our narcotics problem and that of the foreign nations named. As pointed out earlier in this chapter, United States statistics on narcotics are grossly unreliable and tend to understate the problem. In countries in which addiction is not a criminal matter, reliable statistical data are relatively easily obtained from official records kept by drugstores and doctors. In addition to having more accurate statistics, many of the countries named include medical addicts in their totals. In some of the countries the addicts consist to a substantial extent of persons who are receiving narcotics in connection with disease and chronic pain, and of addicted doctors, nurses and pharmacists. Such addicts are not ordinarily included in American estimates. The Chicago estimate, for example, does not include them. West Germany in 1960 reported to the United Nations that of 4,334 registered addicts, 863 were connected with the medical and ancillary professions, 470 were war invalids and disabled pensioners, and that in 3,102 cases the addiction was therapeutic in origin. This suggests that if the American system of counting addicts were applied to Germany the total would be much lower than the one cited above.

During hearings before congressional subcommittees studying the drug problem it was frequently estimated by police officers from various large cities of the United States that nearly half of the crimes in their communities were linked with drug addiction. One may well be inclined to regard this as gross exaggeration, since official crime statistics certainly do not support it, but if one considers actual crimes committed rather than merely those that happen to find their way into the official statistics, and if one considers that, unlike other criminals, addicts necessarily violate the criminal law many times daily, then the conclusion does not seem so absurd. The importance of addicts in crime is far out of proportion to their numbers, but in the nature of the case no reliable figures are available upon which definite estimates can be made.

Needless to say, the American addict is ordinarily impoverished, degraded, and demoralized. This fact, and its repercussions upon the families and relatives of addicts, is part of the human cost of the narcotics problem. In this respect the United States again leads the Western world, for nowhere else are addicts as impoverished, degraded, and demoralized as they are here.

If we disregard the question of numbers and focus our attention exclusively on those evils connected with addiction which are the result of the way in which the problem is dealt with rather than the necessary consequences of addiction itself, then we may say that the drug problem of today is largely one that has come into being since 1914 when the Harrison Act was passed and largely because of it. Before 1915 addiction was a problem mainly in a numerical and personal sense; today it has become in addition a substantial social problem. Before 1915 there was no significant illicit traffic, criminality and addiction were not linked as they are now, the number of addicts in jails and prisons was negligible, and there was no problem of juvenile addiction. It should also be remembered that the vast majority of all present-day drug users became addicted after the Harrison Act was passed.

RECRUITMENT OF NEW ADDICTS

There are two main ways in which addicts are added to the ranks: (a) one is through the therapeutic use of the drug either because of a doctor's prescription or because of folk belief and popular custom; (b) the other is through association between addicts and non-addicts with the drug being used for other than therapeutic purposes. Each of these patterns of recruitment tends to select different kinds of persons. Which of the patterns dominates seems to be determined mainly by the kind of control policy in effect. When the policy is one of prohibition and punishment for addicts, the second pattern is ordinarily dominant and the number of addicts relatively large; when addicts are handled as patients and are given access to legal drugs, the number of addicts tends to be smaller and most of them have first used drugs for medical reasons.

From a knowledge of the demographic characteristics of a nation's addicts it is usually a simple matter to infer what that nation's policies are, and vice versa. Thus if there are relatively many addicts and they are overwhelmingly young urban males from the lower classes and the slums, one may infer that the control system is one of prohibition and punishment, as in the United States, and that the habit is being spread through underworld association between addicts and nonaddicts. On the other hand, when the addicts are older, so that few are under thirty, for example, and when they are rather evenly distributed by classes, by sex, and in rural and urban communities, one may usually conclude with confidence that addicts are handled as medical cases and are recruited primarily through the therapeutic use of drugs. In this case it is also usually true that the number of addicts in proportion to population is comparatively low and that addicts from the medical and allied professions constitute a large percentage of the total. In 1960, to cite two examples, Britain reported that 63 of 437 addicts were connected with the medical profession and West Germany that more than 850 of 4,334 in that country were so connected.[29]

Medical recruitment accounted for the largest proportion of new addicts in the United States during the nineteenth century, as it also does today in most European countries where addicts are supplied with drugs by doctors. During the nineteenth century in the United States the spread of addiction was largely determined and decisively influenced by conditions and developments within the field of medicine. Among these influences were the discovery of morphine near the beginning of the century and of heroin near its close. Both of these drugs were at first believed not to be habit-forming and were liberally and carelessly used by physicians. During the Civil War, the hypodermic method of injection came to be widely known and it was at first thought that opiates administered in this way were not habit-forming. Opium and its derivatives played a much larger role in medical therapy in those days than now and were used in the treatment of a great many ailments. They were, for example, extensively used during the Civil War in the treatment of dysentery, which was so common in the Army that it was sometimes called "the soldier's disease."

A factor of special importance in the spread of the drug habit during the nineteenth century in this country was the extraordinary dimensions of the patent medicine industry. Many of the nostrums sold during the patent medicine era in large quantities contained opium or addicting drugs derived from it. The sale of these medicines was largely uncontrolled and the persons who bought them rarely knew what they contained. As the drug habit spread and became a matter of personal concern to more and more people, the patent medicine industry rose to the occasion with many medicines which were guaranteed to cure addiction. Most of these remedies themselves contained the addicting drug so that the patient simply transferred his addiction to the remedy. When heroin first appeared, it was sometimes used by physicians to cure the morphine habit.

There was little or no regulation of the distribution of addicting drugs in any of the countries of the Western world during this period, but in the older, more mature countries of Europe, medical practice was more sophisticated and more closely regulated and the consumption of drugs in patent medicines and other forms did not develop as it did here. The per capita consumption of drugs in this country, as shown by the quantities imported, rose rapidly throughout the nineteenth century until about 1900, when it began to decline. The reasons for the decline were that control measures had begun to be enacted on a local basis, medical practice had become more sophisticated, and the public had become more aware of the danger of addiction. The Pure Food and Drugs Act of 1906 put a crimp in the patent medicine industry and in 1909 the importation of smoking opium was forbidden by congressional action.

In the years immediately preceding the Harrison Act various types of control measures were enacted by different states. As a consequence of these early measures small numbers of narcotics offenders and addicts began to show up in jails and prisons and studies were made of them. Invariably these studies revealed the characteristic pattern of underworld recruitment by association, such as youth, criminality, slum origins, and a large preponderance of males. During the same period and before, studies of those addicts receiving drugs from legal sources usually showed an approximately three to two preponderance of females, a high average age, and an even distribution among the socioeconomic classes.[30]

The smuggling and illicit use of drugs, which began in a small way before 1914, went into high gear when the Harrison Act was passed. The effect of this Act may be indicated by noting that the Census Bureau reported a 2066 per cent increase in the number of narcotics violators committed to all types of penal institutions in 1923 as compared with 1910. In 1910, the total of such commitments was given as 314.[31]

The Harrison Act had the effect, along with other measures, of drastically reducing the flow of new addicts from medical practice or through the use of legal drugs. On the other hand, by shutting off the supply of legal drugs for the countless users without criminal records it forced them to the illicit traffic and into the underworld. The illicit traffic expanded enormously and there was a large increase in the rate at which new addicts appeared within the underworld. The appearance of large numbers of the new type of addict, recruited from the underworld and its fringes and from a younger urban generation, was observed and commented upon as early as 1921 by E. S. Bishop. They were motivated by "curiosity" and "search for adventure," he said, and stimulated by "unfortunate spectacular publicity."[32] At present, more than forty-five years after the Harrison Act, the trends set in motion by it have had time to work themselves out. The old type of addict who first used drugs in connection with illness or by smoking opium has now been replaced by another type of user who takes up heroin looking for kicks and who is evidently attracted to it in the first place by the glamor of its illegality and expensiveness.

An outstanding feature of the changing nature of the addicted population has been the spectacular increase of addiction among Negroes, particularly in northern cities. Before 1915, surveys generally indicated that there were few Negro addicts and that the Negro population as a whole, in proportion to numbers, had about as many or somewhat fewer addicts than the white.[33] Since that time the proportion of Negroes among narcotics law violators has increased to around half of the reported national totals. This trend has been especially pronounced in some northern cities, where arrest rates of young Negro males for narcotics offenses have in some instances increased by several thousand per cent in a period of twenty years.

Whatever other factors may be involved, it is clear that it is the illicit traffic which makes the drug available to Negroes in the slums, and also supplies an easy but dangerous way of raising the money with which to buy it. Increased addiction among Negroes cannot be accounted for in racial terms, since the trend appeared only after the Harrison Act was passed, and then primarily among urban Negroes in the North. Two other minority groups which have become involved in recent years are Puerto Ricans and Mexicans.

Another minority group which formerly contributed disproportionately large numbers of narcotics law violators was the Chinese. It was the Chinese who came to this country in the second half of the nineteenth century who introduced opium smoking to America. The habit was picked up from them by American criminals, among whom it became something of a fad. Opium smoking thus became the first natural target of control measures. The Chinese, who imported the opium, smoked it, and operated the early opium joints, constituted a considerable proportion of the offenders against the antiopium measures of the late nineteenth and early twentieth century. When the traffic became big business after 1914 it passed out of Chinese hands. As the years have passed the Chinese contribution to the problem has steadily diminished. In 1957 only 13 persons of Chinese origin were reported in a total of more than 7,000 offenders.

It is a common belief that addiction is deliberately spread by drug pushers to enlarge their markets and that they give away free samples to nonaddicts to get them hooked. This idea is false. If instances of this sort do occur they are very infrequent. Peddlers do not give drugs away because they are too expensive and because it is too dangerous. If an ambitious entrepreneur were to start giving away free samples in the manner depicted by some writers, word of this would flash through the addict community and he would be besieged by willing victims, most of them addicts claiming never to have touched heroin in their lives. A considerable number of addicts have testified before congressional committees and most were asked how they became addicted. None of them said it had been through free samples distributed by a pusher, although most did say that their first shots were obtained without cost from friends. Some of the confusion and controversy on this question arises from the tendency of addicts to blame other persons for their addiction when they think they can get by with it or when there is some advantage to be gained by it as, for example, in court before an unsophisticated judge or jury.

As I have said, the process of initiation into the drug habit today usually presupposes intimate friendly relationships between a user and a nonuser, such as those between lovers, close friends, or gang members. The nonuser is not forced to take his first shots or even ordinarily urged to do so. He does so of his own volition, often against the advice of his friends. The human relationship in which addiction is established and in which the preliminary psychological preparations for becoming addicted take place are of such a nature that they are rarely observed. Ordinarily we learn about them only afterward when a new addict is discovered. One of the most favorable environments for the spread of the drug habit in addition to the city slum is, paradoxically, the jail or prison. Unprecedented numbers of addicts are now to be found in our penal institutions. Nonaddicted prisoners become acquainted with them and listen to them talk about dope. Curiosity is aroused. When drugs are successfully smuggled in they may try a pop, or they may do so after release when they meet their addicted prison pals. Nonaddicted criminals often despise and distrust addicts but such prejudices tend to break down in the intimacy of prison life.

Another important element in the creation of new addicts is the lure of easy money from the traffic. Persons who go after a fast buck in this way sometimes end up using the product which they sell. The traffic brings them into association with addicts, familiarizes them with the lore and the necessary techniques, and arouses their curiosity. The step to actual experimentation is easy, especially so because like most nonaddicts the beginner usually believes that he has sufficient will power to resist the drug or to draw back in time.

CHAPTER 5

THE NARCOTIC CLINICS

THE Senate subcommittee under Price Daniel devoted a three-day session in September 1955 to a plan proposed by the New York Academy of Medicine to establish narcotic clinics throughout the country where addicts could receive supplies of drugs legally. This plan was worked out with considerable care and with numerous safeguards to prevent abuses, such as fingerprinting and photographing of addicts, and the suggestion that the fact of an applicant's addiction and his daily drug needs be established by medical observation in a hospital. The clinics were then supposed to operate as out-patient dispensaries providing addicts with low-cost supplies pending complete withdrawal. In the case of incurables it was proposed that they be allowed to obtain their supplies indefinitely from this source. The purposes of the plan were to take the addict out of the hands of the drug peddler and to make it unnecessary for him to commit crime to maintain his habit. Cures were to be voluntary rather than compulsory.

Because no country in the world at present deals with addicts in this manner, a good deal of the argument concerning the system is hypothetical. While most of the Western nations allow addicts access to legal drugs, none of them have clinics. For a brief period of time from about 1919 to 1923 some forty clinics of this general type were set up in the United States. The subcommittee, relying largely on the testimony of federal officials, took it for granted that these clinics had been abject failures and had been closed for that reason. This assumption evidently prejudiced the New York Academy of Medicine plan from the outset, and the subcommittee findings strongly opposed it.

The subcommittee's findings on the clinic idea were formulated in ten propositions:

1. Addicts must be hospitalized, in an atmosphere free of narcotic drugs, or treatment will fail.

2. Ambulatory treatment, where a supply of narcotics is either handed to the drug addict or where he must come to the clinic for shots, is totally unsatisfactory.

3. The plan fails to consider the "tolerance" factor, which causes the addict to demand ever-increasing doses of narcotic drugs.

4. The illicit market would not be eliminated, as the tolerance factor would drive the addict to supplement his "clinic" supply from peddlers.

5. The legalized distribution of free drugs would create new addicts and increase the narcotics problem in the United States.

6. Successful rehabilitation of drug addicts cannot be accomplished under the "clinic plan."

7. "Clinics" would maintain drug addiction, as the addict who failed to respond to rehabilitation would be given "sustaining" doses for life.

8. The "clinic" proposal would necessitate United States withdrawal from international treaties, as well as major changes in Federal and State laws.

9. Experiments with similar "narcotics clinics" in the 1920's showed their abject failure.

10. The "clinic plan" undermines efforts to prevent drug addiction and raises a grave moral issue.[1]

The subcommittee then went on to say of the existing treatment and rehabilitation program that a negligible percentage of present addicts are being cured (less than 15 per cent) and suggested permanent confinement for these incurables, a suggestion which would entail, according to the subcommittee's own estimates, the provision of new prison facilities to accommodate at least 50,000 persons. Federal prisons today house slightly more than twenty thousand inmates.

Objections to the clinic idea were many, but among the most persistent was the notion that the inherent nature of the addict is such that he will under any and all circumstances seek to spread the habit and that punitive coercive measures must be applied to him. The proponents of legalization repeatedly called attention to the fact that these assumptions are invalid in countries like England. This argument appeared to puzzle the Senators briefly but was brushed aside. An interesting comment was a remark by Dr. H. Isbell of the Public Health Service:

... I merely say that England is not the United States; that social conditions in England are far different from those in the United States. Apparently we have an addict-prone population.[2]

That addicts become what they are because of the way they are treated or that the size of the problem is connected with an inappropriate plan for dealing with it are ideas which apparently have not occurred to narcotics officials.

Of the subcommittee's ten propositions concerning clinics, numbers 1, 2, 6, 7, and 10 deal with hypothetical handicaps to the rehabilitation of addicts involved in this plan. But since it is admitted that addicts are not being rehabilitated under present circumstances, these objections amount to contending that the clinic plan would not produce a significant change in this feature of the problem.

The Senate subcommittee's conclusions concerning the clinic plan, and, indeed, on almost all policy questions, were overwhelmingly influenced by the position of the Federal Narcotics Bureau as expressed by its head, Mr. Anslinger, and faithfully echoed by other lesser officials. On the matter of clinics, the Bureau has issued a pamphlet which purports to be an objective evaluation of them, but which is in fact simply a systematic attempt to discredit the clinics.[3] As an historical record this document is highly unreliable and inaccurate. However, its easy availability and official sponsorship, coupled with the fact that the materials which prove its inaccuracy and unreliability must be sought in libraries, has apparently caused it to be generally accepted as the authoritative account of the clinics.

According to this document, during the year 1919 and immediately after, 44 narcotic clinics suddenly blossomed forth in this country only to be promptly closed when local authorities and local communities noted these establishments led to all sorts of evils and abuses including especially an increase of the illicit traffic and the spread of addiction.[4] Actually the clinics were opened upon recommendation of federal authorities and they closed because they were ordered closed under the threat of prosecution by Washington officials. The federal officials who took this action, in the nature of the case, could not have known about the success or failure of the clinics nor of community evaluation of them. It will be recalled that the Harrison Narcotic Act was passed in December 1914 and went into effect early in 1915. The enforcement of the act was at first put into the hands of the collectors of internal revenue, and the brief history of the narcotic clinics is therefore reflected in the annual reports of the Commissioner of Internal Revenue. The annual report covering the fiscal year from June 1918 to July 1919 (the year the clinics appeared) contains the following statement:

It is evident from the enforcement of the law as amended that provision must be made for the treatment and cure of addicts who are unable to obtain supplies of drugs necessary to meet their proper needs, as the ordinary addict, when suddenly deprived of the drug to which he is addicted, suffers extremely both physically and mentally, and in this condition may become a menace to life and property. . . .

To meet immediate demands for the treatment of addicts this matter has been taken up with State and municipal boards of health, and in many instances local clinics have been established to handle this situation temporarily.[5]

The next year's report shows a changed attitude toward addicts and toward clinics; an attitude of moral condemnation replaces the matter-of-fact sympathetic statement of a year earlier:

As a result of the decisions of the Supreme Court in the cases of Doremus and Webb and Goldbaum, in which it was held that the furnishing of narcotic drugs to an addict merely to satisfy his addiction, and not in bona fide medical treatment of disease or addiction, is an indictable offense, many physicians, fearing the operation of the law, refused to use narcotics in their practice. The Bureau was flooded with pleas for "permits" from habitual users of narcotics. In many of these cases the continued use of narcotics seemed necessary to preserve the health and lives of the applicants, but there is no authority of law for the issuance of "permits" in such cases. During the month of July, 1919, instructions were issued to collectors of internal revenue to confer with the United States attorneys and local health authorities in their districts with a view to devising some plan whereby bona fide narcotics cases might be properly treated.

As a temporary expedient to relieve this seemingly critical situation a number of narcotic clinics or dispensaries were established. Some of the so-called clinics that have since been established throughout the country without knowledge or sanction of this Bureau apparently were established for mercenary purposes or for the sole purpose of providing applicants with whatever narcotic drugs they required for the satisfaction of their morbid appetites. Little or no attempt was made by some of these private clinics to effect cures, and prominent physicians and scientists who have made a study of drug addiction are practically unanimous in the opinion that such clinics accomplish no good and that the cure of narcotic addiction is an impossibility unless accompanied by institutional treatment. Steps are now being taken to close these

clinics, which are not only a menace to society but a means of perpetuating addiction. In many cases their continued existence constitutes a
flagrant violation of the law.[6]

In 1921 there is only the brief comment:

Results obtained from closing 44 narcotics clinics formerly operated
in the United States have been most gratifying. The action has been
endorsed by the highest medical authorities.[7]

These excerpts make it quite clear that the clinics were opened
on government initiative and closed by government orders at a
period when drug addicts found their access to the medical profession blocked by the Supreme Court decisions referred to. The
rapid rise of the illicit traffic at this time reflected the addict's inability to secure legal drugs and had nothing whatever to do with
the clinics. The Narcotics Bureau document itself contends that
the addicts registered in the various clinics constituted only a small
proportion of the total addict population. Five years earlier, after
all, in 1914 and before, when every drug store was in a sense a dispensary, there was no illicit traffic!

It is also evident that some time between July 1, 1919, and
June 30, 1920, a radical change in the attitude of the government
took place. A clue concerning the explanation of this about-face is
provided by a description, in the 1920 Report of the Commissioner
of Internal Revenue, of a reorganization undertaken during the
year, in which narcotic and liquor law enforcement were merged:

Early in the calendar year 1920 the field force formerly employed
under the direction of the several revenue agents in charge of the enforcement of the Harrison Narcotic Act was placed under the direction of the twelve supervising Federal prohibition agents. . . .
The Prohibition Unit was created for the purpose of enforcing the
National Prohibition Act, approved October 28, 1919. . . . The Prohibition Unit is also charged with the enforcement of the Harrison
Narcotic Law. . . . A permanent form of organization for the unit was
put into effect December 22, 1919. . . .[8]

The change in policy toward narcotic clinics was thus, in all probability, merely a reflection of this reorganization which replaced revenue officers with prohibition agents as the persons in charge of policy. The brief period of existence of most of the clinics, the arbitrary manner in which many were closed, and the moralistic tinge of the 1920 report all fit neatly with the theory that the new officials brought with them a new philosophy—that of prohibition as expressed in the Volstead Act.

One of the more ridiculous arguments advanced against the clinics in the Bureau's pamphlet is that they perpetuated an evil habit in persons who could be readily cured of their addiction. In 1921 the Treasury Department issued regulations outlining the treatment of addiction permitted under the Harrison Act. In this publication there is the following statement:

It is well established that the ordinary case of addiction yields to proper treatment, and that addicts will remain permanently cured when drug addiction is stopped and they are otherwise physically restored to health and strengthened in will power.[9]

Following this line, the pamphlet suggests that most of the addicts who attended the clinics could easily have been cured of their habits had it not been for the clinics. Thus,

Buffalo, N.Y.—The doctor in charge expressed the opinion that four-fifths of the addicts could be cured if afforded institutional treatment.[10]

In Syracuse the clinic doctor is reported to have claimed that 90 per cent of the 92 addicts there were curable; in Binghamton, N.Y., 22 of 32 were so described and in Oneonta, N.Y., it was 24 of 37.[11]

Actually, the main difference between the clinic idea and current practice with respect to curing addiction is that in current practice the so-called cure is forced upon the addict usually by arrest and incarceration, whereas under the clinic plan it was proposed that addicts temporarily receiving drugs from the clinics would eventually *voluntarily* submit themselves for institutional withdrawal and attempted rehabilitation. The clinics were never intended as a means of curing addiction, but were from the beginning conceived as emergency devices to prevent the economic exploitation of addicts by drug peddlers. It was recognized that complete withdrawal of the drug needed to be undertaken with the addict under constraint within a hospital.

The clinics were set up hastily and often by persons who knew little or nothing about drug addiction. Some of them undoubtedly were poorly operated and abused as the Bureau has claimed, but others were not. In any case most of the clinics were in operation only for an average of several months. As we have seen, the government announced that it had begun to close the clinics before July 1920 and that they had all been closed by July 1921. (Actually the Shreveport Clinic operated until 1923.) In view of the wide differences between the clinics, and the short period of operation, it is inconceivable that the Washington authorities who ordered them closed acted on the basis of knowledge of how the individual clinics operated.

The experience of the New York City Clinic may actually have been a decisive influence. This clinic was poorly conceived in many respects and the addiction problems in New York City were especially difficult. Daily drug rations were handed out to new applicants at an initial amount of about ten grains a day and were then cut down progressively to the minimum daily dosage that would sustain the user. There were no effective controls or checks to prevent the user from supplementing this dosage. The clinic was located in the New York slums and addicts lined up on the sidewalks waiting for their turn. Under these conditions it is not surprising that many users, particularly those with occupations to attend to and with respectable reputations to consider, did not patronize the clinic. The illicit traffic, which had been negligible before 1915, had already developed to considerable proportions by 1919 and the brief establishment of 44 clinics, in which a grand total of less than 15,000 addicts ever registered, made no substantial inroads on it. The latter burgeoned at this time, not because of the clinics, but because of the Supreme Court decisions which caused medical men to refuse to treat addicts.

The same story applies to the rapid increase of the number of addicts in prisons during this period, cited by the Narcotics Bureau's pamphlet as proof of the nefarious influence of clinics. Before 1915 there were very few addicts in the prisons of the land. As the Harrison Act was interpreted in successive Supreme Court decisions and the illicit traffic became the principal source of drugs for them, addicts appeared in jails and prisons in rapidly increasing numbers. When the clinics were closed this trend was accelerated, as was the growth of the illicit traffic.

In view of the Bureau's claims and the common assumption that the clinics of 1919 and 1920 aggravated the drug problem, a brief glance at the federal statistics of narcotics arrests and convictions for the relevant years is pertinent. In *1918*, the year before any clinics were opened, 888 federal arrests and 392 convictions for narcotics offenses were reported. In *1919*, the year in which the New York Clinic operated and others were opened, arrests totaled 1,008 and convictions 582. In *1920*, when the clinics, including the one in New York, were being closed, arrests rose to 3,477 and convictions to 908. In *1921*, when the Prohibition Commissioner reported in June that all the clinics were closed (one exception), arrests had risen further to 4,014 and convictions to 1,583. The yearly rise continued to a peak in *1925*, when the clinics had been closed for several years with 10,297 federal arrests and 5,600 convictions.

The Narcotics Bureau's pamphlet relies heavily, in its negative evaluation of the New York Clinic, on the statements of two New York City health officials of that time who were associated with it—Dr. Royal S. Copeland and Dr. S. Dana Hubbard. Only negative statements are quoted, but both of these men also had some positive things to say. All of these remarks are omitted in the pamphlet. Copeland, for example, after calling attention to the weaknesses of the scheme, added:

The clinic has served a humanitarian purpose in that it has provided a place for a careful physical examination, advice as to needed medical treatment for fundamental conditions, and careful oversight of the progress of the drug disease. . . . Attendance at the clinic has given the health department time and opportunity for study of the home surroundings, personal characteristics, and reliability of the patients.

The gradual but consistent reduction of the daily dosage at the clinic has shortened the period of necessary hospital treatment. Likewise, it has increased the value of residence in the hospital by sending patients in much better condition to begin with than would otherwise be the case. The clinic has given us a hold on hundreds of addicts who, without it, would be lost to the municipal authorities, and, lastly, it has made possible a steady flow of patients to the hospital, thus justifying its necessarily large personnel, and in every way facilitating the problems of hospital administration.[12]

Dr. Hubbard, who also had extensive experience with the operation of the New York Clinic, disapproved of it in general and argued instead for strict enforcement of the Harrison Act, saying, "If they [addicts] cannot obtain a supply, they will reform. . . ." Nevertheless, he also wrote the following:

The work of reclaiming the narcotic drug addict in this vicinity at least—judging from those we have seen and helped—is more than worth while.

The clinic is not the solution—but it aids in bringing the secretive addict out of his lair. He becomes friendlily [*sic*] disposed and, deprived of his supply, he is willing to be cured. . . . No doubt, with suitable organization and funds to institutionalize and adequately and properly care for them, not only to effect withdrawal of drugs, but to rehabilitate by several months after care in the open country, together with efforts to get the individuals away from bad and demoralizing associates, into new and more useful environments, many will revert to useful and normal lives.

Many of these addicts have never had a square deal, and only need a fair chance to change their ways. Already many of them have been returned to useful lives, and many more can be revamped with proper and necessary help.

With success in many instances, in spite of the disadvantages under which the clinic was operated and under which this study has been made, we report our experiences, that others may be induced to enter into this work, appreciating its difficulties and complexities, but knowing that success is possible, in many cases.[13]

Compared to any program for handling addicts that has since appeared, these remarks are high praise indeed, and it is small wonder that many thoughtful members of the medical profession who have read something besides official handouts should favor a return to the clinic idea.

In January 1922 a Congressman with a medical background, Lester D. Volk from the state of New York, on the floor of the House of Representatives violently attacked a number of doctors from New York City and a small group of followers they had gathered about them.[14] He charged that this group was exerting undue influence upon the Prohibition Commissioner and other Washington officials engaged in the enforcement of narcotics laws, and he accused them of engaging in a propaganda campaign designed to pervert the law and to deprive the medical profession of its right to treat addiction disease according to its own lights.

Representative Volk stated that there had grown up in the United States two schools of thought concerning drug addiction, one of which was the "habit" theory, the other the "disease" theory. The New York group which he assailed accepted and promulgated the habit theory, contending that addiction was merely a vicious indulgence which could be controlled and overcome by an appropriate exercise of will power. In accordance with this theory, the medical men who espoused it advocated and supported the prohibitionist policies adopted by the government in about 1920, opposed all ambulatory treatment, and happily turned the addict over to the policeman. It is from the opinions of this New York group and the proponents of the habit theory that most of the medical opinions cited in the Narcotics Bureau's pamphlet were drawn. Volk specifically named Drs. Copeland, Hubbard, and Prentice as members of the small coterie under attack. The views of Hubbard and Copeland have already been touched upon. Dr. Alfred C. Prentice was a member of an American Medical Association Committee on Narcotic Drugs. According to the Narcotics Bureau's pamphlet a member of this committee, probably Prentice, wrote as follows in 1921:

Public opinion regarding the vice of drug addiction has been deliberately and consistently corrupted through propaganda. Cleverly devised appeals to that universal instinct whereby the emotions are stirred by abhorrence of human suffering in any form, or by whatever may appear like persecution of helpless human beings; lurid portrayals of alleged horrible suffering inflicted on addicts through being deprived of their drug; adroit misrepresentation of fact; plausible reiteration of certain pseudoscientific fallacies designed to confuse the unscientific mind; downright false statement [*sic*], and insidious innuendos assiduously propagated are brought to bear on an unsuspecting public to encourage it to feel pity for the miserable wretches, whose name is legion, we are told, and whose sufferings, hysterically exaggerated, are graphically served up to be looked on as if they were actually being made victims of persecution by the authorities, who would deprive the wretches of even the drug they crave.

The shallow pretense that drug addiction is a disease which the specialist must be allowed to treat, which pretended treatment consists in supplying its victims with the drug which has caused their physical and moral debauchery . . . has been asserted and urged in volumes of literature by the self-styled specialists.[15]

The same author spoke of addiction as follows:

The vice that causes degeneration of the moral sense, and spreads through social contact, readily infects the entire community, saps its moral fiber, and contaminates the individual members one after another like the rotten apples in a barrel of sound ones.[16]

This is the language of the prohibition tract rather than of the medical profession. The appearance of this language and this attitude in various reports and resolutions of bodies within the American Medical Association at that time was undoubtedly directly connected with the influence of men like Prentice and others referred to by Volk and indirectly associated with the triumph of the prohibition movement in general.

In opposition to the habit theory, Volk lists Drs. George E. Pettey and E. S. Bishop.[17] He could also have included Drs. C. E. Terry, M. Pellens, E. H. Williams, and many other figures. As we have seen, the Supreme Court of the United States adopted the disease theory in 1924 in the Linder decision and would certainly not have done so if this view had not had high standing and competent representation in medical circles. Representative Volk notes that while the American Medical Association in a number of official actions after 1920 supported the govenment's program, another important national body, the American Public Health Association, opposed it in action taken in 1921.[18] Numerous editorials and comments criticizing the manner in which the Harrison Act impinged on doctors appeared throughout the country at this time.[19] In a number of instances clinics were sponsored and supported by local medical bodies, which also resisted the govenment orders closing them. All of this demonstates beyond any reasonable doubt that the government's program of closing to addicts all avenues of legal access to drugs did not have the undivided support of medical authorities at the time, and that the latter were in fact engaged in a bitter controversy on the question.

The following remark by Congessman Volk was evidently directed at the narcotics agents who collected the materials cited in the Narcotics Bureau's pamphlet on clinics:

. . . It seems to me that the untutored narcotic agents of this great Government under the last administration might have been better employed than in taking sides in a medical controversy involving the broad subject of what will or will not constitute the proper medication in the treatment of addiction. Yet this was done, and I am sorry to say is now being done by our Government, and will continue to be done until the end of time unless some protesting voice is raised against undue interference by lawyers, policemen, and detectives in the practice of medicine, and the furtherance of its research and study.[20]

Concerning the influence of the New York group on Washington, Volk said:

There has developed a tendency in carrying out the objects of the Harrison law to substitute for the provisions of the act arbitrary administrative opinions expressed in rules and regulations which amount to practically a repeal and nullification of the law itself.

These rules and regulations have been promulgated by those in charge of the administration of the Harrison law upon the representation and statements coming as official pronouncements of the New York City Board of Health, presented by a particular small group or clique among whom stand out prominently the names of Royal S. Copeland, Health Commissioner of the City of New York, Drs. E. Elliot Harris, S. Dana Hubbard, Alfred C. Prentice, and a lawyer, Alfred C. Greenfield. Reliable records, reports, scientific information, and experience have been swept aside by these men and in their place has been set up a campaign of publicity intended in the end to benefit this small coterie who seek to control the avenues of narcotic treatment throughout the country.

The agitation emanating from New York City from these men and the Department of Health is spreading over the entire country and knowingly or unknowingly has evaded and ignored sound medical findings. As a substitute for open discussion of known medical facts there has been set up a propaganda for the incarceration of all drug users, their treatment by routine methods, and complete elimination of the family doctor. An undeniable effort is now being made whereby physicians are to be denied any discretion and power in the prescribing of narcotic drugs and to force all those addicted to the use of these drugs into hospitals exploiting questionable "cures."[21]

Volk, with prophetic accuracy, warned of the "calamitous" effects likely to follow from the government's policy, referring to the daily parade of criminal and noncriminal addicts in the courts, the mistreatment of addicts by the police, and the rapid growth of the illicit traffic. He also commented upon the "mysterious orders" from Washington which closed the clinics shortly after they opened without explanation except that Washington officials had "changed their minds."

TWO VERSIONS OF THE SHREVEPORT CLINIC

No reliable information is available concerning most of the forty-four clinics which were opened in the United States and a full and accurate appraisal of them remains to be written. It is the general impression today that the one in Shreveport, Louisiana, was one of the most efficiently operated. It was also the last to close after an existence of about four years. In order that the reader may judge for himself the reliability of the Federal Narcotics Bureau's pamphlet, we reproduce here in full everything which it has to say about the Shreveport clinic, and following this, there is an account of the same clinic taken from Charles E. Terry and Mildred Pellens, *The Opium Problem*, a recognized scholarly and authoritative work.

Shreveport: according to the Narcotics Bureau.[22]

It was estimated that 75 per cent of the drug addicts in Texas made their headquarters at Shreveport following the operation of that clinic. One addict in Texas was apprehended receiving a package through the mail containing 8 grains of morphine sulphate bearing the label of the Shreveport clinic. The defendant stated that he had a friend in Shreveport who obtained 20 grains of morphine from the clinic daily and that he always received half of it.

Forty per cent of the addicts gave a history of venereal disease or examination showed its presence.

In this clinic many fugitive offenders were caught by the police and sent back to places where they were wanted.

The clinic sold monthly $2,500 worth of narcotics, at a monthly profit of about $1,800.

Several prostitutes attended the clinic and plied their trade on the streets of Shreveport. One, 19 years of age, and another 23, had never been addicts until they registered at the clinic.

The addicts said they would take less drugs if the cost were higher; in some cases daily amounts were increased from 5 to 8 grains to 10 grains daily. Addicts who had used 2 grains daily before coming to the clinic were demanding 10 grains. Addicts who got supplies at the clinic sold to other addicts who would not attend. Many of the addicts came from distant states and said they would be off drugs if it were not so easy to procure them. One addict who had never taken drugs previously was induced to buy drugs from an addict in attendance at the clinic and later was persuaded to accompany her to the clinic. The former made a regular practice of selling narcotics she got from the clinic and of getting morphine from other persons she persuaded to go to the clinic.

One citizen of Shreveport stated: "The clinic is an outrage; it should be discontinued; it brings a lot of bums here; nothing is safe on the streets, and the quicker the clinic is closed the better." Another stated: "One of the greatest things that can be done for this community is to close the narcotic clinic." These statements were typical of the public opinion on the subject.

Evidence showed a continuous traffic in narcotics between the clinic patients and others, and that numerous persons who had never used drugs previously, or who had been cured of addiction over several year periods, registered at the clinic and using as high as 10 grains daily. Many of the persons used fictitious names and addresses, and were without visible means of support. One addict stated that when he came to Shreveport before the clinics were established, the same doctor who was in charge of the clinic had cured him of drug addiction, after which he had discontinued the use of drugs for 18 months. As soon as the clinic went into operation he applied for 8 grains of morphine a day, and when his case was investigated he was receiving 12 grains daily at the clinic from the same doctor who had previously cured him of addiction. Another addict who had been cured of addiction before he registered at the clinic stated that "it would be one of the finest things that ever happened if there were not a grain of morphine obtainable, because the only reason that myself and others are addicts is due to the fact that the stuff is so easy to get in Shreveport."

One addict went direct to Shreveport from Leavenworth Penitentiary where he had served a year for narcotic law violations. He was put on the clinic register and given 10 grains of morphine daily. A woman who had been off drugs for a considerable length of time before she went to the clinic was receiving 11 grains of morphine daily.

There was a continuous illicit narcotics traffic being carried on in Shreveport, both in supplies procured from the clinic, and in narcotics obtained elsewhere by peddlers. It was never possible to procure evidence of illicit sales of drugs as agents were always confronted with bottles bearing the clinic label.

This clinic was conducted not only in violation of the Harrison Act but in defiance of orders of the Louisiana Medical Association a year prior to the date in 1923 when it finally ceased operations.

Shreveport: according to Charles E. Terry and Mildred Pellens.[23]

Historical Sketch

Inception, Development, Municipal Activity, Reasons for Closing

During 1916, four physicians of Shreveport were indicted for violating the Harrison Act. They were not convicted but the incident had a psychological effect upon the medical profession as physicians hesitated, as Dr. Butler says in his report, to care for cases of addiction lest they unintentionally violate the federal law, avoiding the handling of these cases rather than studying the law, the case itself and the problem as a whole.

This state of affairs became apparent to Dr. Butler, the parish physician, as the chronic users of opium applied to him for assistance and very quickly developed a sociologic problem which the community was not equipped to handle. Some of the cases were sent to jail for treatment and either were withdrawn from the drug or supplied by smuggled drugs. A number of them died.

Eventually the use of four rooms in the jail was secured for the treatment of these cases but because of the inadequacy of equipment and of the difficulty in stopping the smuggling of the drug, this work was not successful.

In 1919 the state board of health appointed a physician in Shreveport to take charge of the narcotic situation. He wrote all the prescriptions of these cases, which were filled at one authorized drug store. This arrangement lasted but one month, its failure being due to three factors: first, the expense and trouble to the patient who was required to secure daily prescriptions when he could patronize the peddler more easily; second, the impracticability of one physician's attempting to care for so many cases without assistance; third, the druggist's objection to having his store patronized by a class of people looked upon by the public as criminals.

The physician who had been appointed to handle this situation resigned and Dr. Butler was instructed by the state board of health to care for these cases by establishing a dispensary. That the need of some provision was increasing is shown by the following excerpt from a letter to Dr. Butler from the president of the state board of health:

"We are getting daily the names of patients being discharged from the Army and Navy who reside near Shreveport and who should be sent there for treatment, but as yet we are unable to refer them there."

Dr. Butler organized his dispensary and with the assistance of a pharmacist and special assistants supplied the drug to chronic users according to state regulations which will be explained later. Quarters in the Charity Hospital were secured for the treatment of curable cases. During the first two years the number of patients handled at the dispensary was reduced from 494 to 188, some having been cured and others in one way or another eliminated.

On March 15, 1921, the Louisiana State Board of Health after consulting with the federal narcotic officials discontinued the narcotic dispensaries in New Orleans, Alexandria, and Shreveport. Upon the following day Dr. Butler reopened the Shreveport dispensary and moved the institution for treatment from the Charity Hospital to a house near the business center of the city. He continued to work on his own responsibility as parish physician and through the authority of the city council of Shreveport, expressed in the following ordinance:

"(1) That a public health hospital and out-patient service be, and the same is hereby established for the City of Shreveport.

"(2) That said institution shall be under the charge and control of the City Council of Shreveport and its management subject to the supervision of said Council, shall be under the direction of Dr. Willis P. Butler, Parish physician until such time as it may be otherwise ordained by this body. The purpose of said institution is declared to be for the treatment of narcotic and venereal cases.

"(3) Be it further ordained: That whereas the Police Jury of the Parish of Caddo defrays a portion of the expenses of said institution that said Parish physician is empowered to care for and treat the same class of patients for the Parish of Caddo."

The last clause of this ordinance shows that the Police Jury had already taken action. In fact previous to and anticipating the state board of health's order to close the dispensary and institution, the Police Jury had passed a resolution to continue Dr. Butler's narcotic work.

This briefly outlines the inception and development of the dispensary and institution for treatment. The need of municipal action begins with the indictment of the four local physicians already mentioned and had its final expression in the passage of the ordinance continuing the method that the council had found to be effective. During the years 1921-23 this arrangement controlled satisfactorily the narcotic problem. One hundred and forty patients were given curative treatment while the number of cases attending the dispensary was decreased to one hundred and one.

Early in 1923 a conference was held in the office of the United States District Attorney between Dr. Butler and the federal narcotic agents. As a result of this conference it was decided to close the dispensary. The agent present at the conference stated that he had been sent "to close the clinic because it was the only one left in the United States." In commenting on this Dr. Butler quoted from a letter written by Dr. L. M. Powers, Health Commissioner of Los Angeles, California, who said when the Los Angeles clinic was closed in 1921:

"I have not been able to realize the actual purpose of the closing of our clinic for there has been some unseen motive prompting much opposition to clinics which I have not been able to comprehend."

THE DISPENSARY
METHOD OF OPERATION—RESULTS

The dispensary was located in the director's laboratory in the Shreveport Sanitarium with the following personnel: medical director, chief clerk and bookkeeper, assistant clerk and finger-print expert, pharmacist, dispenser, three inspectors selected with the approval of the police department, the local board of health and the medical director; other assistants for special work were employed when needed.

The dispensary days were Monday, Tuesday, Thursday, and Saturday from 8:30 to 10:00 A.M. and from 4:30 to 6:00 P.M. Where these hours created a hardship on the patient he was cared for at some more convenient time.

Morphin was dispensed in solution, the container being labelled to show the amount in grains and the price. The doses varied from one grain to as much as twelve grains a day for certain patients, the average being eight grains. In each case the amount of morphin dispensed was the least that the patient could take and still remain in "drug balance." Since the dispensary was not intended for curative treatment but as a means of caring for incurables and those physically unable to undergo treatment, no effort was made to reduce the amount finally decided upon as the patient's proper dose.

The cost of morphin as supplied at the dispensary was an important matter as will be explained later. The wholesale price of the drug varied from two to three cents a grain. The dispensary price was six cents a grain as against the druggist's price of ten to twenty-five cents a grain, exclusive of the prescription fee, and the peddler's price of $1.00 a grain. Under the dispensary management the difference between the cost and the selling price paid the actual operating expenses of both the dispensary and the institution for treatment, the entire undertaking being self-supporting.

Patients admitted to the dispensary were carefully examined and recorded. In the beginning any patient applying was admitted but the number was necessarily limited later to residents of the state and again later to residents of Caddo Parish. They were divided through examination into the curable and incurable cases and placed in one of the two classes. Complete medical histories were taken, together with information relating to age, sex, color, length of time during which the drug had been used, former treatment, and the causative factors, together with an exhaustive physical description. Finger-prints with personal description were sent to the local police department, to the local detective agency and to Leavenworth.

Before being dispensed to, the patient was requested to sign a pledge not to sell, give away, lend, borrow, or otherwise obtain any of the drug. His residence and business addresses were secured and frequently checked by inspectors. All patients able to do so were required to work and to secure proper food and clothing. No loafers were tolerated. These rules governed patients who were not infirm, decrepit, or bed-ridden.

A monthly record sheet contained the names of the patients. Upon receiving their medicine patients signed this register, the clerk entering opposite the signatures the amount dispensed in grains and the price paid. This daily record was kept of those coming to the dispensary in person. For those who were bed-ridden or who held a doctor's certificate as to infirmity a special order form printed on safety paper was employed. These were serial in number, dated and signed, and gave the reasons for the individual's inability to come in person, together with the name of the authorized proxy. Only one order form was issued at a time and a strict record kept of each.

The institution for treatment was located at the Charity Hospital until the work was discontinued by the state board of health in 1921 when it was established in another locality. It was called the Public Health Hospital and in addition to treatment for chronic users of opium it provided treatment for cases of venereal disease either free or at the cost of the medicine. This institution had a resident physician, super-intendent, nurses, guard, and attendants.

The rules governing the institutional treatment of the narcotic patients were as follows:

"(1) Institutional treatment is free to any resident of Caddo Parish.

"(2) An addict who is able physically to undergo treatment must sign voluntarily an application for commitment to the institution. (If he is judged physically able and will not take the treatment he is no longer dispensed to.)

"(3) He also signs a request to be placed in the Parish jail to complete the treatment if for any reason this may be deemed necessary by the Director.

"(4) He is required to make a deposit of twenty-five dollars for his own use at the end of treatment, unless he is known to be in good financial circumstances.

"(5) The medical method of treatment is divided into three parts, (1) Previous preparation; (2) the period of narcotic withdrawal under restraint; (3) after care. By the first term is meant, assurance that the physical condition is strong enough to endure the rigor of the withdrawal. The salient features of the treatment proper, are rapid withdrawal and substitution, proper elimination, abundant food, rest and warm baths. By the third term is meant, a place of convalescence, preferably in the country."

RESULTS

Dr. Butler states that the results from the points of view of the users, physicians and druggists, and society at large from a properly operated dispensary and institution for treatment have a distinct medical and sociological value.

First: The patient. Such a treatment prevents or alleviates a great deal of physical suffering. The dispensary and treatment institution treated all cases including the parish prisoners. The curables were treated first for whatever physical conditions they were suffering from and then for their drug intoxication, while the incurables were improved physically and their doses properly regulated. Many cases who had been "down and out" were raised to a plane of decent living. With their drug inexpensive and regularly supplied they were enabled to work and provide for their families. In the opinion of the Associated Charities, federal and parish authorities and the city police department, crime was prevented and the narcotic problem from every angle was ameliorated by the medical care of these patients.

Second: Physicians and Pharmacists. The system was helpful to physicians and druggists in that it saved much of their time and prevented annoyance from the insistent demands of individuals for whom they could not regularly care. It prevented duplication of work for one patient and neglect of others. That the medical profession appreciated this work is shown by its unqualified support and approval of the clinic as evidenced by the passage of resolutions to this effect.

Third: Society as a whole. That the work of the clinic was beneficial to society as a whole is apparent. It reduced the number of future users and the system that made the dispensary effective became an auxiliary to the city's police department. Dishonest and unworthy cases were detected, cut off from the dispensary and because of the absence of peddlers in the city were forced to move away. Thus crime was prevented, as there was no profit possible for criminal addicts or peddlers. A considerable burden of indigency was saved the city by the rehabilitation of these patients.

RELATION OF CLINIC TO:

1. Peddling
2. Federal and state-control measures
3. Other methods of control.

1. It prevented peddling and the pauperizing of the user. It prevented illicit sale by (a) providing for the incurable cases, preparing the curables for treatment and treating them, whereas the peddler deliberately increased his sales by creating new users and (b) eliminating the vicious type of user.

2. The chief manifestation of federal control has been the arrest of users in order to stop the illicit traffic. This method of control, according to Dr. Butler, only aggravates the situation as it makes dependents of the user's family, which thus creates a social and economic problem.

Dr. Butler quotes the United States Marshal as having stated that through taking advantage of the facilities afforded at the clinic he was able to secure quick relief without the unnecessary resorting to red tape required under other circumstances. Through the detective system practiced by the dispensary many arrests of peddlers were made and evidence sufficient to convict them secured, but Dr. Butler states these cases when brought into court were either repeatedly postponed or dismissed.

3. Another method of control that Dr. Butler claims is a complete failure is that of the enforced treatment of users. This procedure results in repeated relapses, deaths, or suicides during the withdrawal, or smuggling of the drug into the institutions in which these cases are confined. In this connection Dr. Butler gives the following acknowledgement from the state board of health president: "Your statistics in cures are decidedly higher than those of any others we have received."

In conclusion he states that federal and other state control measures employed have failed to give such good results as were derived from the operation of the dispensary and the institution for treatment, namely:

One responsible organization to control supply.

Proper facilities for observation, examination, and treatment of patients.

Ability to care for incurable cases without expense to the community and at but slight expense to the patients.

A self-supporting system.

Since the closing of the dispensary, Dr. Butler reports the deaths of several former patients, three of these in jails in other cities, while a number of his patients have been sent to the state penitentiary. Of the remainder of the one hundred and one incurable cases, Dr. Butler continued to care for forty for about a year. The others he states were supplied by peddlers at $1 or more a grain inasmuch as their physicians refused to care for them. Individuals who during the life of the dispensary were leading decent lives and supporting their families reached a condition of wretched poverty. In 1924, the number of incurables attended by Dr. Butler was reduced to twenty-four and then to twenty-one. These were continued until March, 1925, when he ceased prescribing for them. Of the forty cases remaining in his care after the closing of the clinic, four have died, two or three found other physicians to care for them temporarily, a few moved away, and the others have been forced to patronize peddlers.

The organized charities, he states, recognize the evil effects of the closing of the clinic and the city police department and the sheriff report that they are having endless trouble with users and peddlers. Petty crimes are increasing and the peddlers are creating new cases.

The following communications supplied by Dr. Butler from professional groups are of interest in connection with the operation of the Shreveport narcotic clinic:

"To the Shreveport Medical Society:

"This committee appointed to investigate and report on the Shreveport Narcotic Clinic begs to report as follows:

"We had an interview with Dr. Butler at his office on September 29th, and wish to express our unqualified approval of the work being done by Dr. Butler and his associates. We were most favorably impressed by the conduct of the Clinic including the details of complete records of all addicts coming under care, classification of addicts, and treatment according to classification, the elimination of non-residents of La., and the careful treatment of curable cases *Under restraint*, the procuring of employment for addicts who are able to work while attending the dispensary and for cured patients who wish to remain in Shreveport after recovery, are all features of this work that strongly recommend the conduct of this Institution.

"It is significant that Dr. Butler's judicious and tactful conduct of the Clinic has secured for him the unqualified support and cooperation of the Federal, State, Parish and City Authorities, and the State and City Boards of Health.

"In brief we wish to express our unqualified support and approval of the Shreveport Narcotic Clinic and its systematic and effective administration by Dr. Butler.

"Signed: W. H. Billinghaley, M.D.
J. J. Frater M.D.
J. G. Pou M.D.
Committee

"This report was presented to the Shreveport Medical Society at the regular meeting Oct. 5, 1920, and was unanimously adopted.

"Shreveport, La.
"March 15, 1921."

"At a regular staff meeting of the T. E. Schumpert Memorial Sanitarium held at the Sanitarium Tuesday night, March 15, the following resolution was unanimously adopted:

"Resolved that, in the judgment of the Staff of the T. E. Schumpert Memorial, that, for the best interest of humanity and the community, it is advisable that Dr. Willis P. Butler continue the so-called narcotic dispensary and institution as now conducted in the City of Shreveport.

"The following doctors were present at this staff meeting:

J. C. Willis	T. D. Boaz
B. C. Garrett	R. F. Harrell
J. R. Knighton	M. S. Picard
J. J. Frater	M. R. Purnell
J. M. Bodenheimer	I. B. Hougon
J. G. Pou	Thos. Ragan
F. G. Ellis	Dr. Harwell
S. C. Barrow	Dr. Yerger

"Signed: W. S. Kerlin, Sec'y-Treas."

"Dr. Willis P. Butler
Shreveport, La.

"Dear Doctor:—

"The following resolution was adopted by the Staff of North La. Sanatorium, at its regular monthly meeting last night, March 22nd, 1921.

"Resolved that, in the judgment of the Staff of the North La. Sanatorium, that, for the best interests of humanity and the community, it is advisable that Dr. Willis P. Butler continue the so-called Narcotic Dispensary and institution as now conducted in the city of Shreveport, La."

The following Doctors were present:

Dr. D. H. Alverson	Dr. G. C. Rigby
Dr. S. C. Barrow	Dr. J. E. Slicer
Dr. J. M. Gorton	Dr. V. Simmons
Dr. A. G. Heath	Dr. J. F. Tanner
Dr. R. F. Harrel	Dr. Wm. P. Yerger
Dr. L. H. Pirkle	Dr. Thos. F. Ragan
Dr. M. R. Purnell	Dr. C. B. Hicks
Dr. R. A. Pain	Dr. Hearn

"Yours Truly,
"(Signed) J. M. Gorton, M.D."

The striking disparity between these two documents is too obvious to require much comment. Suffice it to say that, in the light of the detailed, factual, and documented account provided by Terry and Pellens there is hardly a single general statement about the clinic in the Bureau's account which can be accepted as accurate or which does not require serious qualification. The opening sentence, for example, contains the assertion that it was estimated that seventy-five per cent of the addicts of Texas made Shreveport their headquarters. It is further stated that many of the addicts came from distant states, presumably other than Texas. Yet, during the entire period of its existence only 1,237 addicts were registered at this clinic, and in one year, 1920, only 331 nonresidents were treated.[24] The reasons given by the Bureau for the closing of this clinic are obviously false.

It is easy to understand that many busy law-enforcement officers would find it much simpler and easier to read the Narcotics Bureau's version, broadcast to them without charge and requiring no special exertion from them, than to dig up the account in Terry and Pellens' book. It is not so easy to understand how it has been possible for other officials to ignore the latter account as completely as they have. Whatever the reason for it may be, the present public version of the history of the United States narcotic clinics of the 1920's is based overwhelmingly on the Bureau's document.

CLINICS AND THE BRITISH PLAN

Finally, it should be repeated that the clinic plan bears almost no relationship to British pactice. English officials become noticeably and justifiably irritated when their scheme is described as the "clinic system," as it often is in the United States. American opponents of drug law reform have adopted the tactic of merging and confusing the two ideas, thus making it possible to discredit both by citing the Bureau's pamphlet and rendering an actual study of the British system superfluous.

CHAPTER 6

NARCOTICS CONTROL IN BRITAIN AND OTHER WESTERN NATIONS

THE writer first became concerned with the narcotics problem about 1935 and a few years later, in published articles, began to make references to the fact that it appeared to be the practice of various European nations to view and deal with addiction, not as a punishable offense, but as a medical problem to be handled by the medical profession rather than by the apparatus of the criminal law. In this connection, special reference was naturally made to the British program both because information concerning it is readily available in the English language and because the program is highly regarded and has sometimes been deliberately emulated by other European nations.

OFFICIAL ATTITUDES

A decade or so ago the idea that it might be wise policy not to apply prohibition tactics to drug addiction was generally regarded as heresy in this country. The narcotics officials of the federal government connected with the Bureau of Narcotics and the Public Health Service generally ignored the existence of anything like the British program, or, if they did take note of it, it was to disparage it and brush it aside as irrelevant to the American problem. This is still the attitude of officials. In the meantime, however, so many descriptions of the British program have appeared in print and been broadcast over radio and television that informed public opinion in this country is now fully aware of the fact that Britain, and most other European and Western nations, permit their addicts access to legal drugs and that none of these nations has a drug problem that represents more than a tiny fraction of the problem in the United States.

When the writer proposed in 1947 that the United States should seriously consider the British system of drug control, Dr. Victor H. Vogel, Medical Officer in charge of the Public Health Service Hospital at Lexington, Kentucky, commented as follows on the proposal:

In spite of known weaknesses of "police" control of narcotic addiction in the United States, which the author proposes to abolish, the fact remains that since the Narcotic Act was passed in 1915 there has been a substantial decline in the number of addicts in this country, although the author leaves one in doubt as to whether he believes a decrease in drug addiction is really desirable. . . .

Professor Lindesmith mentions as an advantage of this free prescription that contraband drug traffic would be wiped out, and the addicts would be able to get their required drugs at a reasonable price, as if that were desirable. Public clinics and free prescription of drugs for addicts have been tried several times with disastrous results. . . .

The proposal for unrestricted prescription of narcotics for addicts is naive in the extreme and dangerous to the public health of the nation. Fortunately, sounder judgment than the author's will prevail and there is no likelihood of the "reforms" which he proposes being carried out.[1]

Another Public Health Service official from Lexington, Dr. Abraham Wikler, remarked:

As for Professor Lindesmith's therapeutic program, one could wonder how many addicts would "voluntarily" enter a hospital and remain sufficiently long for adequate treatment if they could obtain all the drugs necessary to maintain addiction through legal channels at low cost! England is cited as a desirable example of such a practice, but no facts or figures are given to support this contention. The situation in India, Iran, and China is passed over in discreet silence.[2]

In 1948, when these remarks were published, the essential facts concerning European practices were as available to Public Health Service officials, as they are today. It is strange that none of them ever sought to nip the heresy in the bud by describing these practices!

At the White House Conference on addiction in September 1962 very little attention was given to any foreign programs. Professor Edwin M. Schur, who had just published what may fairly be described as a definitive study of British practices on the basis of two years of on-the-spot observation and inquiry, was allotted two minutes at the very end of one session.[3] Earlier in the session another speaker had, in a much longer speech, told the audience that the British program was essentially the same as the American. No attention at all was devoted to any of the many other successful foreign programs. The President's Ad Hoc Committee which met before the 1962 White House Conference, as well as the President's Advisory Commission appointed after the conference, which issued its report in November 1963 gave little attention to foreign experience or dismissed it as irrelevant.

THE BRITISH SYSTEM

The description of British practices which follows will be abbreviated because it is believed that the essential aspects of the program are generally understood in this country and are no longer under serious dispute. It will be noted that British practices are here referred to as a "system," despite the fact that it is alleged by various writers that British officials deny that their program constitutes a system. It is said by these writers that the "so-called British system" was invented by Americans for propaganda purposes. In defense against these critics, it is worth noting that British practices have been called a "system" by a prominent British official, formerly with the Ministry of Health and a Joint Secretary of the famous Rolleston Committee—Dr. E. W. Adams. The Rolleston Committee, by its report of 1926, virtually established the British system through its interpretation of the Dangerous Drugs Laws of 1920—an interpretation which was accepted as official and continues to be so regarded.

Dr. Adams had this to say about his country's program:

The regulations made under the Dangerous Drugs Acts are so strictly and impartially enforced that the person who has had the misfortune to contract a drug habit soon finds it difficult or impossible to get supplies of his drug sufficient to satisfy his craving and he begins to suffer the pangs of partial or more or less complete abstinence. This state is so distressing that he is driven to consult his doctor and to reveal to him the nature of his ailment in the hope that he may at least be furnished, for the time being, with enough of the drug to keep him going. Nor is this hope ill founded, for he will most likely be submitted to the so-called "ambulatory treatment" under which the patient is at large while being treated, and is allowed to receive such supplies of his drug as the doctor thinks to be necessary for therapeutic purposes. For it is never possible at once to cut off the patient from his drug by this method. He takes advantage, in fact, *of what, to speak frankly is neither more or less than a system of legalized purveying.* [Italics added.]

Even where the addict has, from the nature of his profession, special opportunities of access to narcotic drugs, as is the case with members of the medical and ancillary professions, yet, sooner or later, the same difficulty of supply confronts him, for unusual purchases of "dangerous drugs," beyond the reasonable necessities of his professional requirements, sooner or later attract attention and are revealed to the authorities either by inspection of his own records or those of the supplying druggists. He can, therefore, in the long run hardly escape detection and is then constrained to place himself under the care of a brother practitioner to whom the nature of the case will of necessity have to be revealed.[4]

The Home Office annually reports the number of persons known to be using drugs regularly. It maintains a file in which the cases are classified into two sections—medical and nonmedical. The former contains data concerning persons regularly receiving drugs because of disease, such as cancer patients; the latter, persons who are simply addicts—that is, persons who are receiving drugs primarily because they are addicted to them and not because of disease. The number of addicts reported in 1955 was 335, a total which was evidently secured by counting the number of cards in the nonmedical section. Since 1955 the number has risen to over 500. The information recorded in these files is obtained from data voluntarily supplied by pharmacists and doctors, as well as from regular inspection of the pharmacies.

Narcotics Bureau spokesmen in the United States have suggested that British statistics are unreliable and that there are probably more addicts than they indicate. This is true to some extent, for the only figures disseminated by British officials are those pertaining to addicts known to the Home Office. They do not offer estimates concerning unknown addicts except to say that the number is relatively small. British narcotics statistics are, in fact, considerably more reliable than our own, as one would expect from the fact that addiction is handled as a medical matter and that the motives for concealment are correspondingly less. It is also pointed out with respect to British totals that they do not include opium smokers, of whom there are said to be a small number, mainly of Oriental extraction, in a few of the larger cities.

In May 1955 Mr. John H. Walker, the British delegate to the United Nations Narcotics Commission, described the British drug problem and how it is handled to a special committee of the Canadian Senate. On the matter of hidden addiction he commented as follows:

From time to time, the Home Office has received confirmation of its opinion that the degree of hidden addiction is small. One of the leading physicians in the country, who lives and practices in a large provincial conurbation, asked over seventy local practitioners if they had a drug addict among their patients. None of them had. The physician himself was aware of one case in the district, which was of therapeutic origin. The chief constable of a provincial seaport (a city where, if drug addiction flourished at all in the United Kingdom it would certainly be found) in response to allegations about the existence of vice and drug addiction in the city, and in particular among seamen of Asiatic origin, conducted a most thorough enquiry and found no evidence whatever of drug addiction. . . .

There are one or two minor pointers which suggest the same conclusion. For some years the metropolitan police isolated the figures for dangerous drugs in respect of theft from unattended motor vehicles. This practice was discontinued because the number of cases was so small that the information was worthless. The prewar practice of keeping statistics of all drug addicts admitted to prisons fell into partial disuse for the same reason. A recent survey of admissions to the principal prisons in Great Britain revealed less than two dozen addicts were admitted in the two years ending December 31, 1954. . . . The "Criminal" addict, i.e., the addict who is a confirmed criminal apart from his drug addiction, is virtually unknown in the United Kingdom.[5]

These statements have since been fully confirmed by an American sociologist, Edwin M. Schur.[6]

The basic antinarcotic statutes of Britain were passed in 1920 and are known as the Dangerous Drugs Laws. Like the Harrison Act, these statutes make no reference to drug addicts or to addiction, and like the Harrison Act they do not state what is regarded as the proper medical practice with respect to addicts. A memorandum issued to doctors and dentists by the Home Office states that doctors and dentists may have or use drugs only for ministering to the "strictly medical or dental needs" of patients.[7] This rule reflects the attitude of the law enforcement agencies and the Home Office immediately after 1920 until the Rolleston Report appeared. The latter was an official committee consisting of medical men which was appointed in 1924 to resolve what appeared to be a conflict of views between physicians, who were in fact caring for addicts, and law enforcement bodies, which thought that the 1920 statutes prohibited this. The Rolleston Committee resolved the issue in favor of the physicians when it ruled that drugs might be administered or prescribed regularly for addicts when "the patient, while capable of leading a useful and relatively normal life when a certain minimum dose is regularly administered, becomes incapable of this when the drug is entirely discontinued."[8] This rule had the effect of defining as "treatment" the regular provision of drugs for addicts and gave to physicians the final authority in handling addicts.

The above interpretation of the statutes by the Rolleston Committee is the crux of the difference between the British program and ours. It has created a situation in Britain such that the addict is under pressure to go to the physician, for if he does so he not only may obtain regular supplies of pure drugs but he can also avoid all entanglements with the law. There is a small black market in some of the larger cities but all operations on this market, whether by addicts or nonaddicts, are subject to punishment. The penalties generally consist of fines of less than $500.00 or of jail or prison sentences of less than one year. The maximum prison term specified in the statute is ten years, the same as in the Harrison Act.

The British program with respect to addicts is in reality absurdly simple and almost impossible to misunderstand. The addict simply goes to a doctor, confides in him, and is taken care of by the doctor. The latter is under a professional obligation to attempt to cure the addict, but there is no provision for forced cures, and the user must therefore be *persuaded* to submit himself to a hospital for withdrawal of the drug. Under the National Health Act, the addict's habit costs him only the few cents that all patients are charged for each prescription—two shillings, or 28¢. The doctor who cares for the addict takes no risk of criminal prosecution. The addict can be prosecuted for forging prescriptions, going to two doctors simultaneously to augment his legal supplies, or patronizing the black market. The British program has no necessary connection with what is commonly called "socialized medicine," since it was in existence before the latter. The British addict is handled about the way in which a few upper-class addicts in this country are, namely, as a patient afflicted by disease.

The advantages which seem to follow from the British program are numerous and important. Since the demand for narcotics which maintains the illicit traffic stems from addicts, the profits of that traffic are seriously undermined when addicts are largely removed from the market. Legal accessibility to drugs through physicians makes it possible for the addict to avoid the social disgrace and demoralization associated with criminality. The motivation to commit property crimes to pay high illicit prices is removed. The addict is protected from exploitation by peddlers and police alike. Most important of all, perhaps, is the fact that the addict is accorded a decent right to privacy and does not face the constant prospect of seeing the unhappy details of his habit and personal life published on the front pages of the daily newspapers. From the standpoint of costs, the program is also attractive because it involves little expenditure of public funds and does not require a large bureaucracy or many special public institutions. Unlike the program in the United States, the British program has less tendency to draw all addicts and peddlers together to form a self-perpetuating narcotic subculture.

American critics sometimes say that the British program does not put enough emphasis upon curing drug users of their habits. However, there is nothing to indicate that cures are any less frequent there than here. The central difference in this respect is that we attempt to cure by compulsion while the British do not. While it may seem at first glance that a forced cure is better than none at all, it should not be forgotten that there is a price to pay for compulsion in terms of criminality, the illicit traffic, and the demoralizing, self-perpetuating effect that inevitably attends the congregate handling of addicts in large public institutions. As we have seen in an earlier chapter, it is characteristic of Britain and apparently of virtually all countries with this type of program that the number of addicts is relatively low, that there are very few youthful users, and that addiction contributes little to the crime problem in proportion to the number of addicts. If a program of this sort contributes to creating these effects, it deserves more serious consideration than it has yet been given.

OFFICIAL VS. PUBLIC OPINION

For a considerable number of years after 1954 the Federal Bureau of Narcotics circulated an anonymous, undated document attacking the present writer and seeking to discredit the British program or deny its existence. This document opened as follows:

Several years ago a professor of sociology at an American university who is a *self-appointed expert* on drug addiction, after interviewing a few drug addicts, wrote an article in which he advocated that the United States adopt the British system of handling drug addicts by having doctors write prescriptions for addicts. He reported that this system had abolished the black market in narcotics and that consequently there were only 326 drug addicts in the United Kingdom. The professor followed the method used by dictators to "make it simple, say it often"; true or false, the public will believe it. "Adopt the British system" is now urged by *all self-appointed narcotic experts who conceal their ignorance of the problem by ostentation of seeming wisdom.* The statement was recently used by a Columbia University professor on a television program and in a national press release in advocating this system. A Citizen's Advisory Committee report to the Attorney General of California urged the British system. It has appeared in articles by university professors in several states. The Yale University Law Review published a supporting article. It is now accepted as a fact. [Italics added.]

Nothing could be further from the truth. The British system is the same as the United States system. . . .[9]

This states the theme which the Bureau of Narcotics and its followers have been promoting during the last decade. It is a theme which the new head of the Bureau, Henry L. Giordano, has taken over from his predecessor. It is significant to observe that the statement contains a phrase which is used over and over again by Bureau spokesmen and law enforcement personnel—"self-appointed expert." This term is applied by the Bureau, often with the added clause—"who conceal their ignorance of the problem by ostentation of seeming wisdom,"—to most of its critics. This involves tacit recognition of the interesting fact that the demand for basic narcotics law reform in the United States arises from the informed general public and is opposed by officialdom. A narcotics official, even if he disagreed with the Bureau, could not be called "self-appointed."

The tactics followed by the Bureau under Mr. Anslinger were, in the main, to deny that the British program is any different from ours, to equate the program with the clinic system, to disparage the accuracy and reliability of British official reports and statistics, to include Hong Kong in Britain, and to argue that the British program is not a "system." To cite a few examples from Mr. Anslinger, in 1953 he remarked:

No government in the world conducts such clinics, no matter what is said about England. What about all the seizures there? What about the trouble doctors are having keeping their bags from being stolen?

In England, the British Government reports annually only 350 drug addicts known to the authorities—mostly doctors and nurses. When we ask them about the statistics on seizures of opium and hashish [marihuana], they say: Negroes, Indians, and Chinese are involved. In this country, we don't distinguish; we take the situation as a whole. England, during the past year, has had a surge of hashish addiction among young people. A year ago they were looking at the United States with an "it can't happen here" attitude. Suddenly hashish addiction hit the young people. Ordinarily hashish is only something for the Egyptian, the Indian. Now the British press is filled with accounts of cases of addiction of young people.[10]

From these statements one would not suspect that prosecutions for offenses involving marihuana reached a peak of 152 in Britain in 1954, or that in most years no seizures of manufactured drugs and no cases of the theft of legitimately manufactured drugs are reported to the police.

In a review of Mr. Anslinger's 1953 book, a British police official who signed his review with the initials "R.M.H." remarked as follows:

> There are one or two attacks on English complacency about the drug position in this country. On page 279 we read: "Suddenly hashish addiction hit the young people and now the British press is filled with accounts of cases of addictions of young people." This statement is, of course, quite untrue.[11]

Speaking of the distribution of legal drugs to addicts, Mr. Anslinger in 1955 said:

> There is only one place in the world—well, there are three places in the world where that is done. There is a transitory condition there in India and Pakistan, where the eating of opium will cease in 1958, and they have registered their last opium smoker in both of those places. So there is only one. There is only one country which still permits the so-called ambulatory treatment of drug addiction through pipe smoking, and that is Thailand.[12]

The conception of legalized opium smoking as a form of "treatment" and the implication that the opium-smoking den is a type of clinic are interesting. In 1957, Mr. Anslinger was quoted as follows: "There is a great deal of misconception about the so-called British system; the European countries, except Denmark, have the same system as ours, and England does not permit prescribing for a non-medical addict."[13]

From an interview by Pete Martin with the new head of the Federal Bureau of Narcotics reported in the *American Legion*

Magazine, it is apparent that the Bureau is continuing to stick to its guns. The following conversation is reported:

MARTIN: I'd like to begin by asking you about the difference between the American system and the English system of narcotics control. I understand that in England they have free clinics for addicts to get their daily shot; while in this country we discarded that system back in the twenties and are more inclined to grab the addicts and institutionalize them.

GIORDANO: The so-called British system has been discussed many times in this country—and tried as you mentioned—but there's really very little difference between the methods actually practiced today in England and those employed here. Dr. Granville Larimore and Dr. Henry Brill from New York State went over there to study British methods. . . . When they came back they said in effect that they could find very little difference between the control method used in England and here. . . .

Britain has never made a real census of drug addiction. For three years they've published figures, indicating they had 350 addicts, two years ago 400, and last year 500. This seems unrealistic when not long ago they tried and convicted a doctor for selling drugs to hundreds of addicts among his "patients" alone! The only figures they have in the United Kingdom are when a doctor chooses to report them.

MARTIN: Five hundred seems a completely unrealistic figure to me. Just what is this British system?

GIORDANO: As far as we're concerned, there really isn't such a thing, even though everyone talks as if there is. The trouble is they seem to have ignored the problem, apparently have refused to acknowledge it. Now in Hong Kong, where they have an accurate census, they admit having 200,000 to 250,000 addicts, and it is a serious, sizable problem. The British have a growing marijuana problem at home, too.[14]

There are a number of puzzling aspects in the above remarks. For example, if the British program is no different from ours, what does Mr. Giordano mean by agreeing with Martin that the program was tried in this country in the 1920's and abandoned? Also, if the programs are the same, why try to show that the program in England is not as effective as claimed? Giordano's reference to an English doctor who sold drugs to his patients seems to be a reference to Dr. John Bodkin Adams. Dr. Adams, however, was tried for murder, not for selling drugs, and he was acquitted. The assertion that Dr. Adams sold drugs to many of his patients seems to have been based on newspaper reports in this country and not on any facts developed in an English court. The reference to Hong Kong is especially ironic because, as we will point out in a subsequent chapter, the program in use there is essentially the American one of prohibition and punishment. It is true that Britain does not have a census of addicts; but neither does the United States, or Hong Kong.

Narcotics enforcement officials at the state and municipal levels generally follow the line established by the Federal Bureau of Narcotics and if they read any of the literature it is most likely to be materials distributed by the Bureau. Those who read more widely run into the problem of trying to reconcile the Bureau's position with what they read. This is exemplified in a book already referred to, by Lt. Thorvald Brown (now Captain Brown) of the Oakland, California, police department. Following the lead of the federal authorities, Brown makes many disparaging remarks about "uninformed experts," the "many who know so little," and, on the first page of a chapter devoted to "The British System and the American Clinic Plan," flatly asserts: "after serious consideration and study, it is soberly suggested that Her Majesty's government knows little about the illicit traffic in the British Empire."[15]

Lt. Brown, however, is an honest cop, and as one continues to read his account of the British program, the existence of which he at first seems to deny, it becomes perfectly clear that he knows that English addicts are provided with drugs legally by physicians. He comments, for example:

The government makes no demands of proof that addicts who are furnished drugs are leading normal and useful lives, or that drugs are essential or given in the minimum doses necessary for this purpose.

Physicians receive a government subsidy for writing narcotic prescriptions and the high consumption of legal drugs suggest the existence
of much hidden addiction.

A survey made in England indicates there are probably close to one
thousand addicts rather than the 350 known to the Home Office. . . .[16]

As we have seen, many spokesmen for the Bureau's curious position on Britain's policies preface their comments on it by deploring
public misconceptions of it in this country. As a matter of fact,
however, the American public probably has a much clearer picture
of the British program than of the American. After all, the former
is extremely simple and consistent and its essentials can be spelled
out in a paragraph. Millions of Americans, moreover, have listened
to top British officials explaining their system on national television
programs in this country. The American program, on the other
hand, is extremely complex, inconsistent, and varied, as anyone
quickly discovers when he tries to comprehend it.

THE LARIMORE-BRILL REPORT

This report on British practices with respect to drug addiction
was submitted to Governor Rockefeller of the state of New York
in 1959.[17] Its authors were two officials of the state government,
from the Departments of Health and of Mental Hygiene. It will be
recalled that the present head of the Bureau of Narcotics has cited
this study in support of his contention that there is no distinctive
British program. Since the Larimore-Brill report was made, it has
been reprinted in quantity and widely circulated free of charge by
the Public Health Service and the Federal Bureau of Narcotics.
The writer, for example, has received four unsolicited free copies
of it! No other report on this subject has been accorded this honor.

The central distinctive aspect of the Larimore-Brill report is that
these authors, after accurately stating the fact that English physicians legally provide addicts with regular supplies of drugs, nevertheless conclude that the program is little different from that in the

United States. The logical processes involved in reaching this conclusion have never been divulged and are not understood. At a conference in Los Angeles at the University of California in April 1963, Leslie T. Wilkins, well-known statistician, student of delinquency and crime, and Home Office official, indicated with unmistakable clarity that he regarded this conclusion of Larimore and Brill as nonsense.[18] The New York Academy of Medicine reached a similar conclusion.[19] Both Mr. Wilkins and the Academy agreed that the description provided by Schur is a more cogent and accurate one than that of Larimore and Brill.

An argument presented by these authors and picked up by Americans who favor the status quo is that the admittedly small extent of the British narcotics problem is the cause of the program rather than the reverse. The implication is that the nature of the program has nothing much to do with the number of addicts. From this viewpoint, since the British and American programs are allegedly the same, the British adopted their system because they had so few addicts and we adopted the same system before they did because we had so many. The number of addicts in a country, according to Larimore and Brill, is determined mainly by the number of addiction-prone personalities in the population, not by the system of control. The illicit traffic in drugs, they imply, depends upon the demand for drugs from such addiction-prone persons, not on the demand from those who are addicted. The absence of an illicit traffic in Britain is to them an indication that there are very few addiction-prone people in Britain. The influence exerted on the illicit traffic by taking addicts out of the market is wholly overlooked, as is the influence of the traffic on the factor of availability. An addiction-prone person does not become addicted unless drugs are made available to him, usually through the illicit traffic, and the latter cannot flourish if addicts can secure low-cost legal drugs.

Since virtually all of the countries of Europe have programs substantially the same as that in Britain, and since all of them also have relatively small numbers of addicts, the Larimore-Brill argument must be that they have medical programs for addicts because they have so few of them. If this position is taken seriously in conjunction with the contention that the extent of the drug problem is determined by cultural and personal susceptibilities to addiction, there could be no possible objection to American adoption of the British program which, in any case, is said to be the same as the American, because this would have no effect upon the number of addicts in the country, just as it allegedly has had no such effect in Europe.

The Alice-in-Wonderland nature of the reasoning in this report is well exemplified in the following remarkable statement by Larimore and Brill in the condensed version of their report:

In England what appears to be the major gap in the epidemiologic picture, probably for cultural reasons, is the susceptible individual. Certainly the drugs are available (even though limited) through medical channels and by our standards an environment conducive to spread exists in certain areas although admittedly there is no environment which appears to be as heavily seeded with narcotics as are certain areas in this country. The lack of organized crime with a criminal element interested in the narcotic traffic is, of course, a factor. However, the fact that traffic is carried on in marihuana in spite of efforts to control it does not lend credence to the belief that it is superior law enforcement that is the sole reason that narcotic addiction does not flourish in England. There is also little to suggest that the availability of drugs through medical channels is the only reason why there is little or no criminal activity in connection with narcotics. While theoretically narcotics are available through medical channels, they are, as one British official told us, actually quite "hard to come by" in England so that if there was widespread susceptibility to addiction and a consequent demand for the drugs criminal activity might be able to supply the demand. Law enforcement is obviously good in England, but it has sufficient failures, such as the control of marihuana, to indicate that it would not be omnipotent in coping with criminal forces bent on supplying a real demand for narcotics if such actually existed. Thus the answer must lie, for the most part, in the British people themselves and their apparent lack of a cultural susceptibility to narcotic addiction.[20]

The authors seem to say that narcotics are simultaneously available and unavailable in Britain and obviously do not recognize that bootleg narcotics, like bootleg liquor, depend on prohibition. The reference to marihuana is totally beside the point because it, unlike heroin and morphine, is prohibited in Britain as in the United States. It is precisely for this reason that there is a fairly brisk illicit traffic in marihuana and almost none in heroin and morphine.

It is unfortunate that the Larimore-Brill report has received so much attention by virtue of the fact that is has been circulated so widely by agencies of the government. Nevertheless, for those who actually read the original 31-page document it can serve a useful purpose, for its factual content is detailed and accurate. Its authors evidently allowed their preconceived biases to distort their interpretations of the facts. It is also possible that, as members of the Health and Mental Hygiene departments of the state of New York, the writers may have come in contact with unusual types of addicts from the upper classes or the medical profession and so may not have had too clear an idea of how the average American drug user is in actuality dealt with.

Another source which the Bureau has relied on in the past is the writing of a Canadian, G. H. Stevenson, who, like Larimore and Brill, states that British addicts receive their supplies of drugs legally from physicians and that they are handled the same as users in the United States. Stevenson has also published articles denouncing the clinic plan and he was asked by Senator Daniel whether his conclusions were not based on a study of all available material concerning clinics. Stevenson replied: "No. Those statements are made in that booklet published by the United States Government entitled, 'Nar-

Narcotics Control in Britain

Narcotics Control in Britain 179

cotic Clinics in the United States.' "[21] Asked by Senator Daniel if
he agreed with the findings stated in the pamphlet, the Canadian
expert responded: "Well, I had no reason for disagreeing with
them. They were stated as facts."

OTHER BRITISH-TYPE FOREIGN PROGRAMS

Most of the nations that are members of the United Nations Organization make annual reports to the Commission on Narcotic
Drugs of the Economic and Social Council of that body. These reports are summarized in an organized form and published annually
in English under the title, *Summary of Annual Reports of Governments*.[22] It is a common practice of the reporting nations to describe briefly their systems of handling addicts in one report and
not to repeat this description annually but instead to refer back to
the earlier description. From the perusal of these annual summaries
it is evident that most Western nations follow a program of narcotics control which, in broad terms, is like that used in Britain in
that addicts are permitted to have regulated access to legal supplies
of drugs provided them by physicians. A frequent pattern of control is that such distribution is supervised by public health authorities, that a register of known addicts is maintained, and that addicts
are required to patronize only one doctor and one pharmacy.

In view of the evident tendency in the United States to regard
Britain as a unique instance of a country which has succeeded with
a program not suitable for the United States, it is important to observe that in actuality the punitive treatment of addicts as practiced here is the unusual and exceptional type of program. From
an examination of the *U.N. Summaries* for the years from 1949 to
1956, it appears that the nations listed here, among others, handle
addicts as medical cases. Each of these nations also provided an estimate of its addicted population. The approximate population of
the country is supplied to facilitate comparisons:

Country	Approximate Population	Estimated Addicts
Netherlands	11,000,000	300
Luxemburg	300,000	12
Norway	3,500,000	700
Spain	29,000,000	1,000
Israel	2,000,000	73
Argentina	19,500,000	212
Belgium	8,900,000	112
Austria	6,900,000	300
Finland	4,300,000	300
West Germany	53,000,000	4,784
Switzerland	4,000,000	109
New Zealand	2,200,000	70
Australia:		
New South Wales	3,500,000	13
Queensland	1,400,000	102
Totals	149,500,000	8,087[23]

While some of the above estimates of the numbers of addicts are no doubt too low, a compensating tendency is that of including "medical addicts," who are not included in American official estimates.

It will be observed that the above list represents a great variety of cultural conditions and a considerable range in the extent of the problem, with Germany seeming to have the most severe one. It is pertinent to inquire whether the experiences of any of these nations is relevant or can be applied to any aspect of our problem. Or must we take the view implicit in the manner in which this foreign experience is disregarded by our lawmakers and officials, that the United States is so absolutely unique culturally that none of the many successful foreign programs now operating in dozens of Western nations have any relevance for us? Is it enough to argue that the small number of addicts in most of these countries is caused by a lack of "cultural susceptibility" to addiction, or that the relatively large number of addicts in Germany contributes very slightly to that nation's crime problem because they happen to be of the "medical" rather than "criminal" type?

The following excerpts from a few of the annual reports of the listed nations to the United Nations are presented as examples to give a more concrete picture of characteristic attitudes and programs.

The Netherlands

The number of suspected patients, including addicted medical practitioners, is approximately 300.

Addicts are generally of middle age and, in most cases, women. Medical practioners constitute approximately twenty-five per cent of the total, which also includes a few nurses. . . .

Where a case of addiction is established on the basis of excessive medical prescriptions, the Inspector of Pharmacies informs the Medical Inspector of the Health Department and they make a joint investigation. In some cases the medical practitioner concerned is required to make an attempt to cure his patient; in other cases an attempt is made to persuade the addict to discontinue the use of drugs. A number of patients have been requested to select a special pharmacist in the town in which they live, and other pharmacists have been forbidden to sell them drugs. Once each month the Inspectors interrogate these pharmacists concerning the quantities of drugs prescribed and dispensed.[24]

Spain

The number of drug addicts who have been registered is about a thousand. . . . Most drug addicts suffer from this vice because of the extreme pain endured from cancer or malignant tumors, or because they have previously endured some suffering or a surgical operation.

A detailed register is kept of patients and addicts needing special supplies of narcotics; each is given an "extra-dose book" and is registered on an index card bearing his photograph and such particulars as his age, status, medical history and the name of his physician and of the dispensing pharmacy. Pharmacies are required to submit monthly returns on these persons.[25]

Israel

There was no compulsory treatment of addicts. Each addict was connected with a pharmacy where he received his daily dose of a narcotic solely by a prescription issued by a medical officer through the above health office [District Health Offices of the Ministry of Health].

The majority of the drug addicts were immigrants who had come from North Africa, the Middle and Far East and had indulged in the abuse of narcotic drugs in their native countries.[26]

Austria

There is no general obligation to report addicts. All persons who obtain narcotic drugs on long-term prescriptions and for whom the prescribed dosage exceeds the normal maximum daily quantity allowable by law, are registered. . . .

Disintoxication treatment is given only in closed institutions. . . . This type of treatment is compulsory only for the addict who is a danger to himself or to others.[27]

Germany (West)

There is no compulsory registration of addicts. The view prevails that addicts or persons requiring narcotic drugs should be regarded as sick persons whose dignity is to be respected unless the patient infringes on the rights of others or jeopardizes his own safety or public order and security.[28]

Switzerland

The number of addicts remained the same, with 109 persons, of whom 52 were women and 57 men. Their ages range from 27 to 80 years. They are practically all therapeutic addicts. A list of their names is available to every physician and pharmacist to prevent them from obtaining narcotics illicitly. When necessary, addicts who are considered sick persons receive the doses they need from the official physician or a physician appointed by the authorities.[29]

Australia (Queensland)

The registration of all addicts is compulsory. . . . There are 34 addicts to manufactured drugs. . . . The sources of supply of these addicts were authorized medical prescriptions, and the addictions were all of therapeutic origin. . . . In addition to the addicts to manufactured drugs, there are 68 elderly Chinese [ex-opium smokers] who were authorized to receive tincture of opium in doses varying from nine to sixteen ounces.[30]

THE PRESIDENT'S COMMISSION DISREGARDS FOREIGN EXPERIENCE

After the White House Conference in 1962, a presidential commission of citizens was appointed to examine the narcotics problem and make recommendations. In this Commission's final report three-fourths of one page is devoted to the British program, with no mention of any other foreign system.[31] This program is referred to as the "so-called British system," as is customary among those who would rather not talk about it. The Commission did dare to admit that the British system differs basically from the American and that the crucial difference was in the authority exercised by the British doctor "to treat the addict as he deems best in his medical judgment." Two pages earlier, the Commission recommended that the definition of proper medical practice with respect to addicts be determined by the medical profession. This, of course, is exactly what is done in Britain.

Nevertheless, the Commission went out of its way to suggest that the British program really had little significance for the United States. "The British addict," they said, unlike his American counterpart, "appears to have sufficient motivation to pursue an ordinary life." The national policy, however, has nothing to do with this point or with the fact that there are so few addicts in Britain, according to the report. The reason for the small number of addicts, they say, lies outside of the system and is attributed to "British abhorrence of narcotic drugs and the lack of cultural susceptibility to drug taking." This nonsense is clearly drawn from the discredited Larimore-Brill report.

The Commission points out that most British addicts are "medical addicts," explaining that they first experienced the effects of drugs when they had been prescribed for them by a physician in connection with illness and had later become addicted. It is argued that the British have their program because their addicts are "medical." The fact that before the Harrison Act most addiction in the United States was also therapeutic in origin, or that it is characteristically so in nearly all countries with the British-type program, was either ignored or not known by the Commission. It was not pointed out that persons who acquire their addiction therapeutically in the United States are given no special consideration by the law and are ordinarily forced to become "criminal addicts."

MIGRATION OF CANADIAN ADDICTS TO BRITAIN

The most decisive refutation of the position that the British program is no different from the American, or that it has no applicability to the American problem, is probably provided by recently published evidence which suggests that substantial numbers of Canadian addicts are going to England to avoid harsh punishment in Canada and to be treated. As we have seen, the Canadian system is essentially the same as ours: addicts are arrested and sent to jail for possession of illicit drugs, as they are here. In a Canadian medical journal published early in 1964, Lady Frankau, a psychiatrist who operates a clinic in London, reports on fifty Canadian drug addicts who received treatment from her.[32] Most of these had left Canada to escape the Canadian system.

It was noted earlier that during the last several years the reported total of known addicts in Britain has increased from something over three hundred to more than five hundred. The article indicates that a substantial portion of this increase is accounted for by an influx of Canadian users who had heard about the "British system."

Even more illuminating is the story of what happened to the fifty Canadian users under Lady Frankau's care. Eighteen are reported to have been freed of their habits and to have been off drugs at the time the article was written. Nineteen were getting regular daily allotments of heroin and were at the same time working regularly at jobs and were not known to their associates or their employers as addicts. Seven got into trouble with the British police or were headed for such trouble by reason mainly of attempts to secure narcotics by illegal means. The remaining six were either dead or their status was ambiguous.

The fifty Canadian users were grouped in three categories. The first of these consisted of ten persons with good family and cultural backgrounds, who came to the clinic first. They had either become addicted while living in Europe or had left home immediately after beginning to use drugs. The second consisted of 31 persons who appeared to have no criminal record which antedated their addiction. After being hooked, however, these persons had engaged in criminal activity of various sorts connected with narcotics and with raising money to buy narcotics. The third category consisted of nine persons who had criminal records before becoming addicted. All of the seven who had trouble with the British police or were threatened with it came from this last group.

The forty addicts in the last two categories came to England during the two years before the article was written. They were described as follows:

Few of these patients had ever worked steadily, all had been dependent on an illicit supply of drugs and none had been normal, gainfully employed members of society. Two reasons were given to explain their inability to work steadily: (a) they would not be able to earn enough money to maintain the necessary supply of drugs, and (b) if they did find work their employers were informed, sooner or later, that they were drug addicts. The few who had money belonged to the upper hierarchy of the drug peddling world, but at one time or another the majority had been involved in selling drugs to support their addiction.[33]

This is a reasonably standard description of what is known in the United States and Canada as the "criminal addict." The reasons given for not working would probably be viewed here as transparent rationalizations. The apparent fact that a large proportion of these persons became self-supporting and law-abiding in England when they were on a regular daily heroin allotment is of considerable significance. In the face of this report by Lady Frankau it is difficult to see how the position that British experience is irrelevant for the United States because we have "criminal addicts" can be any longer maintained. As we have seen, this is the position taken by the President's Advisory Commission on Narcotic and Drug Abuse.

The system used by Lady Frankau in treating addicts is also of considerable interest in connection with the belief in this country that compulsion and authoritarian handling are necessary. The first step in the program was to establish a daily dosage for each of the Canadian addicts which was just sufficient to keep him comfortable. At the same time the patients were repeatedly assured that they need not fear for a lack or shortage of heroin and that a supply was always available and would be furnished if needed. They were also assured that they would not be forced to do anything against their wills and no attempt to achieve final withdrawal of the drug was ever made without the consent and full cooperation of the patient. The addicts were advised not to seek contacts with other users. In general all phases of the program including the medical techniques were explained to the addicts so that they knew what to expect.

The article by Lady Frankau evidently grew out of a talk which she had made in 1963 before a Canadian conference in which she described the results obtained in treating some 350 narcotics addicts.[34] A Canadian policeman objected to her "permissive" approach and offered as evidence that his agency knew of eight Canadian addicts who had been treated by Lady Frankau and had returned to Canada. Of these he said that one had died of an overdose, three were known to be using drugs and were being sought by the police, and the behavior of the other four indicated that they too might soon be in trouble. It is of interest that one of the important reasons for some of the addicts returning to Canada may well have been that they were deported from England. In any case, the policeman's testimony supports the conclusion that Canadian addicts behave very differently when they are in England. There seems to be some evidence that the Canadian Government is moving toward a more liberal and permissive approach resembling that in Britain.

Materials like those in the article by Lady Frankau and television programs such as one presented by Chet Huntley for the National Broadcasting Company during the summer of 1963 are making it extremely hard to maintain the fiction that there is no British system.[35] In Huntley's program, for example, a Scottish writer and an addict, Alexander Trocchi, contrasted his experience in the United States with his life in England, where he fled to escape the American system. Inspector Leonard Dyke, head of the Dangerous Drugs Branch of the Home Office, explained that one who becomes addicted in Britain can go to a doctor to get the drugs he needs. Viewers must have wondered what Dr. Henry Brill was talking about when, toward the end of the program, he said that there really was no significant difference between the American and British programs and that "there is no cause and effect relationship between the favorable situation which England enjoys with respect to narcotic addiction and the so-called British system."

We have seen in this chapter that there has been a growing interest on the part of the American public in the systems of narcotics control used in Europe and especially in Britain. This interest reflects a growing realization that the American program has not been successful and that it is out of line with the conception of addiction as a disease. Just as vested bureaucratic interests in this country have distorted and misrepresented the problem here, so also have they misrepresented the situation in Britain. Despite this, there is now a large and growing demand from informed public opinion that more attention be given to foreign programs and that the basic assumptions of our present policy be reexamined and over- hauled. The 1963 report of the President's Advisory Commission was a relatively weak expression of this trend.

A perusal of reports to the U.N. over a period of the last ten years overwhelmingly suggests that there is a close relationship be- tween the type of control program used and the characteristics and origins of the addicted population. There is a distinct pattern in all of the European countries and other Western nations with medical programs for addicts, which tends to be repeated almost monotonously. In the next chapter we shall see that in the Far East, where the prohibition system of control has become the usual one since the end of World War II, new addicts are recruited mainly from segments of the population which correspond closely to those which are currently most susceptible to addiction in the United States. All of this strongly indicates that a national control policy is, in fact, a matter of decisive importance in determining both the nature and extent of the narcotics problem. The effects of policy appear to be determined by its tendency to encourage or discourage a secret illegal traffic.

CHAPTER 7

DRUG CONTROL IN THE FAR EAST

THE opium poppy was introduced into the Orient
in the early centuries of the Christian era, presumably by Arab
traders from the Middle East.[1] The therapeutic virtues of opium
were known to Chinese doctors and the drug was used by them
for centuries before the practice of smoking opium made its appearance. This practice spread in conjunction with the adoption
of tobacco smoking and the introduction of the tobacco plant into
the Far East by the Spaniards. Opium and tobacco were evidently
at first smoked in combination. The practice of smoking opium first
took root in the Dutch East Indies, from where it spread to Formosa. From Formosa it spread to the Chinese mainland during the
sixteenth century. In subsequent years, up to and including the
present, the smoking of opium has been a peculiarly Chinese problem, in the sense that the habit became extremely widespread in
that country and that it was carried to other Far Eastern countries
by Chinese migrants. As the League of Nations Commission of
Enquiry said in 1931, "At the present time the habit of smoking

189

opium is spread mainly among the Chinese. . . . In all countries subjected to the Commission's enquiries are found smaller or larger Chinese communities which are invariably addicted to opium smoking to a lesser or greater degree." From these communities the habit sometimes spreads to the indigenous populations.[2]

The history of antiopium measures in the Far East may be conveniently divided into three periods: (1) the period before 1912, which was the date of The Hague Convention in which agreement was reached by the powers with interests in the Far East to attempt a gradual suppression of opium smoking, a vice which was subject to no serious control before this time; (2) the period from 1912 to World War II, characterized by the prevalence of government monopolies which controlled legal production and distributed opium to consumers, who were often registered or rationed; (3) the third period, after World War II, characterized by the elimination of government monopolies and the triumph of prohibition. The latest country to prohibit opium smoking was Thailand in 1959.[3] Before 1912, with some exceptions, opium was in the main handled like other commercial products for the sake of profits which it offered. There was little effort to control consumers or to reduce consumption.

At the International Opium Conference in Shanghai in 1909, the United States, seconded by China, advocated immediate prohibition and suppression. The European "colonial powers," on the other hand, favored a policy of gradual suppression, and it was this view which was accepted and later implemented at The Hague Convention of 1912.[4]

The period of government monopolies was marked by a wide variety of schemes for controlling and limiting production and distribution, presumably with a view to reducing the problem gradually in preparation for complete suppression or prohibition at some indefinite later time. The government monopolies were subjected to considerable criticism on the ground that they functioned pri-

marily to raise revenues rather than to reduce the problem. While
there were good grounds for this criticism in many instances, some
of the programs were relatively successful. In fact, the most effective Far Eastern program of any type seems to have been that
imposed on Formosa by the Japanese after they took over the island
in 1895. This program, a government monopoly, in forty years
reduced opium smoking in Formosa to a small fraction of what it
had been. Nevertheless it was not adopted by other nations nor was
it continued in Formosa after the war when the island passed out
of Japanese control.

Prominent among the influences which led to prohibition of
opium smoking in the Far East was political pressure upon the colonial powers by the United States, by the League of Nations, and
by the United Nations. Anticolonial sentiment among native peoples of the Far East made it easy for them to accept the idea that
the government monopoly system was a vicious form of exploitation, and that the only morally defensible program was one of
immediate and complete suppression. Practical objections to this
which emphasized that prohibition would encourage the illicit
traffic were of no avail in the face of the charge that the European
powers were interested only in their own revenues. The American
position on the side of China and the colonial peoples gave the
United States important political and moral advantages.

The two most important exceptions to the trends sketched in
the preceding paragraphs were China and the Philippines. In the
former, as will be indicated in detail later, the prohibition system
of control was the main one used after 1729. In the Philippines,
prohibition was established in 1908 after the United States took
over the islands from Spain.

Smuggling has been rife throughout the Far East for centuries
in all countries where there are opium smokers, and they are found
almost everywhere. With few exceptions this has been true regardless of the system of control. Official connivance and police com-

plicity in the traffic have always been widely reported and are still probably the rule rather than the exception.

With the single exception of Formosa during the period of Japanese control (1895-World War II), the prevalence of smuggling has made it virtually impossible to form reliable estimates of the extent of the problem in any part of the Far East. Figures that are released are ordinarily highly unreliable and require a great deal of interpretation to be understood at all. They are sometimes doctored in order to create the desired impression and to put officials in a good light. During the era of government monopolies statistical data ordinarily pertained only to registered smokers and ignored those who relied upon smuggled supplies. Where prohibition is practiced, the only available figures are those which reflect police activities, so that the extent of the illicit market and the spread of the habit can only be vaguely estimated. Under these circumstances conflicting claims covering a wide range are made, depending upon the interests of those who make them. The problem itself is subterranean, often largely out of sight and out of control.

The effect of the present prohibition era in the Far East upon the number of addicts is impossible to estimate. However, abundant supplies of smuggled opium and manufactured drugs such as heroin continue to be available. During the era of government monopolies, when sporadic local attempts were made to reduce consumption by such devices as reducing rations progressively (e.g., 10% per year) or by raising government prices, it began to be noticed that smokers sometimes resorted to the use of manufactured drugs such as heroin or morphine as substitutes. This trend has been greatly accelerated since the late war, throughout the Far East, by the adoption of prohibition. The hypodermic method of use is also gaining ground.

Like opium, heroin was first introduced to the East from the outside, by manufacturing countries of the West. In the 1920's or earlier heroin pills began to be manufactured in Shanghai and other parts of the Far East. Heroin is now exported in quantity from that part of the world. Increasing consumption of heroin, morphine, and other manufactured equivalents of opium is being regularly reported in most Far Eastern countries.

International discussions of the Far Eastern opium and drug problems have often been highly charged with emotion and filled with political crosscurrents, mutual recriminations, charges and countercharges. During the eighteenth and nineteenth centuries, when the East India Company encouraged the cultivation of the poppy in India and sold opium in the Calcutta auctions for eventual shipment to China, Great Britain and India were heavily censured. When China expanded opium production and began to export it, she came under heavy attack. All of the European powers with Far Eastern possessions in which opium smoking was permitted were assailed by prohibitionist-minded critics in the United States and elsewhere, and particularly by nationalistic, anticolonial natives of the Far East. The European colonial powers retaliated as best they could by pressing the United States to report on the success of its own prohibition scheme in the Philippines and by blaming the continuation of the smoking habit on the excessive supplies of opium being produced in China. After the Japanese invasion of China, Japan became the favorite target of attacks. After World War II, when opium smoking had been prohibited in most areas, Thailand was widely criticized for not following suit and it was alleged that opium produced legally in that country was nullifying the efforts of Thailand's neighbors to control their problems. Communist China is regularly accused by the United States and Nationalist China of deliberately encouraging and exploiting the illicit sale of Chinese-produced opium for political ends. Countries in which there is an illicit drug traffic with supplies originating outside the country invariably blame the country of origin for their problems; no blame appears to attach to those countries which provide the markets for illicit supplies.

OPIUM IN CHINA

By 1000 A.D. opium was already being widely used in China and the Far East as an indulgence, and when Portuguese traders showed up in that part of the world many centuries later they found in existence an old and well-established opium trade being managed by Arab and Indian merchants. The Portuguese took over this lucrative trade, to be subsequently displaced by the Dutch, who were in turn displaced by the British.

It is of special historical interest that China has had a longer experience with the prohibition system of control than any other nation, for its first prohibitory laws were promulgated in 1729. The Emperor's edict of that year provided punishment for all parties in opium transactions except the user. The punishment decreed for keepers of opium shops was strangulation after brief imprisonment. As the practice of smoking opium continued to spread, other edicts appeared, and the punishment was increased for lesser parties in the transactions including the users. This prohibition system lasted until well after the Opium War, to the year 1858, when the trade was legalized.[5] During the twentieth century the Chinese government sporadically returned to the traditional system of prohibition backed by savage punishment for all offenders and for addicts.

What the program of opium control is in Red China seems to be hard to learn, even for informed persons in Hong Kong. In that city it is said that there is no opium problem in Red China.[6] While there is a lively smuggling trade between Hong Kong and China involving a variety of items, opium is evidently not important among them. There appear to have been few addicts among the millions of refugees who migrated to Hong Kong from the mainland after World War II and after the Communist take-over. On the other hand, there is a huge smuggling racket in Hong Kong which involves opium and locally manufactured heroin. The source of some of this opium may well be Communist China, for it is reported that much opium is grown in the general region of the borders of Thailand, Laos, Burma, and China.[7] Supplies from this region, which is relatively inaccessible and inhabited by tribal peoples, easily move across the national boundaries to reach the big coastal distribution centers such as Hong Kong, Bangkok, Singapore, and Rangoon.[8]

American soldiers who fought in the Korean conflict have told the writer that there were opium addicts among the Chinese prisoners that they took. These Chinese soldiers allegedly carried supplies of opium which were issued to them by the military. This suggests that there may be some sort of licensing of addicts in Red China with legal distribution of supplies. If this were the case it would account for the impression that there is no opium problem there. Prior to the Communist victory it was generally estimated that there were more than 5,000,000 addicts in China. These users could not have vanished into thin air, but what happened to them is not clear.

While no reliable statistics are at hand concerning the development of the problem in China, it appears that opium smoking increased in popularity during most of the eighteenth and nineteenth centuries. By 1715 the British had taken over the opium trade from the Dutch, and the East India Company was organizing poppy cultivation in India for the Chinese market. In the meantime, as the demand mounted, Indian opium found itself in competition with that being grown to an increasing extent in China itself. By 1800 it was estimated that domestic production of opium in China was equal to the amounts imported from India.[9]

Although the governments of Great Britain and India were severely criticized for exporting opium to China, the fact was that Chinese officials were deeply involved in the illicit traffic and were making fortunes from it. Calcutta opium was brought to the coast of China by the opium clippers and delivered there to Chinese smugglers, who carried it into the interior. High Chinese officials who were charged by the Emperor with the duty of preventing the importation of the drug in some instances owned their own fleets of smuggling vessels, which they used to accept delivery from foreign ships in the harbor outside of Canton, where the bulk of imported illicit opium was delivered. When the opium ships had made their deliveries it was the custom of Chinese officials to go through the motions of chasing the opium ships to sea and reporting to the Emperor that the nefarious foreign opium traders had been repelled and would probably not return.[10]

Domestic production of opium in China was stimulated by the numerous taxes and fees levied upon imported Indian opium. By 1900 the poppy was being grown in all the provinces of China and domestic production was thought to be about six times that imported from India.[11] In the period from 1729, when the first prohibition edict was issued, to 1900, China had increased her annual consumption of smoking opium more than an estimated one-hundred fold and her nationals had carried the habit to nearly all countries of the Far East and had even introduced it into the United States via San Francisco's Barbary Coast during the decades following the California gold rush.

Early in the twentieth century, in 1906, the Chinese emperor again became concerned over the prevalence of opium smoking and again a prohibitory edict was issued proclaiming the intention of suppressing both the native and the foreign product within a period of ten years.[12] India agreed to reduce its exports with a view to ending them within the allotted period, and did so in advance of the stipulated time. There followed a period of harsh enforcement with stern punishment of offenders that included beheading. By 1917 the British minister at Peking was able to state that opium cultivation had virtually disappeared, although some opium was still being produced in the remote provinces. Large numbers of addicts remained, however. The richer ones were able to provide themselves from secret caches and from smuggled supplies, while the poorer ones began to turn to the use of morphine and heroin pills, which began to be imported in large quantities and were smuggled into the interior.

In a matter of a few years after this apparent victory, when many observers believed that China was on the verge of eliminating her opium problem, political turmoil and the greed of local military governors brought about a rapid revival of poppy cultivation and by 1924 the situation was as bad as it had ever been. Local warlords and troops, often little more than bandits, encouraged and even forced the cultivation of the poppy in order to collect taxes or "fines" from the cultivators, as well as to reap the profits from sale.

Chinese representatives at Geneva placed the blame for the situation in their country upon extraterritoriality and foreign interference.

In 1934-35 a new plan under the direction of Generalissimo Chiang Kai-shek was announced by the Central Committee of the Kuomintang. This plan proposed to suppress the cultivation of the opium poppy by stages and to establish prohibition in six years. Cultivation of the poppy was to be suppressed at once in the inner or coastal provinces and gradually in the outer frontier provinces. Smokers were required to register and to submit to a gradual program of cures. Where poppies were cultivated, strict supervision was to be enforced and heavy penalties were provided for all violations. After January 1, 1937, not only manufacturers and dealers in narcotic drugs, but also uncured addicts were given life imprisonment or executed, and the death penalty was prescribed for government employees who protected offenders or accepted bribes. Some thousands of offenders were executed under this program.

Despite these efforts, and despite the establishment of numerous hospitals to cure smokers, the demand of addicts for their supplies continued to be met either by smuggled supplies of opium or by heroin and morphine tablets which were again smuggled into the country on a vast scale. Revenues from the sale of opium continued to be high in many provinces and numerous officials continued to connive in the illicit trade and to line their pockets with the profits.

In 1941 Generalissimo Chiang Kai-shek circulated a statement throughout all of Free China to mark the end of the six-year period of suppression. This statement forbade any further indulgence in opium and provided the death penalty for anyone guilty of cultivating the poppy, manufacturing opium or narcotics, or offering them for sale. Drug users were to be shot if caught taking injections or smoking heroin pills, while opium smokers were made subject to imprisonment for terms of from one to five years. Persons instigating or encouraging resistance against the uprooting of poppies were made subject to life imprisonment or execution.

In the meantime Japan had invaded China in 1937 and the opium racket in the occupied portions of China passed into her hands and was exploited by her military governors to raise revenues for the prosecution of the war. The deterioration of economic and political conditions in China during the war and afterward, during the struggle between the Nationalists and Communists, make it impossible to estimate what the consequences of Chiang Kai-shek's program might have been. In view of the history of the problem in China, the millions of smokers, the inability of the Central Government to control the outer provinces, where cultivation of the poppy was never stopped, and the extreme difficulty of controlling the smuggling of opium and heroin, there are few grounds for optimism. In all probability, had the program continued, the illicit manufacture and distribution of heroin and morphine would have grown more rapidly then they did.

THE "AMERICAN SYSTEM" ESTABLISHED IN HONG KONG AND THE FAR EAST

Hong Kong became a British colony after the first Opium War between Britain and China, in 1841. The population of the colony is in excess of three million, and in 1961 was about five times what it was in 1945. The population is almost wholly Chinese; in fact, in all respects except the political, Hong Kong is a part of China. This is true of its opium problem.

In 1914 there was established a government monopoly system under which government opium was sold to the smokers, who were permitted to smoke legally except that the operation of opium dens, or divans as they were called, was illegal. The government for a time made a serious attempt to eradicate the illegal opium dens that flourished in the area but more or less gave up the hopeless struggle after a few years. The government opium was sold by vendors who were paid a monthly wage and who made no profit of their own from it.[13]

The main feature of the system which it was hoped would discourage consumption was the high price charged for the superior quality opium sold by the government. In 1924 this was estimated at about four times the black market price.[14] Under these conditions it was inevitable, considering the income level of the population, that most users patronized the illicit market. The latter was large, well organized, and had been in existence in Hong Kong before the British had acquired it. Around the beginning of the twentieth century manufactured drugs such as heroin and morphine began to be imported into China from Western countries, and later began to be manufactured in China.[15] Red and pink heroin pills were commented upon in the 1920s and factories devoted to their manufacture began to be discovered.[16] The overwhelming proportion of narcotic addicts in Hong Kong had always consisted of opium smokers, and this continued to be the case until after 1949, but the use of heroin pills steadily gained ground.

On one occasion only in the history of Hong Kong's government monopoly was there an experiment with low-priced opium.[17] This experiment was the result of a large seizure of high quality imported illicit opium. It was proposed to distribute this to smokers at a low price in order to determine what effects this would have on (a) the illicit traffic, and (b) the number of smokers who would buy legal rather than illicit opium. The latter figure increased by several hundred per cent but the experiment was discontinued before any conclusion could be reached about the effects upon the illicit traffic. Subsequently, government opium continued to be sold at much higher prices than those on the black market and the number of legal purchasers declined.

In the period between the two world wars Hong Kong officials generally considered the prohibition system of control over opium smoking as impractical and unenforceable.[18] Emphasis was placed on the impossibility of checking the illicit traffic, on the prevalence of corruption among enforcement officials, and on the failure of prohibition in the only two Far Eastern countries that had experimented with it up to that time, i.e., China and the Philippines. By the time that World War II began there were fewer than 1000 smokers in Hong Kong who purchased government opium in contrast to an estimated several tens of thousands who relied on the smuggled product. In addition, there were thousands of addicts who used heroin pills which were cheaper than opium and made detection by the police more difficult. In 1938 about 3,500 persons were imprisoned for violations of antinarcotics laws.

In 1943, the American Government called a conference in Washington with representatives of Britain, The Netherlands, and a number of other interested nations, to consider what Allied policy with respect to opium would be in Far Eastern areas wrested from the Japanese. The Federal Bureau of Narcotics account of the results of this meeting sheds considerable light on how it happened that opium smoking was prohibited in Hong Kong after the war, and why the prohibition system of control was generally adopted in the Orient.

The announcement on November 10, 1943, by the British and Netherlands Governments of their decision to suppress opium smoking in their Far Eastern colonial empires following the liberation of those areas from Japanese domination constitutes one of the most important developments of all times in international drug control. The United States has been urging this policy since the convocation of the Shanghai International Opium Commission in 1909, which was the first attempt to deal internationally with suppression of the abuse of opium. Such action should cut off illicit traffickers from post-war access to what has in the past been one of their leading sources of supply. Opium was purchased freely at small cost by the smuggler across the counter in the Far East and then smuggled into the United States and other victim countries. Curtailment of the opium traffic there has become a matter of even more immediate concern to the United States in view of military operations in the Far East and the large number of young Americans deployed in that area.

The Japanese are maintaining these monopolies in the areas which their armed forces now occupy and are deriving enormous revenue therefrom. Two per cent of the entire revenue of the Netherlands East Indies is derived from smoking opium. In British Burma, 5 per cent of the country's revenues are similarly derived. In the British Federated Malay States, 6 per cent. In British North Borneo, 10 per cent. In British Sarawak, 11 per cent. In the British Unfederated Malay States, 12 per cent. And in the British Straits Settlements, 20 per cent. Before the Japanese conquered Hong Kong there were in that city 5,557 rationed government smokers and an estimated 90,000 illicit smokers, which illustrates the failure of the sale of opium by governments. . . . The smoking of opium under prescribed conditions has been legal in the Netherlands Indies, British Malaya, the Unfederated Malay States, Brunei, Formosa, Kwantung Leased Territory, Burma, India, Ceylon, British North Borneo, Hong Kong, French Indochina, Thailand, Kwanchow-wan, Macao and Iran.

Beginning in January 13, 1943, a series of informal meetings were held in the Treasury Department office of the Commissioner of Narcotics in Washington, attended by representatives of Great Britain, Canada, Australia, New Zealand, The Netherlands, and China; also by representatives of the State Department and the Foreign Policy Association, regarding the question of what would be done in case some island or territory where a smoking-opium monopoly exists is occupied by the military forces of the United Nations.

From the standpoint of the health and safety of the men of the armed forces of the United States this Government was convinced that it will be imperative immediately upon the occupation by the United States forces of a part or the whole of any one of the Japanese-occupied territories to seize all drugs intended for other than medical and scientific purposes which may be discovered, and *it therefore instructed American expeditionary forces under American command to close existing opium monopolies, opium shops and dens.* That was the immediate problem. The long-range problem was what should be done in regard to the opium monopolies and the opium problem in general. Another question was, What will happen if the British or the Chinese alone should reoccupy Burma, for example? Would the British license the sale of opium for nonmedical needs, while the Chinese refused to license the opium smokers?

The competent authorities of the United States were of the opinion that there would be an increase in addiction among Americans after the war because of the close association of American troops with opium in Far Eastern areas. . . . As long as opium smoking is permitted in the Far Eastern war theatre, it is probable that troops would acquire addiction and that drug smuggling would continue from countries in the Far East to countries in the West, unless some counter action is taken. *It was pointed out that the Americans had never allowed the sale of opium in the Philippines and when the Japanese moved in it is not likely that the United States would have gotten the support which it did get from the Filipinos if the United States Government had been selling the Filipinos opium for a generation as had been done, for instance, in Far Eastern territories under control of European governments.*

At the conclusion of the informal discussions it was apparent that the representatives of the governments present were in agreement as to the final objectives to be reached; viz., total prohibition of opium smoking, and that any differences of opinions expressed concerned only the methods to be applied to attain this objective. It was pointed out that monopolies did not reduce the number of smokers; that international cooperation would be the solution to the problem, and that the production of opium had a bearing on the control of the monopolies. . . . The belief was expressed that *one way of making sure that the narcotic traffic is controlled is to increase the penalties;* unfortunately in the areas of the Far East where opium monopolies exist the penalties are low.

The observation was made that in some countries the command might shift from the Americans to the British and that in such event the Americans did not want a situation to arise in which some other country would say that opium was in and the Americans would say it was out; therefore, it was desirable that agreements be reached.

As a result of these discussions the United States Government on September 21, 1943, addressed an aide-memoire to the British, Netherlands and other interested governments on the subject. On November 10, 1943, as stated above, the British and Netherlands Governments announced their intention to abolish the legalized sale of opium in their Far Eastern territories. [Italics added.][19]

The Bureau of Narcotics then went on to say that it was the opinion of the Government of the United States "that the interested governments, acting in concert, can now solve the problem of smoking opium." The French and Portuguese Governments also accepted the American proposal in 1944.

The italicized portions of this statement are especially interesting as indications of the position taken by the Bureau of Narcotics toward the Dutch and British representatives. The latter were obviously presented with a *fait accompli*, besides being lectured on the moral and practical superiority of the American system of prohibition. This system was adopted in Hong Kong in 1949. In view of the Bureau's confidence in 1943, that the opium smoking problem "can now be solved," let us look at subsequent developments in Hong Kong.

We have already quoted the present head of the Federal Bureau, Mr. Giordano, to the effect that there are now from 200,000 to 250,000 addicts in Hong Kong. (A more common estimate in Hong Kong is 50,000.) It is interesting that these figures were cited by him to discredit the "British system" which he and others say prevails in Hong Kong. As we have seen, the system in use there is actually the American one. In 1943 Mr. Anslinger placed the number of addicts in Hong Kong at around 95,000. Since that time it is true that there has been an enormous influx of refugees and the population has increased by over five hundred per cent. However, investigations in Hong Kong show that while most current addicts were born in China and migrated to Hong Kong, the overwhelming majority of them contracted the habit in Hong Kong.[20]

When opium smoking was prohibited in 1949, most smokers had been obtaining their supplies from the illicit trade, as has been indicated. After 1949 they continued to do so. Except for the small number of licensed smokers who could afford to pay the high government prices, the 1949 change in policy meant relatively little. There has never been any close connection between the medical profession and addicts in Hong Kong and the addicts there do not and cannot go to doctors as they do in Britain.

The prohibition of opium smoking has, in a relatively few years, transformed Hong Kong's opium smoking problem into a heroin problem as it has also done throughout the Far East. In 1961, for example, the authorities of the Tai Lam prison for addicts in Hong Kong commented:

The problem is complicated by the fact that, in recent years, attempts by the Hong Kong Government to suppress opium smoking have resulted in traffickers and addicts turning increasingly to heroin, a drug much easier to smuggle and conceal.[21]

The Federal Bureau of Narcotics has itself reported on the extensive switch to heroin in Hong Kong and the Far East:

Increasing heroin addiction was reported. *Heroin now displaces opium consumed by most addicts in Hong Kong and Singapore*, where many seizures of small quantities of heroin were made from peddlers and addicts. Macao and Formosa reported increasing heroin traffic. Several clandestine heroin laboratories were seized in the Far East and Middle East. . . .

Large quantities of crude morphine were reported to have been transported from northern Thailand to Lampang and Bangkok and smuggled to Hong Kong, Macao, and Singapore, largely for export. Clandestine manufacture of crude morphine was reported in and near the

Shan states of Burma. Illicit manufacture of morphine base, crude morphine, and heroin occurred in various parts of the Far East and Middle East, especially South Korea, Hong Kong, Lebanon and Iran. [Italics added.][22]

In 1958 there were similar reports:

Steady traffic in crude morphine continued from the north of Thailand through Bangkok to Hong Kong, Singapore, Formosa and surrounding areas. Very large quantities of heroin were illicitly manufactured in the vicinity of Hong Kong, and traffic increased between Hong Kong, Macao, Japan and neighboring areas. *Of 15,540 drug offenses in Hong Hong, 11,528 involved heroin.* [Italics added.][23]

It is interesting to observe that virtually all countries named in these statements, both in the Middle and Far East, have prohibition systems, most of them established since the war and some very recently.

The story was the same in 1960:

Extensive traffic in crude morphine continued through Thailand, Hong Kong, Macao, Malaya, and Taiwan (Formosa). Heavy traffic in heroin occurred through Hong Kong, Macao, Japan, and Taiwan toward North America. Taiwan traced most of its illicit heroin to Communist China. Heroin traffic in the United States, supplied entirely from abroad, came chiefly from Communist China, Hong Kong and Mexico.[24]

On page 34 of the same report Mr. Anslinger named France, Mexico, Italy, and Hong Kong as the sources of most of the heroin seized in the United States.

Since 1949 the pattern of narcotic law enforcement in Hong Kong has paralleled that in the United States in almost all details. Large numbers of addicts are being arrested and confined in jails and prisons. The illicit traffic is in the hands of organized mobs known as "triads" or "tongs" and leaders of these gangs are rarely apprehended. Enforcement methods seem to be much the same. The addicts are mainly young males who have acquired the habit in Hong Kong and use heroin by inhalation; the three methods being known as the "ack-ack," "chasing the dragon," and "playing the mouth organ." The first of these involves smoking a cigarette held vertically with heroin on its tip; the second consists of inhaling heroin fumes from tinfoil on which the drug is heated; the third involves inhaling with the aid of a matchbox held to the mouth. The hypodermic method is also coming to be more popular.

Most of the users are from the poorest classes and many of them initially used drugs in connection with such diseases as dysentery, malaria, typhoid, and pulmonary diseases. Even if these users were permitted to receive prescription drugs from physicians they probably would not do so because of costs—the price of illicit heroin is low. In any case, the medical profession in Hong Kong appears to have next to nothing to do with addicts.

THE JAPANESE OPIUM MONOPOLY IN FORMOSA

The Japanese system of controlling and gradually suppressing the smoking of opium in the island between 1895 and 1938, when the last reports were made on the situation there, appears to have been the most effective system ever devised in the Far East. In a period of about forty years the number of opium smokers, according to the statistical reports issued by the Japanese, was reduced from a total of around 200,000 in 1908 to an estimated total of fewer than twenty thousand. Before the Japanese occupied the island it was estimated that fully one-seventh of the population had acquired the vice. Approximately forty years later opium smokers constituted less than one-half of one per cent of the population.[25]

Information concerning the operation and effectiveness of the system is available largely from official Japanese reports and there have been critics who claimed that the Japanese misrepresented the situation. Nevertheless, the Japanese claims were largely confirmed by an independent investigation by a League of Nations Commis-

sion of Inquiry which visited the island in 1929 and by other observers. Japanese claims were also confirmed by critics of Japanese
opium policies in China and other occupied areas during World
War II. For example, Frederick T. Merrill, in a book published in
1942, refers to the Japanese program in Formosa as follows:

The Japanese have thus demonstrated in their own country and again
in Formosa that if they so desire they are capable of curbing opium
smoking not only among their own nationals but among those of a
subject race.[26]

A similar assertion can probably not be made of any other country
in the Far East. The significance of Merrill's statement is enhanced
by the fact that it was published when we were at war with Japan.
Merrill concluded that:

If the annual reports to the League of the last five years are accepted,
even with reserve, it must be concluded that Japan has done a better
job in Formosa than most European governments of Far Eastern colo-
nies.[27]

He attributed the relative success of the Formosan authorities in
curbing the illicit traffic to immigration restriction, strict penalties,
and the policy of keeping down the price of government opium.

The other government monopolies existing at that time charged
high prices and frequently permitted opium smoking in public
divans or dens. The reason given for charging high prices was that
it was hoped that this would discourage consumption. It was felt
that if government prices were lowered consumption would increase and the habit would spread. The Formosan experience
strongly suggests that the habit is spread primarily by the illicit
traffic rather than by legal and rationed consumers.

When the Japanese took over Formosa it was at first contemplated that the strict prohibition laws which prevailed in Japan
would also be applied to Formosa, but after consideration of the
probable effects upon the large numbers of smokers in Formosa it

was thought that such measures would create a vast smuggling problem and would work hardship in the island since most of the smokers were farmers or working men with dependents.

Having decided that a prohibition scheme was unworkable in Formosa, the Japanese set up a government opium monopoly.[28] Licensed smokers were permitted to buy their supply from government shops at fixed low prices adapted to the income level of the consumers. The opium dispensed in these shops was of good quality, carefully prepared and blended to suit the tastes of smokers and sold in three grades. Licensed smokers were provided with purchase books in which records of amounts dispensed were kept. Rations were established for each smoker after medical examination according to the degree of his addiction and no more than three days' supplies were dispensed at any one time. Smokers who wished to quit their habits had only to announce their intentions and to turn in their purchase books.

The first enumeration in 1900 showed 169,064 smokers. Since the initial register was incomplete, licenses were again offered to secret smokers in 1904-5 and in 1908. Approximately 46,000 additional names were added to the original total by these means. Not all of those who applied were granted licenses; some were refused on the ground that they were only occasional smokers and others, usually younger persons, were required to renounce the habit (or to smoke secretly and illegally). Strict penalties were enforced and measures were taken to prevent an influx of smokers from China. In 1910 there were about 100,000 registered smokers, or about 3 per cent of the population in contrast to about 6 per cent when the program started.

As would be expected, smokers who were refused licenses continued to smoke illegally and new addicts continued to appear as a consequence of the availability of opium smuggled from nearby China. However, after 1908, no new licenses were granted until 1929, when the registers were again opened. It had been estimated that there were, at that time, in the neighborhood of 15,000 illicit smokers. However, approximately 25,500 new applications were received. Of these, only about 5,500 were actually granted licenses. In the meantime, between about 1900 and 1929 the number of registered smokers had declined from about 200,000 to about 27,000. No new licenses were granted after 1929, and in 1938 the number of registered smokers had diminished to approximately 11,000, with an estimated additional 7,000 illegal smokers.

In the meantime, most of these licensed smokers continued to engage in productive labor and to support their families. In 1912 it was reported that 68 per cent of them were married, 19 per cent were widowers or widows and only 10 per cent single. In the same year statistics indicated that 40 per cent were engaged in farming, fishing or forestry, 13 per cent in industry, 23 per cent in transportation and commerce, 11 per cent were public officials or in the professions, 9 per cent reported no occupation. About 85 per cent of the licensees were males. Japanese officials noted that it was the custom of smokers, when the time came for smoking, to take an interval for it and then resume their work. Only in rare instances did they indulge for long hours. Public opium smoking in dens or divans was forbidden and smoking was done in private.

The Japanese practice of refusing licenses to young smokers is reflected in the fact that by 1924 none of the registered smokers was under thirty years of age. New applicants in 1929 who were under forty were compelled to break their habits and were refused licenses and, since no new applications were accepted thereafter, very few of the registered addicts during this period were less than forty years old. The relatively rapid reduction in the numbers of registered smokers during intervals when no new applications were accepted is accounted for mainly by the high average age and the high mortality rate among the smokers and to a lesser extent by the fact that each year a certain small percentage turned in their purchase books and announced their intention of quitting the habit. Persons who quit were not permitted to re-register.

One of the interesting and significant consequences of the Japanese program in Formosa was that it generated reliable statistical data concerning large numbers of addicts. For example, the fact that no new licenses were granted to smokers between 1908 and 1929 made it possible to determine with precision what the mortality rates of the opium smokers at various ages were during this interval. In view of interest in the United States in what is called "maturing out," or the tendency for the number of addicts to be extraordinarily small in the upper age groups, there should be some interest in the Formosa data, which are unique. A study of the matter indicated that death rates for Formosan opium smokers do not differ significantly from those of the general population below the age of forty years.[29] After approximately that point, the death rate among the smokers increased more rapidly than that of the general population. The death rates for opium smokers of various age groups compared as follows with corresponding age groups of the general population:

Age	*Deaths per 10,000 annually among:* Smokers	General Population
35-39	40.90	38.43
40-44	62.17	48.79
45-49	86.84	55.59
50-54	129.14	71.93
55-59	166.07	88.25
60 plus	252.64	183.7

The League of Nations 1930-32 survey indicated that life insurance was sold to opium smokers in most Far Eastern countries, but at higher rates than for other persons.

Japanese awareness of the danger of stimulating an illicit traffic by overcharging addicts was one of the outstanding strong points of the program. As far as registered smokers were concerned, low prices and the standardized good quality supplies made it extremely difficult for smugglers to compete successfully with the government shops. Prices were sufficiently high (a smoking habit cost, on the average, about 30 to 35 cents a day) to produce a profit, but these revenues represented originally only a very small proportion of the Formosan budget and they declined from year to year. The price of opium was raised slightly to compensate for increased costs of production but no attempt was made to keep opium revenues from declining, and while these profits were used for general budgetary purposes it is obvious that no reliance was placed upon them. In 1938 opium revenues accounted for only 0.83 per cent of the total budget, one of the lowest percentages in the Far East.

Throughout the period of the operation of this program, smuggling of opium into Formosa from China continued and numerous arrests were reported annually. This illicit traffic supplied the needs of clandestine smokers and also, no doubt, accounted for substantial numbers of new addicts. Strict rationing of registered smokers prevented supplies from the government shops from being diverted from the intended consumers as did the fact that prices charged for smuggled opium were slightly lower than those charged by the government.

Sagatoro Kaku, former Japanese civil governor of Formosa, commented that:

. . . it became my firm conviction that, although the opium question as such was primarily a question which had sprung up in China, no solution was to be found unless every country which permitted opium smoking set its own house in order.

He then quoted a Japanese proverb:

Do not trouble about the snow which has fallen on your neighbor's garden before clearing away the snow which lies on your own roof.

When Formosa was reoccupied by the Chinese government after World War II, the new authorities enthusiastically adopted the prohibition system, citing with approval the proposal made by the United States in 1943 that the European powers agree to suppress all addiction to opiates in their Far Eastern possessions completely and immediately.[30] As in virtually all of the rest of the Orient, the smokers that remained have frequently switched to manufactured drugs and a crop of new heroin and morphine addicts of the usual type has made its appearance. The Republic of China's report to the U.N. in 1945 included the following:

"As far as could be ascertained in 1945, trade in opium in Southeast Asia was not yet wholly suppressed," which was probably the understatement of that year.[31]

INDONESIA AND THAILAND

The Indonesian Government, when independence from the Dutch was achieved after the war, announced that the abuse of opium was to be abolished there in two years. The Dutch had earlier stated that prohibition of opium smoking would be established when the Japanese had been driven out. After 1947, when independence was granted, Indonesian officials made long, detailed reports to the United Nations which were full of enthusiasm and optimism. The old rationing system of the Dutch was temporarily continued but smokers were rapidly switched to medicinal opium (taken orally rather than smoked) and it was then proposed to reduce the rations progressively so that in two years, it was confidently predicted, the evil would be completely and permanently eliminated. Snags at once began to appear in the program. Subsequently, annual reports of the Indonesian Government commented, somewhat plaintively, on the extent of the illicit traffic and on the increased use of heroin and morphine. Foreign nations, especially China, were blamed for the traffic. The reports became less detailed, less voluminous, and more disillusioned. In 1951 it was remarked that:

In view of the meager results obtained in the treatment of addicts in the country, the fight against addiction may be called past hope, and the only hope seems to lie in combating the illicit traffic, for which the co-operation of all countries is required.[32]

During the period of Dutch rule the system of control, as previously mentioned, was regarded as a reasonably intelligent and effective one despite the fact that the prices charged addicts were too high and that there was a great deal of smuggling.

Thailand's program up to 1959 was the government monopoly system, with the government licensing opium dens where the users were supposed to smoke, and also selling opium at relatively high prices to the managers of these establishments, who resold it to their customers, to whom opium pipes were also rented. Permits to operate opium smoking establishments were sold by the government to the highest bidder. Most of the smokers in Thailand, as is usual throughout the Far East, were Chinese. Because of the high prices charged by the government, smuggled opium was available at a lower price and was used by proprietors of the dens to cut their costs. The smuggling trade originating from the north was a large one and was reputed to have been, to a considerable extent, in the hands of the police, who were said to be making double profits from the trade by collecting monetary rewards for seizures as well as by direct selling of illicit opium.

Before opium smoking was made illegal in June 1959, it was proposed to cure the estimated 72,000 addicts in something like six months.[33] After 1959, reports from Thailand indicate that the illicit traffic has been stimulated. As elsewhere, heroin is rapidly replacing opium. While the narcotics problem has become less visible since the opium establishments were closed and the pipes, opium, and other supplies were burned, addiction is still there. Undoubtedly the profits of the illicit traffic have increased. The police are still said to be deeply involved in it.[34]

There is anti-Chinese prejudice in both Indonesia and Thailand. In the former this brought about the deportation or expulsion of considerable numbers, which may have eased the narcotics problem. In Thailand the exploitation of opium smokers as a source of government revenue may well have been tolerated because the smokers were mainly from an unpopular minority group. The eventual outlawing of smoking in 1959 was evidently in large measure a response to outside pressure from the United Nations.

ADDICTION IN JAPAN

Before World War II Japan was invariably cited as one of the few countries of the Far East without a drug problem. Explanations of this strongly resemble those now being offered by American officials of the situation in Britain. Herbert L. May, for example, explained the Japanese situation as follows:

The Japanese are a temperate people, and are accustomed to discipline and obedience to the governmental requirements. The above may serve to explain in part why the Japanese have been singularly free from the evils of opium and "drug" addictions.[35]

Merrill commented upon the absence of opium smoking in Japan and upon the small number of addicted persons in that country:

The reason for this amazing rejection of a habit which has been so prevalent for two centuries in neighboring China lies in the overwhelming pressure of public opinion against opium addiction. [Compare with "British abhorrence of drug taking."] An opium user in Japan is a social outcast. Moreover, the opium problem there has never been one of curing addiction, but of preventing it. Strict prohibition is thus possible, and because Japanese people as a whole are extremely law abiding people, preventive efforts are exceedingly effective.[36]

Since the end of World War II heroin addiction has become a serious problem in Japan. The practice of smoking heroin on the tips of cigarettes is said to have been brought in from the mainland during and after the war. Use by inhalation is usually quickly followed by intravenous hypodermic injection in the manner customary in the United States. As in the United States, Japanese heroin addicts of today are primarily young urban males who acquired the habit through underworld associations and the quest for kicks.[37] It is possible that the problem would have developed in this way after the war regardless of Japanese internal policies, but it is of considerable interest to observe that, as a matter of fact, the United States set up in occupied Japan a system of narcotics control closely modeled after the American. Japanese narcotics squads were organized and trained in American techniques of enforcement, and new legislation was enacted which more or less copied that in the United States. Government reports to the United Nations speak of two types of users in Japan: (1) older addicts, often doctors, who are relatively few in number and usually use morphine, (2) young heroin addicts from the large cities. Most of the latter now coming to police attention have evidently acquired the habit since the end of the war.

The number of addicts in Japan is estimated at about 40,000 at present.[38] Of 1,856 users who came to the attention of the police in 1959 the great majority, 1,358, were under thirty-five years of age. Japan's addicts use heroin by hypodermic injection and secure their supplies from a flourishing illicit market which smuggles drugs to Japan from various places on the continent of Asia, especially Korea, Hong Kong, Bangkok, and Singapore. Now and then, drugs which were manufactured in Red China are seized in Japan. The Federal Bureau of Narcotics, which set up the postwar Japanese program, has remarked on the spread of heroin addiction there:

... Japan, which before the war claimed not one case of drug addiction is now found to have an illicit narcotic traffic equal that in other so-called victim countries.[39]

The Japanese, it appears, have developed a cultural susceptibility to addiction.

AN EVALUATION AND CLASSIFICATION
OF CONTROL SYSTEMS

Mr. Herbert L. May, an outstanding American authority on conditions in the Far East, who long served as a member of the Permanent Central Opium Board of the United Nations, in 1927 reported on conditions in the Far East to the Executive Board of the Foreign Policy Association. This was during the period of government monopoly. May's comments on these monopolies and on the prohibition system in the Philippines are of special interest. They were based upon Mr. May's visit to the countries concerned and they conform closely to the more detailed findings of an impartial committee which was sent to this area by the League of Nations during the same period.

Mr. May listed the main methods of control of opium smoking at that time as follows:

1. No restriction on sale, but simply a tax, or customs duty, or both, as in Persia.

2. Government monopoly, "farming out" to individuals, or to licensees, the right to sell all they can. This system is employed in Macao (Portuguese).

3. Government monopoly, the government operating its own shops with government employees engaged at a fixed salary; in force in British Malaya, Netherlands East Indies and elsewhere. This removes the incentive to push sales.

4. Government monopoly with the smokers registered, licensed and rationed to consume a limited amount, but permitting new names to be added from time to time to the list of registrants, as in some of the Netherlands East Indies. [Also Formosa.]

5. Same as (4) except that the list is closed and that no new names may be added; in effect a sort of limited prohibition applying to all except addicts. This system is in force in some other parts of the Netherlands East Indies. When the addicts are supplied through public hospitals or dispensaries, this becomes an almost complete form of prohibition, with the treatment of addicts considered as medicinal use of prepared opium.

6. Prohibition. There are two classifications which should be recognized as distinct: Prohibition in a district where the vice has never been practiced, and prohibition where it has.[40]

Noting that prohibition had failed in the Far East Mr. May made the following observation:

. . . I should say that the "prohibition countries" would gain by a temporary change to some form of government monopoly, subject to the conditions I am about to describe, particularly regarding profit. Under evaded prohibition they do not know who their addicts are, where their supplies come from or anything about the evil; it is all subterranean. *As a preparation for real prohibition, the government should have control of the sources and the outlets to enable it properly and progressively to dry up the stream, and to identify or "tag" the addicts.* [Italics in original.][41]

The plan favored by Mr. May as the most practicable one and the one most suited to conditions in Asia was the government monopoly system described earlier (numbers 4 and 5). He suggested that the following conditions be imposed upon the government monopoly:

(1) There should be a clear and unequivocal statement by the government as to policy of administration beneficial to the addicts;

(2) There should be no reliance upon the revenue for general budgetary purposes;

(3) As definite a time or contingency as possible should be fixed when prohibition will take the place of a monopoly;

(4) In the meantime there should be prohibition for nonaddicts, and addiction (smoking or "drug") should be treated as a medical problem —this involves a registration plan, with registration easy at first and eventually some form of rationing until cure or death.

(5) The monopoly should be under the control of a public welfare, social welfare, or health department and not in a finance department;

(6) To dispense with the revenue, the government could supply addicts at cost (not a good plan), or could use the profits for treatment of addiction, educational and propaganda work, social amelioration for the victims, and preventive social institutions.[42]

Concerning the prohibition system in the Philippines, Mr. May remarked:

To students of prohibitory laws as a means of bringing a vice under control it will be no surprise to learn that prohibition of opium smoking in the Philippines does not in fact prohibit. Anyone who wishes to buy prepared opium can buy it at a moderate price.[43]

He then quotes the prevailing illicit prices in Manila for various grades of smuggled opium—from China—and adds:

Frequent arrests and convictions by the local police and constabulary, and seizures by the customs authorities, must of course have some deterrent effect, and influence the price somewhat; but a comparison of the price with that prevailing in other parts of the Far East would indicate that there is no difficulty in having the supply keep pace with the demand. Opium is not the only thing smuggled in on a considerable scale; there is a "market price" for smuggling in a Chinaman via British North Borneo, and apparently he is privileged to bring in a supply of opium with him on his person.[44]

Reasons given to Mr. May for the failure of prohibition in the Philippines included graft, "some believing that prohibition law corrupts officials and others taking a more cynical view." From Hong Kong the following report was made in 1925:

In one case, three mail bags belonging to the USA Post Office were seized in the General Post Office; the whole of the contents proved to be prepared opium and drugs; investigations proved that employees in the General Post Office here and in Manila had been suborned, and that parcel post had been extensively used for the conveyance of prepared opium and drugs. Evidence was also found pointing to a large trade in morphia pills between Amoy, and Manila and Cebu. Frequent references were found, in documents discovered, to the aid rendered by the employees of the Post Office and Customs in the Islands in aiding the introduction of opium and drugs.[45]

In other reports Mr. May was told that men in the preventive service of the Philippines were offering to deliver opium to any address in Manila, and that there was a flourishing illegal trade in opium between British North Borneo and the Philippines in which American revenue boats manned by Filipinos participated.

Among the countries with government monopolies, Mr. May noted that the percentages of the total government revenue which were derived from opium sales were as follows:

Dutch East Indies	5%
Straits Settlements	37%
Federated Malay States	14%
Unfederated Malay States	20% to 28%
Sarawak	18½%
British North Borneo	23%

Mr. May's evaluation of the mixed system of control in the Dutch East Indies was relatively favorable.

In all of the localities covered except Formosa, the prices charged for government opium were relatively high. As a consequence, the government-monopoly countries also had to contend with a large volume of smuggling, which was frequently estimated to be as large or larger than the volume of the legal trade. In Formosa, where the cost of government opium was low, there was also considerable smuggling; in this case, to supply smokers who were denied licenses. Mr. May remarked that:

Smuggling is the chief obstacle to any form of government control of smoking, but particularly to prohibition because smuggling increases as barriers are raised against the commodity; prohibition where a demand exists is the highest possible barrier. Smuggling, generally speaking, exists where there is overproduction in one country and a demand in another, with a barrier against its satisfaction.[46]

Elsewhere, commenting on conditions in China, Mr. May observed:

The ideal situation, the world over, for "squeeze" (graft) is just this: a big supply, a big demand, and prohibition law.[47]

It will be seen from this and the preceding chapter that what appears to be the most effective system of control used in the Western world, that of handling addicts as medical cases and giving them regulated access to legal drugs, is the least common system in the Far East. The punitive-prohibition system, which is used in only a few Western countries, is the one which has been adopted by most Oriental countries. As we have pointed out in the preceding pages, American influence and pressure, especially upon Britain, the Netherlands, France, and Portugal was an important factor in this development. In the Philippines and in Japan the American-type program was established directly by the United States. The influence of the United Nations has also been in the same direction, perhaps again because of the weight of American opinion in that body. Thus while the prohibition system has come under increasingly severe attack within the United States, it has been successfully exported to the Far East, where it does not work any better than it does at home.

It is altogether consistent that American narcotic policy in the Far East should be what it is, for this country began to advocate the immediate and complete suppression of opium smoking in the Far East many years before the Harrison Act was passed. In the early part of the nineteenth century American merchants participated in the opium trade with China, competing unsuccessfully with English firms and the East India Company. It may well be that the subsequently adopted attitude of moral indignation toward the colonial powers of Europe, and the uncompromisingly prohibitionist position taken by American representatives to all of the international conferences, stemmed in part from a realization of the political advantages which these views gave to the United States in Asia.[48] Having urged the "corrupt colonial powers" of Europe to suppress opium abuse completely and immediately, the United States could hardly have done anything less when the Philippines were acquired.

The effect of the spread of prohibition in the Far East since World War II has been to convert the opium-smoking problem into a heroin and morphine problem and to drive it even further underground. The hypodermic method of injection has already become the chief method of use in Japan and is gaining ground elsewhere. The new addicts being recruited are, like those in the United States, young urban males from the slums and from the underworld and its fringes. The Far Eastern narcotics problem, is in short, being Westernized and Americanized. It has been forgotten in Taiwan that the Japanese program in that country between 1895 and World War II was the most effective program the Far East has seen. These countries are now sending increasing numbers of officials to the United States to find out how to "cure" addicts and how to cope with the gigantic illicit traffic of the East. In the meantime, Hong Kong is cited as an example of the failure of the "British system" and the spread of heroin addiction in the Far East seems to be viewed as an act of God, or perhaps as part of the inevitable price to be paid for the blessings of Westernization.

One of the reasons for the influence of American opinions in international discussions of narcotics questions is the sheer fact that there are so many more addicts in this country than there are in any other Western nation. Large numbers of addicts means that we also have a proportionately large number of experts with experience that cannot be matched elsewhere in the world. The number of these official experts continues to increase. When their advice is asked for by foreign governments, these officials quite naturally recommend the system with which they are familiar and which they have been taught to regard as the best and even the only possible one. It might seem more logical to pay maximum attention to the control programs in those countries having the fewest addicts, but this evidently happens very rarely since, with a small narcotics problem, there are few officials with expert knowledge or impressive experience to tout the program.

CHAPTER 8

THE MARIHUANA PROBLEM— MYTH OR REALITY?

THE primary fact about marihuana which ought to be taken into account by legislators but is not, is that it is not a habit-forming drug. By this is meant that the regular use of marihuana does not produce tolerance, and its abrupt cessation does not lead to withdrawal distress. As a consequence the problem of controlling or regulating its use is sharply different from that presented by the genuine drugs of addiction, i.e., the opiates such as heroin and morphine and their synthetic equivalents. Nevertheless, by federal legislation in 1951 and 1956, the increased penalties imposed on opiate users and peddlers were also applied to the users and distributors of marihuana. This extension was made casually with little discussion or investigation and with no apparent appreciation that the use of marihuana is something almost totally different from the use of heroin.

EFFECTS OF SMOKING MARIHUANA

Marihuana is ordinarily used in this country by smoking. The effects it produces are experienced as exhilaration, loss of inhibitions, a changed sense of time, and other psychological effects which have sometimes been described and extravagantly praised by those who have experienced them. These effects are in a general way comparable to the stimulating effects produced by alcohol in the sense that they are intoxicating, although they differ qualitatively from those of alcohol.

Intrinsically, however, marihuana is less dangerous and less harmful to the human body than is alcohol. It is, for example, not habit-forming, whereas alcohol is. While the alcoholic commonly substitutes alcohol for food, marihuana sharply stimulates the appetite. Chronic alcoholism is associated with various psychotic conditions and diseases such as Korsakoff's psychosis and cirrhosis of the liver. In comparison, the smoking of marihuana produces relatively trivial physical effects, although it does appear that immoderate use of the more concentrated products of the hemp plant also produce deleterious bodily effects. Such effects, however, are not conspicuous among American reefer smokers, probably because of the relatively small quantities of the essential drug that are ingested from the poor quality marihuana ordinarily consumed in this country. The American marihuana smoker who inadvertently uses too much when he switches, let us say, to the more potent ganja plant raised in Mexico and the West Indies is likely to experience nothing more alarming than going to sleep and waking up hungry.

USE OF MARIHUANA IN OTHER COUNTRIES

Marihuana consists of the dried and crumbled stems, leaves, and seed pods of a plant known as Indian hemp or *Cannabis sativa*. These materials are often mixed with tobacco and in the United States are ordinarily smoked. In many other parts of the world a special type of hemp plant of unusual potency, known commonly as *ganja*, is used in a similar manner or it may be brewed and drunk as ganja tea—a common practice in the West Indies, where this drink is prized for its alleged therapeutic efficacy. In India the un-cultivated hemp plant is smoked as marihuana is here and is also drunk. It is known there as *bhang*. The essential drug of the hemp plant is *cannabis indica* or *cannabinol* and it, of course, can be taken in this form. This essential drug is derived primarily from the resin of the female hemp plant. This concentrated hemp resin is commonly known as *hashish* and is immensely more powerful than either ganja or marihuana. The comparison of hashish and mari-huana is like that between pure alcohol and beer. Lurid accounts of the psychological effects and dangers of hemp are often based upon observations made by and upon hashish users. The mixture smoked as marihuana ordinarily contains very small quantities of the drug and its effects are correspondingly less spectacular, less dangerous, and less harmful than those of hashish.[1]

The medical use of *cannabis indica* has declined in Western medi-cine but it is still extensively used in the Ayurvedic and Unani systems of indigenous medicine in India. In various parts of the world folk beliefs attribute great therapeutic and even divine vir-tues to the drug. In Jamaica it is known to many persons of the lower classes as "the wisdom weed" and it is alleged that it stimu-lates good qualities in the person who uses it and brings him closer to God. The use of ganja there is supported by references to vari-ous Biblical passages which recommend the "herbs of the field." The same passages, incidentally, are taken by the devotess of peyote (a cactus containing mescaline) to refer to that plant. A back-to-Africa protest cult in Jamaica, known as the Ras Tafari, has adopted ganja as a symbol of the movement and its members sometimes refer to themselves as the "herb men." In defiance of the Govern-ment, members of this cult, and others who are simply impressed by the fact that ganja is a more profitable crop than any other, grow and harvest the plant and use some of it themselves. Ganja tea is regarded as a prime ameliorative agent in the folk treatment of many diseases including asthma, tuberculosis, venereal disease, and many others, especially all types of respiratory ailments. Ganja cigarettes are extensively used by the workers in the sugar cane fields and some foremen of the sugar producing companies state that, were it not for ganja, they would have difficulty finding workingmen to harvest their crops.[2]

On the book jacket of Professor Robert P. Walton's 1938 book entitled, *Marihuana: America's New Drug Problem*, Frederick T. Merrill and Mr. Anslinger are quoted. The latter observed: "It is a new peril—in some ways the worst we have met, and it concerns us all." Merrill was even more emphatic and alarmed: "If the abuse of this narcotic drug is not stamped out at once, the cost in crime waves, wasted human lives, and insanity will be enormous." Quoting Walton, Merrill notes that marihuana often produces "uncontrollable irritability and violent rages, which in most advanced forms cause assault and murder." He continues: "Amnesia often occurs, and the mania is frequently so acute that the heavy smoker becomes temporarily insane. Most authorities agree that permanent insanity can result from continual over-indulgence." Marihuana has had no noticeable effect in increasing the population of our mental institutions and whatever crimes of violence it may instigate are as nothing when compared to those that are linked with the use of alcohol.

Norman Taylor notes that the hemp plant, called *Cannabis sativa* by Linnaeus in the eighteenth century, probably originated in Central Asia or in China, where it was described in a book on pharmacy written by one Shen Nung nearly three thousand years before the birth of Christ.[3] The euphoric potential of the resinous female plant was known then and troubled Chinese moralists, who called it the "Liberator of Sin." Nung, however, recommended the medicine from this plant for "female weakness, gout, rheumatism, malaria, beri-beri, constipation and absent-mindedness." From China the use of hemp spread westward to India, to the Middle East, and along both sides of the Mediterranean, and ultimately reached Eu-

rope and the Western hemisphere. Nowhere has its use been eradi-
cated, even after thousands of years of effort in some instances.
Recent publications of the United Nations comment on the apparent continued spread of the practice.

The evil reputation of hemp was enhanced when, during the
eleventh century, it became linked with a cult headed by one
Hasan which initiated a new political tactic of secret assassination
to cleanse the Moslem world of false prophets. Hasan's full name
was Hashishin and he was called the Old Man of the Mountain.
The terms *hashish* and *assassin* are linked with the name of *Hasan*
and his cult.

USE BY LOWER CLASSES

It is possible that the bad reputation of marihuana and other
forms of this drug reflects in part the bias of upper classes against
an indulgence of the lower strata. Since hemp grows luxuriantly
without cultivation in many parts of the world, it is available to
many of its devotees at extremely low cost—in India, for example,
at about one-twentieth the price of good quality whiskey in 1894,
when the English carried out an extensive inquiry into the subject.[4]
Denunciations of the weed come characteristically from persons
of those classes which prefer whiskey, rum, gin, and other alcoholic
beverages and who do not themselves use marihuana. Such persons,
overlooking the well-known effects of alcohol, commonly deplore
the effects of hemp upon the lower classes and often believe that it
produces murder, rape, violence, and insanity.

Despite the prevalence of these beliefs among the drinkers of
rum and whiskey and the upper classes generally, impartial investigations invariably have shown no such results. The moderate use
of hemp, according to the Indian Hemp Drug Commission in 1894,
does not produce significant mental or moral injuries, does not lead
to disease, nor does it necessarily or even usually lead to excess any
more than alcohol does. Excess, the Commission said, is confined

to the idle and dissipated.[5] Many years later in New York City similar conclusions were stated on the basis of experimental study and from an examination of violent crimes committed in that city over a period of years.[6]

In Jamaica, where the lower classes regard the drug with favor, persons of high social status commonly assert that ganja is a potent cause of much of the personal violence which is relatively frequent there among the working classes. This is staunchly denied by the ganja users, who contend that the effects are usually in the opposite direction but admit that ganja may bring out the evil in some persons who are already evil. Police examination of violent crimes in Jamaica suggest that ganja has little connection with them and that they arise rather from sexual jealousy and the highly informal manner in which sexual matters are arranged on that island among the simpler people of the lower classes.

MARIHUANA AND ALCOHOL

In general, virtually all of the charges that are made against marihuana tend to shrink or dissolve entirely when they are closely examined by impartial investigators. The present tendency of the rank-and-file policeman, despite the enormous penalties attached to handling marihuana, is to regard it as a minor problem hardly deserving serious attention except for those who handle the weed in large amounts for mercenary purposes or who promote its use among the uninitiated.

Ironically, the accusations that are leveled at marihuana are all applicable to alcohol, as has been demonstrated by innumerable investigations. These studies indicate that much murder, rape, and homicide is committed by persons under the influence. The special psychoses and ailments of alcoholics are numerous and well delineated in countless scientific and literary productions. The menace of the drinking driver of automobiles is well understood by all and is more or less accepted as one of the inevitable hazards of life in the modern world. It is well known, too, that the manufacturers of alcoholic beverages advertise their products and seek to enlarge their markets and that the use of alcohol spreads from those who already have the practice to those who do not. Why, then, so much excitement about marihuana? It is said that marihuana sometimes causes girls and women to lose their virtue and innocence, but the role of alcohol in this respect is infinitely more important. It seems inconsistent, therefore, that while the decision to drink or not to drink is viewed as a personal moral decision, the use of marihuana should be viewed as a heinous crime subject to long prison sentences.

Among those who have never used hemp or seen it used by others the belief is often found that marihuana acts as a sexual stimulant or aphrodisiac. Actually its effects, like those of opiates, are in exactly the opposite direction, tending to cause the user to lose interest in the opposite sex. Users more frequently than not report the absence of ideas of sex or say that Venus herself could not tempt them when they are under the influence of this drug.

THE EFFECTS OF ANTI-MARIHUANA LEGISLATION

In 1937 the Congress passed a Marihuana Tax Act, modeled after the Harrison Act. It was designed to curb the use of marihuana by the use of the federal police power, and like the Harrison Act imposed penalties upon both buyers and sellers. This Act was the result of a publicity campaign staged by the Federal Bureau of Narcotics under Mr. Anslinger's direction and leadership. The bill was passed with little discussion after brief hearings on the ground that marihuana was a highly dangerous drug inciting its users to commit crimes of violence and often leading to insanity.[7]

The beliefs concerning marihuana which led to this legislation may be represented in a pure and extreme form by turning to the writing of a hyperactive reformer and alarmist of the period, Earle

Albert Rowell.[8] He claimed in 1939 that he had spent fourteen years campaigning against this weed, delivering more than four thousand lectures in forty states and personally pulling up and destroying many flourishing hemp fields. Mr. Rowell's zealous opposition to marihuana was only slightly less intense than his disapproval of alcohol and tobacco. The use of tobacco, he correctly observed, invariably precedes the smoking of the deadly reefer. Mr. Rowell came into disfavor with the Bureau of Narcotics around 1938 and this agency spent considerable energy and manpower in an attempt to silence and discredit him. This may have been because of Mr. Rowell's view that opiate addiction is a disease or perhaps because of his repeated allegations that the police were not sufficiently diligent in destroying marihuana.

Mr. Rowell summarized the effects of marihuana as follows:

We know that marihuana—
1. Destroys will power, making a jellyfish of the user. He cannot say no.
2. Eliminates the line between right and wrong, and substitutes one's own warped desires or the base suggestions of others as the standard of right.
3. Above all, causes crime; fills the victim with an irrepressible urge to violence.
4. Incites to revolting immoralities, including rape and murder.
5. Causes many accidents both industrial and automobile.
6. Ruins careers forever.
7. Causes insanity as its speciality.
8. *Either in self-defense or as a means of revenue, users make smokers of others, thus perpetuating evil.* [Italics in original.][9]

In 1939 when Rowell published his book, marihuana was regarded as a relatively new drug menace in the United States. Mr. Rowell thought that he had already detected an increase of the population of mental hospitals because of it:

Asylums and mental hospitals in this country are beginning to see and feel the influence of marihuana, and are awaking to its deleterious effects on the brain. As we traveled through the various states, superintendents

of these institutions told us of cases of insanity resulting from marihuana.[10]

"The baleful mental effects of marihuana," he said, "begin soon
after the first reefer is smoked. . . ."[11]

When Mr. Anslinger appeared before the Senate subcommittee
which was investigating the illicit drug traffic in 1955 under the
guidance of Senator Price Daniel, there were only a few offhand
discussions of marihuana. Mr. Anslinger observed that the Bureau
in its national survey was "trying to keep away from the marihuana
addict, because he is not a true addict." The real problem, he said,
was the heroin addict. Senator Daniel thereupon remarked:

"Now, do I understand it from you that, while we are discussing
marihuana, the real danger there is that the use of marihuana leads many
people eventually to the use of heroin, and the drugs that do cause complete addiction; is that true?"[12]

Mr. Anslinger agreed:

"That is the great problem and our great concern about the use of
marihuana, that eventually if used over a long period, it does lead to
heroin addiction."[13]

Senators Welker and Daniel pursued the subject, and Mr. Anslinger, when prompted, agreed that marihuana was dangerous.
Senator Welker finally asked this question:

"Is it or is it not a fact that the marihuana user has been responsible
for many of our most sadistic, terrible crimes in this nation, such as
sex slayings, sadistic slayings, and matters of that kind?"

Mr. Anslinger hedged:

"There have been instances of that, Senator. We have had some rather
tragic occurrences by users of marihuana. It does not follow that all
crime can be traced to marihuana. There have been many brutal crimes
traced to marihuana, but I would not say that it is a controlling factor
in the commission of crimes."[14]

Eighteen years earlier, in 1937, the year in which the federal antimarihuana law was passed, Mr. Anslinger had presented a very different picture of marihuana. Prior to 1937 Mr. Anslinger and the Bureau of Narcotics had spearheaded a propaganda campaign against marihuana on the ground that it produced an immense amount of violent crime such as rape, mayhem, and murder, and that many traffic accidents could be attributed to it. During the 1937 hearings before a House subcommittee, Representative John Dingell of Michigan asked Mr. Anslinger: "I am just wondering whether the marihuana addict graduates into a heroin, an opium, or a cocaine user."

Mr. Anslinger replied: "No, sir; I have not heard of a case of that kind. I think it is an entirely different class. The marihuana addict does not go in that direction."[15]

A few months later in the same year, before a Senate subcommittee which was considering the antimarihuana law which the Bureau of Narcotics had asked for, Mr. Anslinger commented: "There is an entirely new class of people using marihuana. The opium user is around 35 to 40 years old. These users are 20 years old and know nothing of heroin or morphine."[16]

The theme stated by the Commissioner of Narcotics in 1955, that the main threat in marihuana is that it leads to the use of heroin, is now ordinarily cited as the principal justification for applying to it the same severe penalties that are applied in the case of heroin. Reformer Rowell in 1939 was more logical and consistent than either the Senators or the Commissioner when he emphasized that cigarette smoking invariably preceded reefer smoking. Mr. Rowell told of a shrewd gangster whom he engaged in what now appears as a prophetic discussion of the prospects of the dope industry.[17]

The gangster remarked: "Marihuana is the coming thing."

"But," I protested in surprise, "marihuana is not a habit-forming drug like morphine or heroin; and, besides, it's too cheap to bother with."

He laughed. "You don't understand. Laws are being passed now by various states against it, and soon Uncle Sam will put a ban on it. The price will then go up, and that will make it profitable for us to handle."

The gangster, according to Mr. Rowell, then commented on the shrewd manner in which the tobacco companies had popularized cigarettes among the soldiers of the First World War and on the enormous increase in cigarette consumption by young persons. He grew eloquent: "Every cigarette smoker is a prospect for the dope ring via the marihuana road. Millions of boys and girls now smoke. Think of the unlimited new market!"

Mr. Rowell got the idea and commented as follows to his readers: "Slowly, insidiously, for over three hundred years, Lady Nicotine was setting the stage for a grand climax. The long years of tobacco using were but an introduction and training for marihuana use. Tobacco, which was first smoked in a pipe, then as a cigar, and at last as a cigarette, demanded more and more of itself until its supposed pleasures palled, and some of the tobacco victims looked about for something stronger. Tobacco was no longer potent enough."

Mr. Rowell was not optimistic about the future: "Marihuana will continue to be a problem for both police and educators, because it is so easy to grow, to manufacture, and to peddle, and is such a quick source of easy money. The plant can be grown anywhere; it can be harvested secretly, prepared in twenty-four hours without a penny of investment for equipment; and every cigarette user is a prospect. As our laws are enforced and the weed becomes scarcer, the price will rise, and greater profit accrue to venturesome and successful peddlers. Whereas now it is usually peddled by lone wolves, as soon as the weed becomes scarcer and the price rises, organized crime will step in and establish a monopoly."[18]

While Mr. Rowell, in the manner of reforming alarmists, exaggerated the evil with which he was preoccupied, the above appraisal of the effects of the Marihuana Tax Act has been reasonably well borne out by subsequent events. Certainly it was a more realistic assessment of the law's effects than any that were made by the legislators who passed the bill or by the officials who promoted it. Mr. Rowell was also completely right in pointing out that virtually every marihuana smoker graduated to this practice from cigarette smoking. His gangster informant was correct in his calculation that state and federal laws prohibiting marihuana would make the weed more expensive and more profitable for peddlers to handle, and also correctly foresaw that with the same merchants handling both marihuana and heroin it would become a simple matter for marihuana users to switch from the less to the more dangerous drug, as they have done.

In the United States during the nineteenth century, and the early decades of the twentieth, addiction to opiates frequently developed from the abuse of alcohol. This still occurs to some extent and is frequently reported from other parts of the world, for morphine provides a potent means of relieving the alcoholic hangover. An American doctor once advocated as a cure of alcoholism that alcohol addicts be deliberately addicted to morphine, arguing with considerable plausibility that of the two habits the latter was obviously the lesser evil.[19] Moreover, he practiced what he preached and recommended his technique with considerable enthusiasm for use by others.

The truth of the matter, of course, is that very few cigarette smokers go on to marihuana, very few marihuana users go on to heroin, and very few alcohol users graduate to the use of heroin. Since some barbiturate and amphetamine users progress to heroin it should be added that it is also only a very small proportion who do. If all of these substances were to be prohibited because they are sometimes involved in the progression toward heroin addiction there is little doubt that the illicit traffic in marihuana and heroin would be expanded to include the other offending substances and that the movement from less to more serious habits would be greatly facilitated.

No one, of course, recommends the use of marihuana nor does anyone deny that there are evil effects and consequences associated with using it. The fact that the use of marihuana is outlawed, for example, means that it is often obtained through association with unsavory types, often used in an underworld environment, and the user takes the risk of criminal prosecution. It is also undeniable that marihuana intoxication may sometimes lead to automobile accidents and to irresponsible or criminal acts. The controversy with respect to marihuana is solely concerning the relative prevalence or frequency of such results in comparison to similar consequences following from the use of alcoholic beverages. All empirical investigations indicate that alcohol constitutes a far greater social danger than does marihuana.

MAYOR LAGUARDIA'S COMMITTEE ON MARIHUANA

Mayor LaGuardia's Committee on Marihuana, on the basis of a close examination of the matter in New York City, stressed the relative triviality of the effects of marihuana use in a report published in 1945.[20] In the July 1943 issue of the *Military Surgeon*, the editor, Colonel J. M. Phalen, commented as follows in an editorial on "The Marihuana Bugaboo":

> The smoking of the leaves, flowers and seeds of *Cannabis sativa* is no more harmful than the smoking of tobacco or mullein or sumac leaves. . . . The legislation in relation to marihuana was ill-advised . . . it branded as a menace and a crime a matter of trivial importance. . . . It is hoped that no witch hunt will be instituted in the military service over a problem that does not exist.[21]

Similar statements have been made by many other competent investigators and observers.

On the other hand, as has been pointed out, a sharply divergent view has been presented by law enforcement officials, particularly by the Federal Bureau of Narcotics, and also by many individual writers. The sharp divergence of views among the scientifically oriented evidently depends upon the manner in which the research is done. Investigators who rely on the opinions of high echelon officials, who have no direct acquaintance with the use of marihuana and who base their opinions on anecdotes rather than actual statistical data, usually reach the conclusion that marihuana is a highly dangerous drug which produces much violent crime and insanity. These conclusions, as we have suggested, may be a reflection of upper-class hostility toward an unfamiliar lower-class indulgence. More critical and skeptical investigators, who look for basic statistical evidence, invariably fail to find it and end up writing debunking articles for which they are roundly abused by the moralists.

It is often felt that, even if the dangers of marihuana are exaggerated, these exaggerations and misstatements should be allowed to stand so that they may frighten adolescents away from the drug. The implication that adolescents are influenced to any appreciable degree by articles appearing in scientific journals is probably absurd. Those who use marihuana probably come to do so on the basis of personal associations and direct observations of their own.

The deliberate circulation of false information is self-defeating in that the adventurous, experimentally inclined youth can quickly discover for himself, by trying the weed or talking to those who have smoked it, that much of the officially circulated view is false. He is then prepared to believe that everything he has been told about narcotics is equally wrong.

When Mayor LaGuardia's Committee on Marihuana made its report, it was strongly attacked by those committed to a belief in the marihuana menace. The *Journal of the American Medical Association* in 1943 published a letter from Mr. Anslinger in which he criticized an article by Drs. Allentuck and Bowman on findings derived from the New York study in which they had participated.[22] There were rumors that the New York marihuana study was to be suppressed, but after considerable delay, it was ultimately released in 1945. On April 28, 1945, the *Journal of the American Medical Association* editorially assailed the report, using language and arguments of a type not ordinarily found in learned journals:

For many years medical scientists have considered cannabis a dangerous drug. Nevertheless, a book called "Marihuana Problems" by the New York City Mayor's Committee on Marihuana submits an analysis by seventeen doctors of tests on 77 prisoners and, on this narrow and thoroughly unscientific foundation, draws sweeping and inadequate conclusions which minimize the harmfulness of marihuana. Already the book has done harm. One investigator has described some tearful parents who brought their 16 year old son to a physician after he had been detected in the act of smoking marihuana. A noticeable mental deterioration had been evident for some time even to their lay minds. The boy said he had read an account of the LaGuardia Committee report and that this was his justification for using marihuana. He read in *Down Beat*, a musical journal, an analysis of this report under the caption "Light Up, Gates, Report Finds Tea a Good Kick."

A criminal lawyer for marihuana drug peddlers has already used the LaGuardia report as a basis to have defendants set free by the court. . . .

The book states unqualifiedly to the public that the use of this narcotic does not lead to physical, mental or moral degeneration and that permanent deleterious effects from its continued use were not observed on 77 prisoners. This statement has already done great damage to the cause of law enforcement. Public officials will do well to disregard this unscientific, uncritical study, and continue to regard marihuana as a menace wherever it is purveyed.[23]

Despite the fact that this editorial continues to be cited and reproduced to discredit the New York study, the conclusions of the report enjoy considerable status and are undoubtedly far closer to the realities of the situation than is the view represented by the A.M.A. editorial. Indeed, if one judges the law enforcement agencies by their actions rather than their words, it appears that even the police, to a considerable extent, have swung over to the viewpoint of the Mayor's Committee.

MARIHUANA ARRESTS

After 1951 the budget and field force of the Federal Bureau of Narcotics were substantially enlarged. Nevertheless, the number of marihuana arrests has steadily declined and by 1960 it was close to the vanishing point, with only 169 such cases. In previous years the numbers of federal marihuana violations were reported as follows: [24]

1952	1,288
1954	508
1956	403
1958	179

Of the 169 federal marihuana violations reported in 1960, 88 occurred in California, 16 in Maryland, and 13 in Kentucky. No other state had as many as ten, and no violations were reported from 28 states. We have already noted that the Bureau does not bother to count marihuana users in its national survey of addiction and does not regard marihuana as an addicting drug. The above figures on enforcement suggest that, at the federal level at least, the marihuana laws are being largely ignored since it is not claimed that the use of marihuana is diminishing.

Statistics on marihuana prosecutions as such are extremely difficult to obtain and data that are available are very unreliable and incomplete. The Federal Narcotics Bureau presented to the Daniel Subcommittee a summary of marihuana prosecutions for the year 1954, giving both federal and nonfederal cases. It is not claimed that the latter are complete; they are merely figures from some of the main cities in the indicated states.

TABLE 5

Marihuana Arrests—Federal and Local by States—1954[25]

State	Arrests Federal	Local	State	Arrests Federal	Local
Alabama	2	6	New Hampshire	0	0
Arizona	25	4	New Jersey	5	26
Arkansas	2	0	New Mexico	23	10
California	51	1,101	New York	5	407
Colorado	28	1	North Carolina	0	0
Connecticut	2	6	North Dakota	0	0
Delaware	0	1	Ohio	25	23
District of			Oklahoma	2	13
Columbia	3	17	Oregon	1	8
Florida	4	30	Pennsylvania	3	50
Georgia	4	1	Rhode Island	0	0
Idaho	0	2	South Carolina	4	0
Illinois	13	327	South Dakota	0	0
Indiana	0	14	Tennessee	11	1
Iowa	0	8	Texas	325	612
Kansas	2	0	Utah	4	0
Kentucky	39	8	Vermont	0	0
Louisiana	17	105	Virginia	0	1
Maine	0	0	Washington	22	10
Maryland	2	30	West Virginia	0	0
Massachusetts	5	1	Wisconsin	0	47
Michigan	30	270	Wyoming	4	0
Minnesota	0	5	Alaska	5	0
Mississippi	0	1	Hawaii	14	23
Missouri	9	15		—	—
Montana	0	6	Totals	713	3,205
Nebraska	1	13			
Nevada	16	2	Grand Total		3,918

From this table it will be seen that 3,263 of the total of 3,918 arrests were made in the six states of California, Texas, Illinois, Michigan, New York, and Louisiana. These states are, in one way or another, centers of the marihuana traffic. High arrest rates in California, Texas, and Louisiana no doubt arise from the fact that considerable quantities of marihuana are smuggled into the country there from Mexico and the Caribbean area. The rates in Illinois, Michigan, and New York reflect mainly police activity in the three large cities of Detroit, Chicago, and New York, all of them narcotics distribution centers. Heroin arrests are also highest in the states of California, New York, Illinois, and Michigan, while Texas and Louisiana are farther down on the list.

The penalty provisions applicable to marihuana users under state and federal law are about the same as those applied to heroin users. These penalties are entirely disproportionate to the seriousness of the offending behavior and lead to gross injustice and undesirable social consequences. For example, it is well known that many jazz musicians and other generally inoffensive persons use or have used marihuana. To send these persons to jail is absurd and harmful and serves no conceivable useful purpose. The moderate or occasional marihuana user is not a significant social menace. Jails and prisons, chronically overcrowded, should be used for those who present a genuine threat to life and property. The absurdity is compounded when an occasional judge, ignorant of the nature of marihuana, sends a marihuana user to prison to cure him of his nonexistent addiction. The writer was once in court when a middle-aged Negro defendant appeared before the judge charged with having used and had in his possession one marihuana cigarette during the noon hour at the place where he had worked for a number of years. This man had no previous criminal record and this fact was stated before the court. Nevertheless, a two-year sentence was imposed to "dry up his habit."

The President's Advisory Commission which reported on narcotic and drug abuse in 1963 took cognizance of the relatively trivial nature of the marihuana evil by suggesting that all mandatory sentences be eliminated for crimes involving it and that judges be granted full discretionary power in dealing with offenders.[26] These suggestions are excessively timid and not entirely logical, for there is no good reason why a mere user of marihuana should be subjected to a jail sentence at all. The marihuana user probably ought to be dealt with by the law along the same lines that are used with persons who drink alcohol.

If it is deemed in the public interest to punish smokers of marihuana, such punishments should ordinarily consist of fines only, up to some maximum of perhaps $500.00, depending upon the offense and the defendant's ability to pay. These fines might be scaled down or eliminated entirely for persons who provided information concerning their source of supply. Police efforts should be focused primarily on the traffic rather than on the user. Persons driving automobiles under the influence of the drug might be fined and deprived of their driving licenses for a period of time. Crimes which could be shown to the satisfaction of a court of law to be linked with the use of marihuana ought to be dealt with about the way that crimes arising from the use of alcohol are handled.

Laws such as this, with penalties of a reasonable nature, would probably be more effective than those now in effect because they would be more enforceable and more in accord with the nature of the problem being dealt with. They would have the effect of reducing the discrepancy that now exists between the laws as written and the laws as they are actually enforced. A more matter-of-fact and realistic handling of the marihuana problem would also probably reduce the aura of sensationalism which now surrounds the subject and diminsh the illicit glamor which is now attached to the hemp plant.

It is argued by some that the marihuana industry should be brought under control by legalization, taxation, licensing, and other devices like those used to control alcohol—and to exploit it as a source of revenue. Advocates of this view might well argue that there should be no unfair discrimination among vices; that if the greater evil of alcohol use is legal, the lesser one of marihuana smoking should be so as well. Since the smoking of marihuana will undoubtedly continue regardless of legislation against it, it can also be argued that it would be better to accept the inevitable than to wage war for a lost cause.

In opposition to this extremely permissive position, the more conservative reformer can call attention to the fact that, outside of a few Asian and African countries, the use of this substance is everywhere disapproved of and subject to legal restrictions. It is possible that legal sanctions exercise some deterrent effect and that without them the use of this drug might spread even more rapidly and assume more virulent forms. Should the use of marihuana become anywhere nearly as widespread as that of alcohol it might be too late to talk of effective restrictions since the users would command too many votes. A legal marihuana or ganja industry which advertised its product and sought to improve it through research and experimentation would be a distinct embarrassment to the nation as a whole as well as being a direct economic threat to the alcoholic beverage industries and possibly to the tobacco industry. A final and decisive argument seems to be that public opinion is not likely in the foreseeable future to accept indulgence in marihuana as an equivalent of, or substitute for, indulgence in alcohol.

The long history of the use of marihuana, the spread of the practice throughout the world in the face of determined and sometimes fanatical opposition, and the persistence of the practice once it is established—all suggest that the smoking of marihuana will continue in the United States for some time to come. The practical question seems to be one of minimizing and controlling the practice while avoiding the extreme tactics of prohibitionists. A comprehensive, impartial public inquiry into the matter, based on the assumption that marihuana is *not* the same as heroin, might help to bring about a more sober and rational approach to an indulgence which merits some concern but which is far less serious than is presently suggested by the harsh inflexibility of current laws.

CHAPTER 9

OBSTACLES TO REFORM

In an editorial entitled "Dismantling a Narcotic Theory," the *Wall Street Journal* early in 1964 commented favorably on the recommendation of the President's Advisory Commission that the Federal Bureau of Narcotics be eliminated in its present form and that its functions be turned over to other agencies.[1] The Bureau, said the editorial, "has become a symbol of a single theory of dealing with drug addiction. This theory rests on the premise that addiction is a crime and, for all practical purposes, little more than that." Observing that this theory has been followed by the government for nearly half a century, the *Wall Street Journal* suggests that it be dismantled along with the Bureau of Narcotics. As presently organized the Bureau depends for its very existence upon the status quo, and it is therefore easy to understand that it has come to be the symbol of a punitive approach and the most important and influential obstacle to reform.

Mr. Harry J. Anslinger became head of the Bureau when it was first organized in 1930 and was not replaced until 1962, when Henry L. Giordano was named as his successor. The new head has given some indications of a more flexible and liberal position but in the main seems to share the views of Mr. Anslinger. Even if Mr. Giordano wished to alter the public image of the Bureau it would be a difficult matter after the thirty-two-year reign of his predecessor. The Bureau's policy of harassing and intimidating those who disagreed with its views appears to have been largely abandoned by the new Commissioner, who has also initiated a policy in 1962 of listing new publications even when they are not in line with the Bureau's views.[2] On the other hand, as late as 1963 a district supervisor of the Bureau told the writer that he attended all publicly announced speeches given in his area by two prominent critics of the Bureau's position. This may perhaps be defended on the ground that the Bureau needs to keep itself informed of latest developments and new research, although this could also be done through the mail.

Under the reign of Commissioner Anslinger, any individual investigator who found himself at odds with the comprehensive official line laid down by the Bureau had to contend with the solid, monolithic phalanxes of the government bureaucracy. The latter, with the mass media and government printing presses available to them, could readily brand the heretic as an irresponsible "self-appointed expert," or inspire a stooge to attack him or to label his work "unscientific." As a result, discussion of the narcotics question during the Anslinger era was a dialogue between two schools of thought, those who agreed with the Bureau and those who did not.

The President's Advisory Commission recommended in 1963 that the government actively disseminate information concerning addiction and the drug problem in order to counteract mistaken popular ideas.[3] At the White House Conference in 1962 a constantly recurring theme was that popular misconceptions greatly increased the difficulty of dealing with the problem and various remedial programs were suggested. The ironic aspect of this was that, to a very large extent, popular stereotypes in this area were based on ideas disseminated by the government, i.e., the Federal Bureau of Narcotics.

At the same time that the Bureau was promulgating a philosophy of addiction and harassing or maintaining surveillance over its critics, it conspicuously failed to provide reliable statistical information on its own enforcement activities or on the narcotics problem in general. It does not seem credible that the extremely poor statistical reporting of the Bureau could be due to lack of funds, for Congress was extremely generous to it in this respect and has apparently never questioned the Bureau's substantial public relations expenditures. It would appear that if the Bureau is not to be dismantled, it would be highly desirable that it put more money and manpower into improvement of its statistical services. If it is dismantled, as recommended by the President's Commission, this matter would automatically be taken care of, since the Federal Bureau of Investigation would then take over this duty and might then publish comprehensive statistical data on narcotics in its regular issues of the Uniform Crime Reports.[4] This effect alone, of incorporating the law enforcement activities of the Narcotics Bureau into the F.B.I., could be of very considerable long-range significance in that it would provide the American public, for the first time, with relatively reliable data about the problem.

While it is too early to know what the policies of the Federal Narcotics Bureau will be under its new head, Henry L. Giordano, it is of practical and also of historical interest to remind the reader what the Bureau did under Mr. Anslinger's direction. When Mr. Anslinger was retired as head of the Bureau he continued to be the United States representative to the Commission on Narcotic Drugs of the United Nations. While he cannot now use the facilities of the Bureau to promote his views, the point of view which he represents and which he vigorously promoted for more than thirty years is still very much alive and is still the major obstacle to fundamental reform.

On April 4, 1961, the Federal Bureau of Narcotics sent a narcotics agent to Indiana University to question its officials and those of the Indiana University Press concerning the proposed publication of a book on the narcotics problem which expressed views contrary to those of the Bureau.[5] The agent inquired minutely into all the details of the publication, wanting to know how many copies were being printed, how the book happened to be published by the Press, and so on. He was especially interested in knowing the details of how it was being financed, whether funds of the state of Indiana were being used, and what funds would be used to make up the deficit if the publication were to lose money. When pressed to explain his presence on the campus he extracted from his pocket teletyped orders from Washington and said he was simply following orders and that he presumed that his boss in Washington would like to stop the publication of this work.

When the visit of the narcotics agent to the Press became known, a reporter of the *Washington Post*, as well as reporters from other newspapers, addressed inquiries to the head of the Bureau of Narcotics. When asked what his agent was up to on the Indiana University campus, Mr. Anslinger was first reported to have said that he would have to get in touch with him to find out. Later he apparently said that he presumed that it was simply "a routine investigation," and still later he suggested that the agent had made the hundred-mile round trip to buy an advance copy of the book. The agent made his visit on April 4, 1961. The records of the Indiana University Press show that the legal division of the Federal Bureau of Narcotics had ordered the book in March. When the *Washington Post* reporter asked the agent how it happened, if his purpose was only to purchase the book, that he had talked to so many University officials, the agent referred the reporter to his superiors for "the real story."[6]

The book which stirred the Federal Bureau of Narcotics to take its action is entitled *Drug Addiction: Crime or Disease?*, and consists of the Interim and Final Reports of the Joint Committee of the American Bar Association and the American Medical Association on Narcotic Drugs, with a brief introduction written by the present writer. The Joint Committee consisted of six distinguished members of the two associations. The bulk of the volume is made up of special studies by Judge Morris Ploscowe, former Chief Magistrate of New York City, and Rufus King, a Washington attorney, then head of the Criminal Law Division of the American Bar Association and well known for his writings on the narcotics problem. The work of the Committee was supported financially by the Russell Sage Foundation, which also financed the printing of a limited edition of the interim report in 1958 for the use of the Committee and the Houses of Delegates of the two associations— both of which accepted the report.

The Interim Report was presented to Mr. Anslinger for his comments and criticisms in 1958 when it was completed. Mr. Anslinger condemned it, stating in a letter to Judge Ploscowe: "I find it incredible that so many glaring inaccuracies, manifest inconsistencies, apparent ambiguities, important omissions, and even false statements could be found in one report on the narcotic problem."[7] When asked for a bill of particulars, Anslinger refused to provide one but instead said that he was going to appoint his own advisory committee to make a report. Mr. Anslinger also discussed the report with officials of the Russell Sage Foundation.

The so-called Advisory Committee to the Federal Bureau of Narcotics which Mr. Anslinger created to reply to the Joint Committee's Interim Report consisted mainly of police and prosecuting officials and others throughout the nation who agree with the Bureau's conception of the drug problem. The result of their work was a symposium of intemperate and vituperative criticism of the Joint Committee, its work, and of other persons known to be in some degree sympathetic with its viewpoint. This report was published in 1959 with a title, format, and color which made it hard to distinguish from the Interim Report itself. It was sold by the Superintendent of Documents for sixty cents and distributed gratis by the Bureau of Narcotics and by some members of Congress. Official circulation of the document was discontinued when the *Washington Post* in 1960 gave publicity to a criticism of the Supreme Court which it contained.[8] Unofficially, according to Benjamin De Mott, this publication, which he suggested "may well be the crudest publication yet produced by a government agency," continued to be circulated. In a copy secured after official circulation had ceased, the offending sentence had been crayoned out with black crayon but was still legible. It was a statement made by Mr. Malachi L. Harney, a former assistant of Mr. Anslinger's: "We are presently the victims of a Supreme Court majority which to me seems almost hysterical in its desire to suppress all freedom of action by law enforcement officers."[9]

According to De Mott, the Bureau's efforts to discourage the publication of the Interim Report were terminated by an order from the White House.[10] It is possible that the publicity given the incident by the press was also an important factor, for it was picked up by countless newspapers and commentators. De Mott also stated that the Bureau had consulted with officials of the Russell Sage Foundation, apparently attempting to exert pressure upon them.

PHYSICIANS AND JUDGES AS SCAPEGOATS

Professor Benjamin De Mott, who has provided a description of the top officials of the Federal Narcotics Bureau of the Anslinger era, refers to the "fury of the Bureau's anti-intellectualism." This rage was directed particularly toward doctors, judges, professors, sociologists, and, of course, the Supreme Court. Mr. De Mott finds the roots of the Bureau's attitudes in what he calls the "cop mentality." "Bureau officials," he says, "have a taste for public propaganda that panders to provincial superstition of 'un-American' types. . . . [T]he Bureau's dismissal of its critics is often accompanied by an appeal to everything that is mean, ignorant, and illiberal in the American consciousness. . . . Narcotics Bureau propaganda reeks with station-house hints that any man who interests himself in the problem of 'known criminals' must have unsavory reasons for doing so."[11]

It has been pointed out that the Bureau has hammered away at the idea that judges were responsible for the postwar rise of addiction because of excessive leniency in imposing sentences, and, on the other hand, that the police are to be credited with the alleged decline of addiction during the decades before the war, when judges were just as lenient as later. These outrageous and inconsistent attempts to pass the buck have largely gone unchallenged and appear to have been accepted with little question by Congress. The underlying conception seems to have been that the competence of a judge is directly proportional to the severity of the sentences he imposes, regardless of individual circumstances, and that it is his duty in handling narcotics cases, at least, to follow the advice of the police.

An example of the Bureau's tactics in dealing with recalcitrant judges is provided by the following news release on February 27, 1962, which was printed in the *Fort Wayne News* in the form of an editorial:

JUDGE UNDER ATTACK FOR CUT IN BAIL
OF THREE RACKETEERS

Washington (UPI)—Members of a House subcommittee have demanded the Justice Department inquire into the fitness of a federal

judge who reduced the bail of three racketeers charged with conspiracy in an internationl narcotics ring.

The demand was contained in Congressional testimony made public
today.

The judge is Edward J. Dimock of the Federal Court in New York
City.

The three racketeers, who have been linked with the late underworld
czar Salvatore (Lucky) Luciano, are Frank Caruso, Vincent Mauro and
Salvatore Maneri.

They skipped the country late last year after Judge Dimock reduced
their bonds from $250,000 to $50,000 each. Three months later they were
arrested in Spain and returned to the United States.

Federal Narcotics Commissioner H. J. Anslinger told a House appropriations subcommittee that Judge Dimock "hated" the narcotics law
under which the trio was arrested.

"He thinks it is too severe," Anslinger said, "and because of that
many of these defendants . . . try to maneuver their cases so they come
before that judge, and of course they naturally waive a jury trial and
are tried by the judge himself."

Anslinger's comments made at a closed hearing late last month,
prompted several Congressmen to voice bitter criticism of the judge.

Chairman J. Vaughan Gary, D-Va., said Dimock "should be removed
from office" if the bonds were not collectible. [It later turned out they
were and the money was forfeited.]

Gary said he would demand the Justice Department look into the
whole matter.

Rep. John R. Pillion, R-N.Y., agreed and said any such review should
include whether there was a possible "abuse of discretion."

Pillion said the department also should inquire into "the judge's fitness and competence to preside over cases involving narcotics offenders."

Rep. Hugh O. Alexander, D-N.C., said he thought "every avenue
ought to be followed up."

Anslinger noted that Judge Dimock was retired but still hears cases
occasionally.

Rep. Otto E. Passman, D-La., said: "It might possibly be suggested
to the judge himself, that in the circumstances, maybe he should be
put in complete retirement."

Federal Judge Edward J. Dimock was one of the six members of the Joint Committee of the American Bar and Medical Associations which issued the report that was sponsored by the Russell Sage Foundation and published in 1961 by the Indiana University Press.

Readers who wonder why a judge would reduce bail in a case like this one should note that the Eighth Amendment of the Constitution specifies that excessive bail shall not be required of persons charged with noncapital crimes and recall that judges are sworn to uphold the Constitution. The purpose of bail is, of course, to permit the defendant to be free before the trial in order to facilitate his preparation of a defense, and reasonable bail is usually thought of as an amount which is not beyond the defendant's reach.

Bureau hostility to the medical profession, Mr. De Mott has suggested, is indicated by the violence of the attack upon the A.B.A.–A.M.A. report as well as by insinuations that the doctors are seeking to cover up addiction in their own ranks. It is further exemplified by the kind of attention that some of the most important congressional committees have given to the private practitioner's relations with addicts. The Senate subcommittee which was chaired by Price Daniel and managed by W. Lee Speer of the Bureau conducted what amounted to something resembling criminal trials of Philadelphia and Washington physicians who had prescribed drugs for addicts.[12] The record of the hearings on one of these cases alone extends to more than a hundred pages, another occupies about seventy. Throughout the hearings repeated references were made to improper prescription of drugs by medical men. The net effect was to suggest irresponsibility on the part of the profession and the need for continued police surveillance.

On the other hand, almost no serious attention whatever was given to securing representative medical opinions from private practitioners concerning policies of dealing with addicts. The bulk of the medical testimony was from Public Health Service officials who supported the Bureau's position.

These hearings and others have made it evident that the congressional committees have, on the whole, not wished to listen to views they might have obtained from judges and doctors which might have weakened or modified the simple philosophy with which they were indoctrinated. A pertinent aspect of this disinclination may have been their realization that the police conception, oversimple as it is, is more useful politically than any other. While politicians may run for office on platforms which promise death for dope peddlers and jail for addicts, none has yet run on one advocating justice and medical care for drug users. Sensational newspapers and pulp magazines also find the police conception congenial to them, for it provides an inexhaustible source of sensational stories featuring cops-and-robbers episodes, extraordinary degradation and depravity, undercover intrigue, plot and counterplot, diabolical Communist schemes, and wealthy gangsters—always with the bad guys, who are in favor of dope, sharply distinguished from the good ones, who are against it.

THE BANNING OF A CANADIAN DOCUMENTARY FILM

In the late 1940's a documentary film was projected by the Canadian Department of National Health and Welfare on the subject of addiction. The film was prepared by the National Film Board of Canada with the cooperation of the police, who provided drug addicts to act in it. The film won for its director, Robert Anderson, a National Film Award.[13] Mr. K. C. Hossick, the Canadian counterpart of Mr. Anslinger, brought the film to New York for a showing at the United Nations before the members of the Division of Narcotic Drugs, who later published a statement in the *U.N. Bulletin* of November 15, 1948, that, "It is the best technical film relating to the control of narcotic drugs which has yet been shown to them. The enlightened treatment of the problem of the drug addict must receive specially favorable criticism."

Prior to the U.N. showing, Mr. Hossick was prevailed upon to show the film to a number of narcotics agents and officials in New York. When word of the nature of the film was conveyed to Mr. Anslinger he asked the State Department to request the Canadian authorities not to show the picture in the United States. This request reached the Canadian officials at about the same time as the statement from the United Nations to the effect that it was the best film on drug addicion that had been shown to that body.

Inquiries addressed to the State Department elicited a reply which read in part: "At Mr. Anslinger's request, the Department informed the Canadian Department of External Affairs that the Commissioner of Narcotics objected strongly to the showing of the film anywhere in the United States because the position it takes concerning the handling of drug addiction is contrary to the long-established policy of the United States. . . . The Public Health Service concurred in the attitude of the Commissioner of Narcotics."[14]

A Reuters dispatch to the *Chicago Tribune* indicated that among the objections to the film the most important was that it insisted that addiction should be viewed as a disease rather than a crime.[15] Another objection was that the actors were too personable and attractive and might thus make addiction seem attractive. We have already noted that the actors were actual addicts. It was also contended that the role of the police was not properly emphasized.

It was evidently hoped that there would be no publicity attached to this incident, for when news of it was published in a column by Jacob Weiler in the *New York Times*, he was immediately visited by agents of the Treasury Department who flashed their badges and demanded to know the source of the item.[16] Mr. Weiler cited a Toronto film trade journal as the source. The incident was subsequently discussed in the *Saturday Review of Literature*, the *New York Times*, and other publications. In reply to protests it was contended that the picture violated the Motion Picture Code. It was never permitted to be shown in this country except in a few special cases, and a scheduled showing at meetings of the American Psychiatric Association in Montreal was cancelled.

Mr. Anslinger evidently took steps to investigate the background for the endorsement of the film by the Division of Narcotic Drugs of the United Nations Secretariat, which was at that time headed by an American. When the film was shown this American was not on duty but was being temporarily replaced by an Englishman, B. G. Alexander. Subsequently, in answer to inquiries from a prominent criminologist at the University of Illinois, Mr. Anslinger enclosed a copy of a letter from the American head of the U.N. Division, which stated that the endorsement of the Canadian film was undertaken without authority by a man who was no longer a member of the staff.[17] This was evidently a reference to Alexander, who had been acting as deputy chief of the Division when the film was shown and who subsequently returned to Britain.

THE BUREAU ATTACKS A "CRIMINAL" ORGANIZATION—1939

That the Federal Narcotics Bureau has long made it a practice to conduct routine investigations of persons holding the wrong views is made evident by an incident in which I was involved. In 1939 a federal narcotics agent approached a member of the Board of Trustees of Indiana University and later the President of the university (of whose faculty I was, and still am, a member), with the word that I was a member of or associated with a disreputable organization. I was told of the agent's visit by telephone. It was alleged that I was connected with what was described as a "criminal" association.

When the agent called on me he indicated that he was acting on orders from Washington and several times gestured toward a fat folder of papers in his possession, evidently sent to him from headquarters. The alleged criminal organization turned out to be one that was being organized on the West Coast called the "World Narcotics Research Foundation." I had been corresponding for some time with a person in Seattle who had recommended this group and urged me to permit it to use my name as one who was interested in its program. My informant wrote me that two brothers, prominent West Coast physicians and writers whose names were familiar to me, E. H. and H. S. Williams, were to be leaders of it.

E. H. Williams was at that time a nationally known writer on the narcotics problem who became involved with federal narcotics agents when he agreed, at the behest of the Los Angeles Medical Association and municipal health officials, to operate what amounted to a narcotics clinic in that city. As described in an earlier chapter (see page 14), he was convicted of a technical violation of the narcotics laws in a much criticized trial and lost the right to appeal through a mistake made by his attorneys. In the meantime, another doctor who was involved in the same incident, Dr. E. H. Anthony, was exonerated upon appeal by Federal Judge Yankwich, who sharply rebuked the Narcotics Bureau for what he regarded as its misinterpretation of the law and its disregard for the Supreme Court's opinion in the Linder case.

The agent called the World Narcotics Research Foundation a criminal body because of E. H. Williams' connection with it. When his attention was called to the books written by Williams and to the numerous honors bestowed upon him, such as being included in *Who's Who* and being an associate editor of the *Encyclopaedia*

Britannica, he remarked that he had never heard of the latter. Concerning *Who's Who*, he made the enigmatic comment that if I were not careful I might end up there too and quoted, "Birds of a feather flock together." He clearly knew nothing about the circumstances of the Williams trial and was unable to discuss it. The only relevant point, he said, was that Williams had been convicted of crime.

The real point of his visit became apparent when he turned his attention to my views of the narcotics problem, which he said were not approved of in Washington and would let me in "for trouble with Uncle Sam." The new organization, he said, was going to have the same kind of trouble. He intimated that I might jeopardize my position at Indiana University by expressing my views and expressed the opinion that I was unfit to teach. I sought to defend my position and indicated that I thought British methods of handling the drug problem were more sensible and effective than our own. He replied that I was living in the United States, not in England, that he didn't like the "damned Limeys" anyway, and that loyal citizens ought not criticize existing laws or policies of the government.

During the two- or three-hour interview the agent relied heavily upon documents in his possession and floundered when he had to depart from his script. From remarks which he made it was clear that investigations had been or were being made of the other persons associated with the organization in question and that dossiers were being collected on them and on me.

A year or so later, in reply to a 7-page article which I published, Judge Twain Michelson of San Francisco published later in the same journal a 27-page vitriolic personal attack upon me and other persons associated with the new organization.[18] The material in this article was largely supplied by the Federal Bureau of Narcotics, for substantial parts of it were identical with things that the agent had read to me. Michelson's article was reproduced in quantity and distributed far and wide by the Bureau for many years, a tactic routinely used. The authors of such articles were invariably described as "impartial experts" and their publications listed by the Bureau in its annual reports under the heading, "Publications of International Interest."

When the visits of the agent became known, interested persons evidently communicated with Treasury officials raising questions concerning the propriety of the action. I was again visited by a Bureau representative, this time by an assistant of Mr. Anslinger's. This assistant explained that the agent who visited me had exceeded his instructions, which did not authorize him to employ threats. When asked why an officer supposed to be engaged in the pursuit of dope peddlers was sent to interrogate a university professor concerning his opinions, the assistant made the following interesting observation: The Bureau, he said, in addition to its law enforcement function also had the duty of "disseminating right information and preventing the dissemination of wrong information." I was informally told many years later that the original incident was interpreted at Bureau headquarters as an attempt on my part to interfere with the civil liberties of the agent, the theory evidently being that his visit was a social one and that he had every right to give free expression to his views.

OTHER INCIDENTS

My correspondent in Seattle, from whom I learned of the proposed organization to be known as the World Narcotics Research Foundation, was the late Everett G. Hoffman, a retired automobile salesman. He had become interested in the drug problem and had obviously devoted a great deal of time and energy to collecting materials and promulgating his views, which I found were fairly close to mine as far as policy was concerned. Like others who have ventured into this field, Mr. Hoffman found himself in conflict with the views of the Federal Narcotics Bureau at many points, one of them being the number of addicts in the state of Washington. The Bureau at that time estimated there were 350 while Mr. Hoffman claimed to have the names and addresses of more than 3,000 which he had dug out of police records.

A letter that I received from him dated February 8, 1938, contained the following:

On January 31, a special friend of mine warned me again (for the third time) that I was to be framed by the Narcotic Bureau in Seattle. They are determined to get me for the information that I have been giving over the radio and speeches on the problem of addiction and the inability of all our law enforcement officials to make any change in the present set up. More especially that the number of addicts is increasing and that my state survey proves it.

I am not worrying, for the reason that I am not a law violator nor will I do something that will put me in this class. What I have to say is based on facts which no one can deny and which is not known generally. That is one reason why I am spreading this information. So that the public can know and make an intelligent decision regarding this work when called upon as they will be during our next legislative session.

This is the third person to warn me, so there must be something to it, and there is.

At 11:00 a.m. Thursday morning, February 3, 1938, I was served with a summons to appear before the Federal Grand Jury. . . . There was no mention, of course, what the reason was. . . .

I cannot disclose what took place in the jury room, but, it was an attempt to establish a charge against me. . . .

I have no desire to go to jail, of course, nor shall I do anything that is illegal—but—I shall continue to speak and work for the only plan which I think will ever help the situation. If doing this, regardless of the fact that I may step on some official's toe at some time, gets me in prison, then I'll take my medicine. . . .

The Grand Jury did not indict Mr. Hoffman. Through him I learned that the Narcotics Bureau was somewhat more successful in silencing Earl Albert Rowell and his son, who were going about the country in the 1930's giving lectures on the marihuana problem. Mr. Earl Rowell claimed to have made speeches in 40 of the states. His disagreement with the Federal Narcotics Bureau seemed to arise from his disposition to criticize the police for inactivity and complacency and from his contention that official handouts were covering up and minimizing a growing drug problem. Rowell's viewpoint was evidently that of an alarmist, a zealot, and a prohibitionist.[19]

According to Mr. Rowell's reports to Mr. Hoffman, which were forwarded to me, the Federal Bureau and its agents utilized the following tactics against Mr. Rowell: In January 1938 he was arrested in Wayne, Pennsylvania, and threatened with prosecution on the ground that the opium pipe and small quantities of narcotics which he used as exhibits constituted illegal possession of narcotics although they had been supplied him by police officers for that purpose. Although there was no follow up of this charge, the Bureau broadcast far and wide that Rowell had been arrested; he was accused of obtaining money under false pretenses, of making a racket of his antinarcotics campaign, and of advocating programs contrary to the policies of the federal government. In Evanston, Illinois, he was threatened with prosecution for failure to pay an amusement tax, allegedly at the instigation of federal officials who were determined to curb his activities; he was followed and watched on his lecture tour by narcotics agents. Derogatory information concerning Mr. Rowell was sent by wire and by mail to influential persons in the communities where speeches had been scheduled, causing some of them to be cancelled; when cancellations occurred and when local citizens made investigations of Rowell after hearing from Washington, such cancellations and investigations were written up and circulated by narcotics officials to discredit Rowell in other communities.

The version of Mr. Rowell's dealings with federal narcotics agents which is given in the preceding paragraph is Mr. Rowell's and is no doubt one-sided and slanted in his own favor. We have seen in our discussion of marihuana that Mr. Rowell was strongly opposed to the use of this "weed of madness," which he thought was a direct cause of insanity and violence, and that he was only slightly less alarmed about alcohol and tobacco. This point of view alone could hardly have brought him into conflict with Treasury Department officials. The real point in this imbroglio is not the correctness of his views or even whether his crusade was a racket or not, but whether it is the function of the federal antinarcotics police force to curb reformers as well as the use of drugs.

The Federal Narcotics Bureau was organized in 1930. The tactics which it has used to deal with critics seem also to have been used by the government agencies which preceded it. Brief reference has already been made to the fact that one of the nation's most eminent medical authorities on addiction, Dr. Ernest S. Bishop of New York City, was indicted in January 1920 for alleged violation of the narcotics laws. Dr. Bishop had been a frank critic of government policies and of the manner in which the Harrison Act was being interpreted and implemented. The indictment issued in 1920 was allowed to hang over Dr. Bishop's head for a period of years before it was withdrawn by another prosecutor, who denounced it as "outrageous." It was strongly condemned by a unanimous vote of the American Medical Editors Association meeting in Cleveland in October 1922, in a vigorous protest resolution which was sent to the President of the United States and to the Secretary of the Treasury.[20] Dr. Bishop was, at this time, of advanced age, and he died shortly after the indictment was quashed.

It is of incidental interest that the American Medical Editors Association, at the same meeting at which it adopted the resolution protesting Dr. Bishop's indictment, also unanimously passed another resolution which was sharply critical of the way in which the Harrison Act was being applied to the medical profession and which called for an investigation of the matter by a select committee of 15 to consist of all the doctors who were then members of the House of Representatives. This was in support of a resolution introduced by Congressman Lester D. Volk, who was also an M.D.

The resolution drawn up by the Medical Editors Association read in part as follows:

WHEREAS, as a consequence of ignorant, misguided, mistaken and all too frequently questionable administration of the Harrison Anti-Narcotic Act, honest and law-abiding physicians are being persecuted, hounded and subjected to unjust and ill founded suspicion and accusation, and

WHEREAS, because of the foregoing, not only have many honest medical men been led by the danger to their reputations, professional standing, and ability to live and support their dependents, to refuse to minister to the medical needs of those requiring the legitimate use of narcotic drugs, but all scientific study and investigation of narcotic addiction have been suppressed, prevented and made impossible for those competent to undertake and pursue such studies and investigations, which thoughtful physicians recognize as one of the most imperative needs in scientific medicine, and

WHEREAS, the sick and suffering are not only being denied proper medical care and treatment, but are being harassed, terrorized and caused untold suffering and distress, while the quacks, charlatans, specific-cure-promoters and illicit dealers are preying upon their hopes, fears and imperative medical needs, and

WHEREAS, the fundamental requirement of efficient medical practice, as well as all progress in scientific medicine, always has been—and always will be—the privilege or right of honorable, conscientious and self-respecting physicians to administer to the disease-stricken and suffering, and to practice their profession without interference or dictation from lay administrators, who are essentially unfitted by their lack of medical knowledge, or experience to interpret or comprehend medical problems, or to regulate or restrict accepted methods of treating disease, and

WHEREAS, it is the consensus of opinion of the great majority of thoughtful medical men that while the original and fundamental purposes of the Harrison Anti-Narcotic Act are commendable and deserv-

ing of support and the results obtained in the early years of its rational
execution promised real and substantial benefits, during the past few
years much or all of the foregoing have been lost by a most regrettable
change and perversion of administrative policies and methods which
have resulted from and been aided and supported by propaganda of a
character warranting the gravest question, if not suspicion of the underlying motives. . . .[21]

Evidently the relations between the medical profession and enforcement authorities were not quite as harmonious and amicable
during these early days as is often assumed at present.

THE POLICY POSITION OF THE
PUBLIC HEALTH SERVICE

With infrequent exceptions, narcotics officials of the Public
Health Service, in their public utterances on policy matters, have
supported the position of the Federal Bureau of Narcotics and
joined forces with it in assailing critics of the status quo. Students
seeking information and bibliographical references on the drug
problem from the Public Health Service have ordinarily been provided with articles written by its officials and with bibliographies
consisting largely of Public Health Service publications plus a few
by Bureau spokesmen and outsiders who support the Bureau's position. Bureau publications are ordinarily deferred to as authoritative with respect to questions of enforcement, while those of the
Public Health Service officials are regarded as authoritative on the
medical, psychiatric, and biological aspects of addiction. The Bureau reciprocates by referring students to Public Health Service
publications and provides them with packets of reprints by its
officials. Neither agency provides references to materials not in
conformity with the official line established by the Bureau.

During the hearings before the Daniel subcommittee the following narcotics officials of the Public Health Service appeared before
the subcommittee in a body: Dr. G. Halsey Hunt, Dr. Robert H.

Felix, Dr. Clifton K. Himmelsbach, Dr. John A. Trautman, Dr. Harris Isbell, Dr. James V. Lowry and Dr. Kenneth W. Chapman. Dr. Hunt introduced the others of this group to the Senators.[22] Senator Daniel remarked:

"Well, Dr. Hunt, these men must have worked with all of the drug addicts who have been in the hospital at Lexington, at least since it was established; is that right?"

Dr. Hunt: "This Group before you, Mr. Chairman, represents a great many years of direct experience in the treatment of drug addiction at Lexington and Fort Worth, and additional years of administrative experience and of overall consultation experience with States and local communities, particularly with States on the part of the National Institute of Mental Health."

Senator Daniel: "What I am getting at is, I believe we have already had this before the committee, that there are about 25,000 individuals as drug addicts who have passed through the hospitals at Fort Worth and Lexington."

Dr. Hunt: "Yes, sir."

Senator Daniel: "Now, these men, one or more of them, have been in the Service in some capacity seeing these 25,000 addicts. In other words, these men together represent all the years those hospitals have been in operation and one or more of these men have been in those hospitals during the entire period of operation."

Dr. Hunt: "Almost entirely, yes."

Senator Daniel: "Almost entirely. Do you know of any panel of men in the country whose experience together has put them in touch with more drug addicts?"

Dr. Hunt: "I think that the Public Health Service does have the greatest concentration of people with long experience in the treatment of drug addiction, and most of these people are sitting before you today."

Having established to his own satisfaction that he had before him the top experts in the country if not in the world, Senator Daniel went on to question these men concerning their views of a proposal made by the New York Academy of Medicine to provide legal drugs for addicts in clinics.

Dr. Hunt then read a prepared statement evaluating the proposal of the New York Academy of Medicine. The statement was surprisingly favorable and ended with the recommendation that the Academy's proposal be tested in a limited way with a small number of addicts. When Dr. Hunt was asked if this was the official view of the Public Health Service he said it was not but that it was the collective view of the officials who had been concerned with the problem. Asked if this is what the Surgeon General would have said had he been there, Dr. Hunt replied:

"I am reading the material the Surgeon General had had prepared in case this question came up."

Senator Butler: "Is it the composite view of this group or others, this group and others?"

Dr. Hunt: "I think I can say this group. There are possibly a few others who may have contributed to it, or who may be involved, but essentially this is the group who are most vitally and directly concerned with these questions."[23]

From this colloquy it is evident that the statement submitted by this group had been cleared with the Surgeon General. In this case a qualified and extremely cautious approval was given to the Academy's proposal, which was surely known to be anathema to the Commissioner of Narcotics as well as to a number of the Senators.

In subsequent questioning by Senator Daniel the Public Health Service officials more or less withdrew even this mild approval of the New York Academy's suggestion. Senator Daniel asked each of the officials if he personally, from the thousands and thousands of addicts he had known, would be willing to administer narcotics to any of them indefinitely solely to maintain their addiction. Each of the men said either that he knew of no such person or that he knew one or two or a few. The upshot was that Senator Daniel's view prevailed and in the subcommittee's report on "Treatment and Rehabilitation of Narcotic Addicts" no mention was made of the fact that the Public Health Service had recommended that the New York Academy's plan be tried.[24]

Thus, while these officials explicitly and unanimously opposed the conception of the drug addict as a malefactor and advocated that he be treated as a patient rather than as a criminal, they did not themselves suggest a plan for accomplishing this and they contributed to discrediting the plan that was suggested. The net effect was that the subcommittee counted them as supporters of the harshly punitive program of legislation which it recommended to Congress and which was enacted by that body in 1956. It is of interest that research done at Lexington on barbiturates and alcohol indicated that these substances create addiction in the same sense that the opiates do, i.e., they produce tolerance and physical dependence. Nevertheless, the narcotics officials of the Public Health Service joined with the Federal Bureau of Narcotics in opposing any legislation which would cause barbiturate addicts to be treated as criminals. These officials have also, of course, not recommended that alcoholism be handled in this way, since this would amount to the reestablishment of prohibition.

In recent years the remarkable agreement between the medical officials of the Public Health Service and the police officials of the Federal Bureau of Narcotics has again been illustrated by their concern with a program of compulsory civil commitments for drug users. Agreement on this issue is puzzling, since in virtually all fields of psychiatry and treatment of behavior disorders, compulsion is being increasingly avoided whenever possible, for example, with the mentally ill. Moreover, the Public Health Service authorities have expressed themselves in opposition to the use of compulsion with barbiturate and alcohol addicts. Why then, one wonders, do they favor it for heroin addicts?

Lexington officials have sometimes admitted publicly that their establishment is in reality a prison. Like other officials with an eye to their budgets, they have sought to present their efforts in the best possible light and to secure favorable publicity for themselves. Exaggerated claims concerning the effectiveness of the program have been allowed to stand uncorrected. In some instances, the cases of prominent persons who were accorded the red carpet treatment at Lexington, as for example that of Barney Ross, appear to have been exploited for public relations purposes.

There is room for a great deal of legitimate difference of opinion on many aspects of the narcotics problem and no student of the problem should be surprised to find himself at odds with another or with a public official. What is noteworthy in this situation is that, with so many reasons for expecting different views, officials should express so little disagreement on the hotly debated policy questions. The consensus among them inevitably suggests that the apparent uniformity of views is artificially imposed from above or that it arises from the nature of the institutional environment within which the officials deal with addicts.

MONKEYS ON THE ADDICT'S BACK

It is axiomatic among students of human behavior that once certain institutional arrangements have been made and are established they tend to be extremely resistant to change. One of the reasons for this is that vested interests develop; persons, groups, associations, and organizations find that they are benefiting in one way or another from existing arrangements. They consequently oppose change, but in doing so rarely mention the real grounds for their conservatism—indeed, they are sometimes unaware of the influence of self-interest. Significant change or improvement in institutional arrangements therefore invariably arouses opposition for the very good reason that such change means that there will be a price to pay, that some persons will lose jobs, power, prestige, or money and that others may gain these things. At the very least, a change that is worth making is likely to cost money. Programs which elicit universal agreement are usually futile for the very reason that nothing is really being changed. It is much easier, for example, to sponsor an anticrime week with posters, slogans, and speeches, than to reform a police department or to establish a rational penal system.

It is evident that there are vested interests in narcotics just as there are in tobacco and alcohol. On the monetary side alone there is a big take which obviously does not go to the addict or to the small-scale peddler. Neither does it go exclusively to big importers and dealers of the underworld. It is not possible to identify exactly all those who manage to share in the illiict profits, but it is easy to guess who they might be.

It is generally impossible or difficult for a profession or a system to reform itself solely from inside impetus. Legal reform and medical reform, for example, have usually been brought about by public pressure. One of the prominent reasons for this is that a feeling of solidarity within the profession makes its members reluctant to attack, expose, or publicly criticize fellow members. The same kind of influence operates among narcotics officials. In private, they may concede that the system of which they are a part has serious weaknesses, but to do so in public is another matter because it would cast discredit upon fellow officials and be interpreted as something akin to disloyalty if it did not put their jobs in jeopardy. This is why building a series of Lexington-type institutions throughout the country would probably delay fundamental reform, for it would greatly increase the size of the narcotics bureaucracy. The greater the number of persons who depend upon the status quo the more difficult it is likely to be to change the system.

Finally, it needs to be noted that the drug addict has become a popular symbol and scapegoat and that politicians have been elected to office on platforms promising more severe punishment for him. Alexander Trocchi, the Scottish writer and addict who sought refuge from "the American system" by returning to Britain and who was the star on Chet Huntley's 1963 television show, has a character in his book say the following about narcotics and narcotic addicts as popular symbols:

It's a nice tangible cause for juvenile delinquency. And it lets a lot of people out because they're alcoholics. There's an available pool of wasted-looking bastards to stand trial as the corrupters of their children. It provides the police with something to do, and as junkies and potheads are relatively easy to apprehend because they have to take so many chances to get hold of their drugs, a heroic police can make spectacular arrests, lawyers can do a brisk business, judges can make speeches, the big peddler can make a fortune, the tabloids can sell millions of copies. John Citizen can sit back feeling exonerated and watch evil get its deserts. . . . Everyone gets something out of it except the junkie.[25]

Speaking of the way in which the arrest of a peddler was described to the newspapers by the police, Trocchi indicates how the addict sometimes manages to mitigate the harsh impersonality of law:

They built it up big for the tabloids so that John Citizen had the impression that Lucky Luciano's first lieutenant had been trapped by intrepid agents and that half the opium smuggled by Mongolian-faced agents of Chou-En-Lai from Communist China to sap the strength of the American people had been seized in the raid; and in return for two Leica cameras they played it down before the judge who, it must be assumed, didn't read the tabloids.[26]

CHAPTER 10

THE PATTERN OF REFORM

Reform of present methods of handling addiction ought to take into consideration a number of objectives concerning which there should be relatively little controversy. The controversy focuses on what are the best methods of reaching the objectives rather than on the objectives themselves. The goal of all drug control measures is, in a general way, the enhancement of the common or social good. When we say this, we should keep in mind that the drug addict is a member of society and that drug control measures ought to take his welfare into account.

AIMS

Concerning the addiction problem as a whole, the following aims would probably be agreed upon as desirable by all parties in the current controversy:

1. Prevention of the spread of addiction and a resultant progressive reduction in the number of addicts.

2. Curing current addicts of their habits insofar as this can be

achieved by present techniques or by new ones which may be devised.

3. Elimination of the exploitation of addicts for mercenary gain by smugglers or by anyone else.

4. Reduction to a minimum of the crime committed by drug users as a consequence of their habits.

5. Reducing to a minimum the availability of dangerous addicting drugs to all nonaddicts except when needed for medical purposes.

6. Fair and just treatment of addicts in accordance with established legal and ethical precepts taking into account the special peculiarities of their behavior and at the same time preserving their individual dignity and self-respect.

Other aims and principles of an effective program which are of a more controversial nature but which are implied by the above are the following:

7. Antinarcotic laws should be so written that addicts do not have to violate them solely because they are addicts.

8. Drug users are admittedly handicapped by their habits but they should nevertheless be encouraged to engage in productive labor even when they are using drugs.

9. Cures should not be imposed upon narcotics victims by force but should be voluntary.

10. Police officers should be prevented from exploiting drug addicts as stool pigeons solely because they are addicts.

11. Heroin and morphine addicts should be handled according to the same principles and moral precepts applied to barbiturate and alcohol addicts because these three forms of addiction are basically similar.

THE PROGRAM IN GENERAL

The most effective program for achieving these ends in Western nations seems to be one which gives the drug user regulated access to the medical profession with the physician determining the mode of treatment in accordance with the circumstances of the particular case. Characteristically, this type of program almost invariably involves, wherever it is used, some sort of supervision and regulation of medical practice with regard to addicts by public health officials. Police measures enter the picture only infrequently when medical controls fail.

The British program has been described in detail because it is an outstanding example of this system which has been emulated by other nations. It is not suggested here that the United States ought to adopt the British or any other program, lock, stock, and barrel. What is suggested is that successful foreign programs, including the British, should be intensively studied and intelligently adapted to American needs and to special conditions existing in this country. Particular attention needs to be given to the manner in which a reform program is introduced into the United States because of the extraordinarily large numbers of addicts in a relatively few large cities. Too precipitous change might well discredit a new program before it was given a real chance.

The final result or goal of the reform program which is implicit in this entire book is a situation in which most of the addicts in the United States would be in the hands of private physicians. The latter would be free to treat addicts in accordance with accepted medical standards without fear of prosecution. The Public Health Service might be the logical agency to exercise a supervisory and advisory control over practitioners with drug users under their care, but a matter of this sort is a detail that should be left to medical officials. The police and federal narcotics agents would be expected to inspect the records of drug stores, drug manufacturers, importers, and distributors as they do at present, and to apprehend persons engaging in the illicit traffic—including any addicts who might do so.

It is absolutely essential, if addiction is to be treated as a medical

rather than as a police problem, that doctors be permitted to prescribe regular supplies of drugs to addicts when this is, in their
judgment, indicated. If this is not permitted, addicts will continue
to be exploited by the underworld as they now are. It should be
realistically assumed that even under relatively favorable circumstances no large percentage of drug users will be permanently and
immediately cured. Nevertheless, the regular administration of
drugs to users should always continue to be regarded as a temporary expedient designed to protect the addict's reputation and to
keep him out of underworld hands pending withdrawal and cure.
It is assumed that physicians would keep the addict's daily dosage
at a minimal level and minimize, as far as possible, the evil physical
effects of addiction while they attempted to persuade him to undergo institutional withdrawal and to try to break his habit. Institutional facilities for withdrawal should obviously be provided in
hospitals, not in jails, and medical authorities should, when necessary, be authorized to employ restraint upon the addict during
withdrawal and for a brief period of time thereafter.[1] Many addicts
currently ask to be committed to jail in order to break their habits.
If humane and intelligently worked out plans and facilities, such as
those at Lexington, were generally available, addicts would quickly
learn of them and would present themselves for voluntary cures
much more frequently than now. Despite assertions to the contrary,
there are very few addicts who do not desire to be freed of their
habits. This is true also in countries where addiction is not a criminal matter.

It needs to be emphasized that the reforms suggested here do
not include the establishment of narcotics clinics, like those of the
1920's, where drugs are doled out or administered to addicts. The
clinic plan has serious disadvantages as a general program, and
there is no country in the world today which has such a program.
On the other hand, the system of placing the narcotic addict in the
hands of the private medical practitioner has been extensively used

for many years in many countries throughout the world with uni-
formly satisfactory results.

It is much more practical to get at the addict through the doctor
than it is to try to handle him at centrally located clinics. The clinic
idea involves the danger of perpetuating the evils of congregate
treatment by bringing addicts together rather than keeping them
separate. There are more doctors than addicts in the United States.
Hence, theoretically if each doctor in the country were to agree
to accept one addict as a patient this would more than take care of
all addicts. Such a program would be difficult to organize, but if
anything could be done to encourage drug users now concentrated
in large cities to move to smaller communities or rural areas, this
would be a distinct gain which would make it easier to administer
the program and also make it easier for addicts to refrain from
relapse after being taken off drugs. An effect of this nature might
be achieved by at first limiting the number of addicts who could be
handled by any one physician in the larger cities where users are
now most numerous.

TRANSFER OF AUTHORITY TO THE MEDICAL PROFESSION

If addiction is a medical problem and the addict is to be handled
medically, it is necessary that the authority to determine what specific program will be applied to the user be placed in medical hands.
This means that power now being exercised by legislators, lawyers,
judges, prosecutors, and policemen must be transferred to the medical profession. This transfer of power will be resisted by some of
those who will have to surrender it, but the issue is clear. It is absurd
to call addiction a medical matter and then permit policemen, prosecutors, and legislators to specify how it shall be treated.[2]

The legal basis for putting doctors in charge of handling addiction already exists in the decisions of the Supreme Court. The basis

in popular opinion also exists, for most Americans today are quite ready to accept the idea that drug addiction, like alcohol addiction, and perhaps like cigarette addiction, ought not be dealt with as a police matter. What is needed is an appropriate plan of action by administrative officials. The first point of attack should probably be the regulations of the Treasury Department which threaten the physician with criminal prosecution for prescribing drugs for users except under the two conditions: (a) terminal disease such as cancer, and (b) an aged and infirm user who might die if the drug were withdrawn. The New York Academy of Medicine has already assailed these regulations and has forcibly pointed out how they have for many years put physicians in a straitjacket with regard to narcotic addiction.[3]

The first step in reform might therefore well be a conference sponsored by the A.M.A. perhaps with the New York Academy of Medicine at the invitation of the Secretary of the Treasury and the Attorney General, with a mandate to revise the existing regulations so as to bring them into conformity with the Supreme Court's doctrine that addiction is a proper subject of medical care. Delegates to such a conference should be predominantly medical practitioners with direct clinical experience with addicts, especially in private practice. There are, and have always been, sharp differences of opinion among medical practitioners concerning the proper treatment of addiction. A statement of standards formulated after a free and open discussion would presumably make allowances for such divergent views. Minority opinions held by substantial numbers within the profession should not be ruled out of court by majority vote. The limits of legitimate treatment for addiction should be determined, in short, in about the same way as they are for venereal disease or for tuberculosis.

A revision by medical men of Treasury Department regulations would certainly either remove entirely or greatly reduce the threat of criminal prosecution to conscientious physicians who undertook to care for addicts. This fact might make it feasible for the medical conference to accept another mandate, namely, that of surveying and bringing into the full light of public examination the facts concerning addicts who are now being handled as medical cases and shielded from the police and punitive action. Little is presently known of these users except that many are thought to be physicians and nurses and that most are members of the upper social classes. Such a survey would facilitate more realistic planning and would serve to enlighten many members of the medical profession concerning the narcotics problem and existing medical techniques being applied to it.

Removal of the threat of prosecution would in all likelihood lead automatically to a gradual increase in the number of addicts under the care of physicians as the latter came to realize that medical judgment, rather than the police or the criminal law, had become the controlling factor. Such gradual expansion of a medical program would be highly desirable because of the large numbers of addicts in this country and because it would permit members of the medical profession to become acquainted with the problem over a period of time rather than having it thrust upon them abruptly. A sudden transition might well lead to chaos and confusion in the large narcotics centers.

The President's Advisory Commission recommended in its report that "the definition of legitimate medical use of narcotic drugs and legitimate medical treatment of a narcotic addict are primarily to be determined by the medical profession."[4] The Commission completely ignored the 1963 report of the New York Academy of Medicine dealing directly with this matter. Instead, it asked the American Medical Association and the National Research Council of the National Academy of Sciences to make a statement on the issue. The result was a masterpiece of diplomacy and noncommittal doubletalk, and was published as part of the report of the Presidential Commission.[5] It stipulated that it is the duty of doctors to obey all laws, rules and regulations at federal, state, and local levels, and simply reiterated the current regulations of the Treasury Department as the definition of proper medical treatment of addicts, without indicating that the definition was drawn from Treasury Department regulations.

The Commission evidently assumed that the A.M.A.–N.R.C. report automatically made the view of the New York Academy unacceptable and illegitimate. But proper medical treatment of diseased persons is not something which is settled by majority vote of A.M.A. officials. That body cannot and does not dictate to physicians how they are to treat diseases. Such questions, like scientific questions, are never settled by majority vote. If they were, and departures from sanctioned practice were prosecuted in the criminal courts as they are in this instance, there could be little progress. The President's Commission, despite its gesture to the medical profession, clearly did not accept the idea of full medical control as advocated by the New York Academy of Medicine. That was no doubt why it made no reference whatever to that organization's position, and why it summarily brushed aside any serious consideration of European programs.

The President's Commission, instead of proposing any plan which would have given physicians the authority they must have if addiction is not to be handled punitively, recommended a program of civil commitment, not as a substitute for imprisonment, but as an alternative to it in selected instances. The Attorney General and the Judiciary, it suggests, should make the "crucial determinations" at the federal level and the Bureau of Prisons, the Public Health Service, and the probation and parole services should manage the actual program.[6] This program explicitly avoids giving any important authority to medical persons. It also leaves the addict's status under the criminal law unchanged, does nothing to remove the threat of prosecution for doctors, and leaves the hapless user in the hands of the illicit traffic. The Commission, in short, did not suggest any transfer of power to medicine, but envisaged the establishment of a rehabilitative medical program for drug addicts within the confines of prisons. Anyone acquainted with prisons knows that they are chronically understaffed, underfinanced, overcrowded, and generally ill equipped to undertake constructive programs of this sort even for inmates who are much less difficult and troublesome than narcotic addicts. Diseased persons are not ordinarily treated for their ailments in jails and penitentiaries.

MONITORING THE PROGRAM

As has been indicated, there are presently privileged addicts to whom the usual penalties and rules are not applied, who are given access to legal drugs and handled medically. Revision of the Treasury Department regulations, it has been suggested, would probably increase the number of addicts under medical care by encouraging doctors to treat users of humbler social status. As the number of users under such medical care increased it would probably be regarded as desirable that the program be monitored by an agency which would continuously collect statistical and other types of data concerning the operation of the plan, perform advisory and inspection services, and continuously evaluate the program. In European countries these functions are generally handled by the public health authorities and there seems to be no reason why the same procedure should not be followed here. In Britain the Ministry of Health uses medically trained inspectors for the job of consulting with and advising doctors in cases where the use of narcotics is an issue.

The proposal advanced here assumes medical control of the program, with changes made in accordance with medical judgment on the basis of experience with the plan. It is therefore, in a sense, presumptuous or pointless to suggest in advance a detailed mode of operation or a specific plan for every contingency. Nevertheless, one may speculate that it might be deemed desirable to establish rules for the guidance of physicians in accepting addicts for medical treatment. The experience of Lady Frankau, as she reports it, suggests, for example, that addicts might be accepted only if they indicated willingness to take and hold a regular job and to maintain a stable residence, and if they gave some indication of a desire to rid themselves of their habits. An advantage of such rules might be to motivate addicts to meet these conditions, and also, conceivably, to prevent the medical practitioners in large cities with many addicts from being overwhelmed by them.

Another conception is suggested by the 1963 Report of the New York Academy of Medicine which points out that there is a variety of medical situations for which the current Treasury Department regulations are inadequate and unduly restrictive.[7] The expansion of medical services to addicts might therefore begin with a gradual relaxation of these regulations, with the following types of addicts being admitted to the program in some sort of sequence:

1. Addicts with non-fatal diseases and chronic illnesses should be among the first to be included.

2. Aged addicts who have been addicted for many years and taken many cures, and for whom cure seems cruel, pointless, and hopeless.

3. Persons who have become addicted in the course of medical treatment. The addicted patient should continue to be a medical responsibility.

4. Addicts who come from good families and cultural backgrounds, have no criminal records, and have regular jobs and stable places of residence.

5. Persons who acquired their addiction in the military service.

6. Any housewife who is a user. This would be for the purpose of making it unnecessary for her to be a prostitute or to help her escape from prostitution.

Ultimately if this scheme were carried out there would remain a residual group of addicts which would probably consist of the hopelessly degraded and demoralized criminal addicts unwilling to give up their illicit way of life, users not interested in quitting, and other hard-core types. For these, civil or criminal commitment would be appropriate and would serve the function of exerting pressure upon them to qualify for the medical program. There would be a residual illicit traffic catering to this remaining group of derelict and recalcitrant types which would be an appropriate object of police attention.

SOME ANTICIPATED EFFECTS

What the effects might be of a program such as that described in this chapter may be indirectly indicated by citing some of the conversations recorded in congressional hearings at which the advisability of subjecting barbiturates and amphetamines to penal controls was considered and rejected. In 1951, for example, Mr. Anslinger commented as follows on the idea that his Bureau handle barbiturates in the same way as heroin:

"It would be worse than prohibition. It would take us years finally to get that under control, and we do not have enough men right now.... It would take $5,000,000 and take five times as many men as we have, and then you would have conditions similar to prohibition. I think it would become a very unpopular bureau in this country.... Certainly it is not a peddling traffic like morphine, heroin and cocaine. It is in the hands of the doctors and druggists. I do not think we ought to take it out of their hands and put it in the hands of the underworld, and certainly it is not in the hands of the underworld today...."

Mr. Simpson: "I would like to get clear on one thing. You would not want morphine and opium, and so forth, in the control of druggists and physicians? That would not suit your purposes, would it?"

Anslinger: "No, Sir."

Simpson: "Then why would barbiturates be safe in their hands? Are they not as dangerous in their hands? That is what I cannot get."[8]

In 1955, again before the Boggs subcommittee, the following exchanges took place:

Mr. Anslinger: "When you are after a peddler he will not sell you barbiturates or amphetamines."

Mr. Boggs: "But there is no reason for him to."

Mr. Anslinger: "That is true."

Mr. Boggs: "Because there is no profit in it. . . . As a matter of fact, if the theory that you can become addicted to barbiturates is true then it seems to me that in that field they are doing just what some of these doctors in New York [the New York Academy of Medicine] have advocated they do in the field of other narcotics, which is a proposal which does not appeal to you at all. . . ."

Mr. Karsten: "Do you have a history, Mr. Commissioner, of barbiturate users graduating, then, later on to narcotics? Do they follow a pattern like that?"

Mr. Anslinger: "We have not seen that pattern, Congressman; that is something which you would think would follow, but they do not go in that direction. The marihuana user is usually the one."[9]

We see in these conversations a perfectly explicit awareness of the conditions that are needed to produce an illicit traffic and of the inconsistency of public policy concerning various types of drugs. Mr. Anslinger's reply to the suggestion that he was not consistent was that the punitive program was necessary with respect to opiates because they are more dangerous and destructive than barbiturates. However, Public Health Service experts had been showing the congressmen films on barbiturate withdrawal and gave them evidence which pointed to exactly the opposite conclusion. We have previously noted that in 1937, before the federal antimarihuana bill was passed, Mr. Anslinger also said that marihuana users did not go on to heroin.[10] Perhaps if barbiturates were prohibited in the same manner that heroin now is its users would also graduate to the latter drug.

The former head of the Federal Bureau of Narcotics has provided other illuminating material concerning the advantages of a program of medical, rather than punitive, treatment for drug users. For example, speaking of the treatment of addicts, he had this to say:

There is no single set way to deal with those trapped in the tentacles. I personally have dealt with many of the individual cases. Each has been different. I am not, for instance, a believer in what doctors call "ambulatory treatment"—giving a patient withdrawal treatment in his office, with no check on what the patient may do, or how much he may use between visits. Yet in one or two exceptional cases, I have, unknown to the addict, employed this method.

The addict in one case was a Washington society woman. I had known her personally for some years. She was a beautiful, and gracious lady. She had become so badly addicted to demerol that no doctor would prescribe for her; her demand was too great.

Word of her case came to me through some of her friends. Was there any way I could help? The woman, I learned, was ready to kill herself. She would not deal with pushers nor would she take a cure or go voluntarily to a hospital herself. Moreover, if I made a case against her, it would destroy her completely—along with the unblemished reputation of one of the nation's most honored families.

I agreed to help her, through a trusted physician to whom she appealed for drugs. She was not to know my role. I also learned that she was so afraid that pharmacists would try to cut the strength of her demerol, with sugar of milk or some other non-narcotic substance, that she insisted on receiving only unopened, sealed bottles of demerol from the druggist.

That complicated the business but I called in a pharmaceutical manufacturer who agreed to work with us. Each bottle of demerol, specially packaged and sealed, delivered in routine fashion from the drug store, on the prescription of the physician, contained less actual demerol than the previous bottle.

Within three months, without the woman realizing, she went from a large daily "ration" of demerol to none at all. What she was getting, in the bottles, was not demerol but sugar of milk.[11]

The woman was subsequently informed that she was cured of her addiction and "broke into tears of joy."

Another similar instance involved an addict who was described as one of the most influential members of the Congress of the United States. This man was completely "intractable," refusing to consider medical treatment and defiant of anything that might be done to him by the police. In this case Mr. Anslinger offered the congressman the proposition that if he would agree not to go to underworld pushers his supply of morphine would be underwritten by the Bureau. It was stipulated that the man was to obtain his supplies from an "obscure druggist" on the outskirts of Washington. The lawmaker naturally accepted the offer and went on using legal morphine till he died with only Mr. Anslinger, the druggist, and the addict himself knowing what was going on.[12]

From the analysis of these two instances we can see that Anslinger had the following desirable effects in mind: (1) protection of the reputation of the addict and his family; (2) making it possible for the addict to escape exploitation by underworld drug peddlers; (3) breaking the habit in an effective and humane manner; (4) preventing suicide on the part of the user; (5) permitting the user to continue in a legitimate occupation and to be self-supporting; and (6) making it unnecessary for users to congregate with other users.

For the medical profession Mr. Anslinger has formulated rules which prevent the physician from handling addicts in this manner:

"Ambulatory treatment of drug addicts should not be tried. Institutional treatment is always required."

"An addict should never be given drugs for self-administration."[13]

The questions raised by Mr. Anslinger's cases include the following: How many American addicts offered the same deal as that proposed to the congressman would accept and abide by it? How many users could be successfully taken off drugs by physicians using Mr. Anslinger's method, and others that medical men might devise? What percentage of American addicts might engage in productive labor, like the congressman, if they were handled in an equivalent manner? On what principles should addicts of lesser status, who are not personally acquainted with prominent officials in Washington, be excluded from the opportunities offered these two?

In chapter 6 we have referred to a report from London on the fate, in that city, of forty Canadian drug users who sought refuge there from Canada's punitive program.[14] From this report one may infer: (1) that there is a probability that a significant percentage of addicts under medical care might work for a living even if they failed to break their habits; (2) that many persons who are addicts first and criminals secondarily would welcome the chance to be law abiding; (3) that an intelligently handled, voluntary program of medical treatment and withdrawal would attract the cooperation of a significant percentage of addicts; and finally (4) that even many addicts who are "criminal" in the genuine sense of the word are not entirely beyond redemption.

EFFECTS ON THE SPREAD OF THE HABIT

In earlier chapters it has been suggested that the spread of the drug habit in modern times has been closely linked with the prohibition system of control and its invariable accompaniment, the illicit traffic. The illicit traffic makes drugs available, but it does more than that. The very facts of illegality and expensiveness give drugs a symbolic significance and attractiveness to some segments of the population which they would not otherwise have. Taking drugs has become for some persons a group way of life, a means of protest, and a way of revolt against accepted values. Nowhere in the Western world are there as many young addicts as there are in the United States, and it is in this country that the so-called "addict subculture" and the drug-using juvenile gang have become especially prominent.

From a study of youthful Negro narcotics users in Chicago, Harold Finestone has provided an excellent analysis of the motivations of a relatively new type of drug user.[15] The title of the article, "Cats, Kicks, and Color," suggests its themes. The Negro "cat," says Finestone, substitutes "hustle" for legitimate work, which he aristocratically disdains; the main purpose of his life is to experience the "kick" from performing acts tabooed by "squares" and beyond their comprehension. The use of drugs, from the standpoint of the cat's revolt against middle-class morality, is the supreme, the ultimate kick. It gives excitement to the cat's life and, in his own eyes at least, sets him off in an elite conspiratorial group:

> It is this limited, esoteric character of heroin use which gives to the cat the feeling of belonging to an elite. It is the restricted extent of the distribution of drug use, the scheming and intrigue associated with underground "connections" through which drugs are obtained, the secret lore of the appreciation of the drug's effects, which give the cat the exhilaration of participating in a conspiracy.[16]

Finestone notes that the young Negro user of narcotics manifests a certain zest in his mode of life, particularly during the initial or honeymoon period. This zest is especially associated with the cat's adventurous and dangerous life on the city streets, with his contest against the whole world to maintain his supply of drugs, and with the game of hide-and-seek that he plays with the police. It is part of this adventurer's way of life to "play it cool" in crises such as those which are represented by withdrawal distress, jails, prisons, and the police.

It is this fact—that drug use in the United States has become a group way of life, a form of protest or revolt against the dominant conventional values of the society—that has contributed heavily to the epidemic character of the postwar drug problem. The meaning of drugs for the adolescent Negro cat is not unlike its significance for "beats" or for many jazz musicians.

Of special importance is the apparent fact that while there are adolescent groups in foreign countries which resemble the American "beats" and "cats," such as the "Teddy Boys" of Britain and the "Bodgies" or "Wedgies" of Australia, the use of heroin seems not to have been taken up by these foreign groups. The reasons for this, one may speculate, are probably connected with the manner in which heroin addiction is handled in these countries. When it is dealt with as a medical problem, the use of heroin evidently does not serve as a symbol of protest or revolt nor does it become a group way of life. Addicts under the care of physicians have no special reasons or need for association with each other or with the underworld. While the direct effects of drugs obtained from physicians are the same as those from illicit supplies, the fact of being under the physician's care no doubt leads the drug user to think of himself more as a sick or diseased person than as a member of an underground conspiratorial group. At any rate, there does not appear to be a single instance of a country in which opiate addiction is handled medically where the use of opiates has acquired the status of a fad or become an epidemic as it has in the United States. This leads to the supposition that a medical attack on addiction in this country would undercut the cat's way of life, as Finestone and others have described it, both by isolating addicts from each other and by changing the significance of drug use.

Dissident, deviant, or antisocial subcultures or groups in foreign countries sometimes emphasize the use of drugs other than the opiates. Marihuana, for example, is used in London by West Indian groups and in certain clubs, as well as by some jazz musicians. However, no appreciable tendency has been noted in Britain to substitute heroin for marihuana. A similar situation exists in Jamaica and other parts of the Caribbean area where marihuana use is very widespread and heroin addiction rare. In Jamaica, in particular, marihuana cultivation and use, both of which are prohibited and heavily punished, have become an important part of a back-to-Africa protest movement promoted by an organization known as the Ras Tafari. It appears that only illegal drugs tend to acquire this kind of symbolic significance. Thus, while there is some morphine addiction in Jamaica, it seems to be completely unconnected with the Ras Tafari and marihuana and is regarded only as a minor medical problem.[17]

The use of addicting drugs by young persons is a matter of especially serious concern. The evidence seems to indicate quite clearly that the situation most favorable for the spread of drug use among young persons is one in which addiction is dealt with as a criminal matter and one which includes a flourishing illicit traffic. It is in this situation that drugs become glamorous and attractive to youth, and these are also the conditions which seem to favor the creation of subcultures of drug users which, by recruitment of new members, tend to become self-perpetuating.

A common argument advanced against a program of the type under discussion is that, with the legal penalties removed, there would be fewer obstacles to becoming addicted and that those already addicted would have a free hand and an open invitation to spread the habit to others. What is overlooked in this argument is that everywhere in the world, availability of drugs for addicts through medical prescription is necessarily linked with nonavailability of drugs for other persons because of the relative absence of a black market. It is true, of course, that the habit tends to spread from users to nonusers but this probably occurs to a lesser extent in countries with medical programs because these programs keep addicts relatively separated from each other, thus giving them a chance to keep their habits secret. The profits of the illicit trade also probably play a part in promoting the spread of addiction.

LONG-TERM ADVANTAGES OF A MEDICAL PROGRAM

From the discussions in other portions of this book and especially from the description of narcotics control programs in other parts of the world in chapters 6 and 7, most of the effects envisaged as long-run consequences of a medical program for addicts are fairly obvious. Some of the less obvious ones should perhaps be specifically stated.

One of the great difficulties in the United States today, as we have seen, relates to the lack of reliable information about our addicts. A medical program automatically generates more reliable statistical data than does a police program. In most European countries figures available from druggists and doctors tell most of the story of addiction, and police data contribute only a minor supplement.

Dealing with addicts by congregate methods in large and expensive public institutions has many obvious evil effects upon the inmates and tends to impede reform and rehabilitation. In addition such a program requires large outlays of public funds and creates a special bureaucracy of narcotics officials. The medical program envisaged here makes use of existing institutions and medical personel, avoids the evils of congregate treatment, does not necessitate the creation of a special narcotics bureaucracy, and costs little in the way of public funds. Under such a program some addicts, certainly many more than now, would be able to work and pay their own way; others might conceivably be covered by insurance for the costs of medical treatment of addiction; others could be subsidized by relatives and friends.

A medical program would reduce the crime problem in a variety of ways, the most obvious being that the user would not have to steal to pay fantastic illicit prices. This fact would in turn react upon the illicit traffic by reducing demand, prices, and profits. The argument that making drugs available to addicts stimulates the illicit traffic and that the clinics in this country around 1920 had this effect is patently false, as we have shown (chapter 5). As Lady Frankau's report from London suggests, a medical program can sometimes motivate the addicted criminal to abandon crime, and in general it makes it possible for an addict to abandon crime even though he may not abandon his habit. Another effect of a similar nature is that the noncriminal who becomes addicted is not forced into crime. For example, if a nurse in a hospital is discovered to be an addict and is arrested and jailed for stealing narcotic supplies from the hospital, the most probable consequence is that she will become a prostitute and an associate of pimps, addicts, thieves, and drug peddlers if she does not commit suicide. Under a nonpunitive program she might be taken off drugs and put on duty in a situation where drugs were not accessible to her.

One of the most interesting therapeutic implications is in the effects upon the general availability of drugs and the repercussion this might have upon the chances of helping users to remain free after breaking their habits. We have already seen that Lady Frankau urged Canadian addicts in London not to seek out other users. Dr. O'Donnell, in a study made in Kentucky of former patients at the Public Health Service Hospital at Lexington, observed that many of those who were abstaining from drugs had moved away from the sources of illicit drugs into communities where there was no illicit market or where they did not "know the ropes." O'Donnell concludes that "This factor of unavailability may go far in explaining the high rate of abstinence in this group [relatively rural], in contrast to previous follow-up studies which were conducted in, or included, large metropolitan areas where the illegal narcotics market has never been completely absolished."[18]

It was long ago that a prominent police administrator, August Vollmer, said:

Drug addiction, like prostitution and like liquor, is not a police problem; it never has been and never can be solved by policemen. It is first and last a medical problem, and if there is a solution it will be discovered not by policemen, but by scientific and competently trained medical experts whose sole objective will be the reduction and possible eradication of this devastating appetite. There should be intelligent treatment of incurables in outpatient clinics, hospitalization of those not too far gone to respond to therapeutic measures, and application of the prophylactic principles which medicine applies to all scourges of mankind.[19]

Giving medical men in general the right to handle addicts would contribute to the end envisaged by Vollmer, making this particular scourge a subject of inquiry and experimentation for many others than a small number of medical men in the Public Health Service. The United States might, in this way, convert into a positive advantage the fact that she now has more heroin addicts than all of the nations of Europe combined.

It may be contended that one of the most important long-range effects and advantages of the medical treatment of addicts is that it is the decent, just, and humanitarian thing to do. Apart from the abstract ethical arguments suggested by this thought, there is the fact that people tend to support programs which they regard as just and fair and to admire their courts and the machinery of justice when they operate to produce real justice and when they seem to promote the basic human values of our society. Official cruelty and disregard for human values tend to lead to the opposite result. It has been argued, in support of severe penalties and the use of compulsion, that such devices have worked well with doctors who are addicts. When faced with the alternatives of staying off drugs or being deprived of their licenses to practice medicine, about ninety per cent are said to have remained free of drugs for five or more years. The others almost invariably committed suicide. Does this represent the kind of ethical values and attitudes toward human life which we wish our citizens to have? Is this suicide rate a fair price to pay for the result claimed?

Another consequence of handling the narcotic addict within the orbit of the doctor-patient relationship is the gain in privacy. Like the details of many other problems that people take to their family physicians, the details of addiction to narcotics are not pleasant. Under existing arrangements the circumstances of addiction are exploited by the tabloids and the addict never knows when the details of his habit and his personal life may appear on the front pages of his community newspaper. With addiction a private matter between the doctor and his patient, the yellow journals would be deprived of raw material and the user would have a chance to keep knowledge of his addiction from becoming public.

CIVIL COMMITMENT OF ADDICTS

The idea of civil commitment of drug addicts is actually quite an old one, for many of the states have long had statutes on their books authorizing such commitment.[20] These laws have been largely unused. One of the difficulties has been that when civil commitment proceedings are undertaken and the user discovers this fact, he can flee the community unless he is forcibly detained. Forcible detention, however, requires that he be charged with an offense, and this means criminal rather than civil procedure.

The new program which has become popular during the last few years avoids the difficulty noted with respect to the older and now defunct program by using the leverage of a criminal charge to keep the addict in custody before commitment. In the New York program under the Metcalf–Volker Act of 1962 the criminal charge is held over the addict's head to encourage him to cooperate in the civil commitment proceedings and the attempted rehabilitation under the direction of the Department of Mental Hygiene. If the addict proves unworthy and the rehabilitation program fails, he can then be brought back to criminal court and tried on the criminal charge. Under the California program adopted in 1961 and amended in 1963, the addict is first tried and convicted, and the civil commitment proceedings are then substituted. When the program fails, the user may then be returned to the criminal court for sentencing. The President's Advisory Commission recommended California procedure over that of New York in this respect, because of the difficulty under the New York plan of trying a case after the lapse of so much time.[21]

Civil commitment as currently conceived and recommended by the President's Ad Hoc Committee, as described at the White House Conference, and as recommended by the President's Advisory Commission on Narcotic and Drug Abuse in 1963, originates from police sources. The logic is as follows: addiction is a dangerous communicable disease; the addict should be "quarantined" to check the spread of the disease; if the addict relapses repeatedly after being taken off drugs he should be quarantined for long periods or for life. The Federal Bureau of Narcotics has long promoted this view and it is this fact which is the main basis for its claim that it favors a medical approach to addiction. In the Bureau's pamphlet on narcotic clinics, it has included in later editions a statement by a retired Canadian policeman who recommends that addicts who are certified as such by three doctors be committed to federally operated narcotics hospitals for a period of not less than ten years. If a user were twice committed it was suggested that he be sent to an institution for life, and that he be provided with a useful avocation "but permanently within the confines of the institution."[22]

The civil commitment program now being urged upon the states and recommended at the federal level does not in fact involve medical control or a real medical program, although it does use some of the vocabulary of the healing professions. The President's Advisory Commission, describing its federal scheme, specifies that "The crucial decisions would be made by the Judiciary and the Attorney General."[23] In California, addicts who are civilly committed are sent to establishments which are operated by the Department of Corrections and which differ from prisons mainly in name. There is no real qualitative difference between the "rehabilitative" program imposed upon addicts and that imposed upon those who are being punished for the commission of crimes. From the addict's viewpoint, he is being punished because he is forcibly deprived of his liberty and suffers the social stigma of the criminal. On the assumption that addiction is a proper subject of medical care the civil commitment program would have to be characterized as a sham, or as a travesty of a real medical plan.

The worst features of the current civil commitment fad may well be connected with its pretense of being something other than punitive. Its current popularity is probably largely due to the fact that it seems to offer advantages to both the police and the medical philosophy of addiction. To the former it offers the continuation of the old practices of locking addicts up and of dodging the constitutional guarantees of the Bill of Rights which are built into the procedures of the criminal law. To the liberals and medically oriented it offers a gesture toward a new and more humanitarian approach and a new vocabulary for old practices. For the addict the situation remains substantially unchanged even if he can qualify as one of the select few eligible for civil commitment, except that he may expect to spend more time in institutions. The price of illicit drugs and the illicit traffic are untouched by this program, and the addict must still commit crimes to maintain himself. He still lives in fear of the police and is still exploited by peddlers. If he seeks to quit his habit voluntarily the only establishments to which he has easy access are jails and their equivalents.

The threat of tyranny and injustice inherent in the rationale of compulsory civil commitment for drug addicts may be illustrated in a variety of ways. Suppose, for example, that we apply the same logic to alcoholics or to those with venereal disease, making them all subject to being locked up. California law applies compulsory civil commitment not only to actual heroin addicts, but also to those who "by reason of repeated use of narcotics or other restricted dangerous drugs are in imminent danger of becoming addicts." Compulsory commitment processes are appropriately applied only when the person to be committed is shown to be dangerous or helpless and satisfactory evidence on this is presented in a court of law. Justice requires that each case be handled on an individual basis. The civil commitment program bypasses the whole concept of due process of law while pretending not to, by prejudging addicts as a group. This is accomplished by leaving unchanged present laws which automatically make virtually all addicts law violators. It is not necessary to demonstrate, for example, that an individual user is a social threat of any kind, nor would it be a defense if an addict could prove in court to the satisfaction of a jury that he was neither helpless nor a menace. Suppose that a druggist who is an addict is discovered because he falsifies his books to conceal the fact that he is diverting drugs to his own use. Civil commitment proceedings against this man would destroy his reputation and his usefulness to society just as effectively as criminal commitment. The civil commitment of addicts is another instance in which "treatment" may well turn out to be more punitive than "punishment."

The civil commitment program is customarily linked with a program of close parole supervision after release, sometimes associated with a nalline testing program. Nalline is a drug which indicates from the effects it produces whether the individual has recently had doses of opiates. Parolees who are required to take these tests are said to relapse less often and quickly than otherwise. With a cooperative addict there seems to be little doubt that nalline could be advantageously used for therapeutic ends. It is presently being used primarily for punitive ends, and sometimes it is part of local programs designed to chase addicts into other communities. Capt. T. T. Brown of the Oakland, California, Police Department, who is one of the staunchest champions of the nalline program, frankly says that "the test is a boon to the community utilizing it and a bane to neighboring metropolitan centers for many addicts flee the area using nalline. . . ."[24]

The following remarks by C. S. Lewis seem peculiarly appropriate to the civil commitment scheme:

But do not let us be deceived by a name. To be taken without consent from my home and friends; to lose my liberty; to undergo all those assaults upon my personality which modern psychotherapy knows how to deliver; to be re-made after some pattern of "normality" hatched in a Viennese laboratory to which I never professed allegiance; to know that this process will never end until either my captors have succeeded or I have grown wise enough to cheat them with apparent success—

Who cares whether this is called Punishment or not? That it includes most of the elements for which punishment is feared—shame, exile, bondage, and years eaten by the locust—is obvious.[25]

Those who hope for basic reform are sometimes inclined to regard the civil commitment bandwagon as the opening wedge of a movement toward more important changes. This view may be right. It may, on the other hand, have the opposite effect because it is often viewed as a nonpunitive, quasi-medical program. If it fails or accomplishes little, ideas like that of locking addicts up in concentration camps may gain ground.

A compulsory civil commitment program of the type now in force in New York and California, if it is linked with a long period of close parole supervision and possibly with a nalline testing program, is an expensive one. During periods of public excitement generated by the mass media there is likely to be greater willingness to spend public funds than during periods of quiescence. That is why it is very likely that some of the more elaborate programs now in use will be abandoned in the future and that others will degenerate, changing from high-minded, rehabilitative, well-staffed programs to routine, poorly staffed, custodial ones.[26] Penologists are thoroughly accustomed to this degenerative process. No matter what arguments are presented from the humanitarian viewpoint concerning the ultimate social advantages of curing addicts of their habits, the fiscal facts are that addicts are relatively difficult and unresponsive and that money spent on them could be spent with greater justification, in terms of results, on others. As long as public funds are limited, this view will be an important one. A proliferation of programs for drug addicts also occurred after the First World War and almost all of them have vanished without a trace.

LIMITED TREATMENT PROGRAMS

In recent years there has been a considerable proliferation of various types of experimental treatment programs for addicts. Some of these are aimed at testing the feasibility of new ideas, as, for example, the selection of addicts to be placed on maintenance doses to determine whether they would be able to work. Others are aimed to reach addicts in prison to motivate them to stay off drugs or to help them when they are released by providing psychiatric and counseling services or helping to secure employment. There has been a considerable expansion of halfway houses which seek to ease the path of the addict as he tries to get used to living outside of prison. Others, handled by medical men or psychiatrists, have included management of the physical withdrawal of drugs followed by aftercare and the attempt to get at the emotional problems which are thought to underlie addiction.[27]

Despite the apparent abundance of these programs, they collectively reach only a small number of addicts and many of them are of a temporary nature, destined to vanish when the funds run out, when the initial enthusiasm disappears, or when the individual who is the center of inspiration for the program dies, moves away, or changes his interests. Most of these programs find themselves faced with heavy odds created by the present policy which inspires strong sentiments of fear, resentment, suspicion, and hopelessness in the users. Sometimes police interest in the users embarrasses these programs, and sometimes, if the program is managed by physicians who think they have the right to prescribe narcotics to addicts, the police may watch the establishment very closely with the idea of putting it out of business. The main objective of the bulk of these private, semiofficial, or experimental programs may fairly be described as seeking ways of counteracting evil effects created by the official program.

Two of the more permanent organizations of this nature are Narcotics Anonymous and Synanon. Both are self-help organizations in which addicts encourage each other to quit and stay off drugs. The former is modeled after Alcoholics Anonymous. The latter has also been influenced by A.A. but has developed a unique and highly interesting program of its own.[28] Synanon's headquarters are in a large old building on the Santa Monica beach. From there it has spread to a number of other localities and the number of members has increased appreciably but does not exceed more than a few hundred. Statistics of a reliable nature concerning the effectiveness of Synanon and Narcotics Anonymous are not available and very extravagant claims are made, especially for the former. Narcotics Anonymous groups exist in a number of prisons as well as outside.

The Synanon program has attracted a great deal of attention from the mass media and a great deal of support. At the same time, it, like other similar groups of addicts, aroused determined opposition from Santa Monica citizens who tried to force it out of that community. It appears to be rather studiously ignored by the narcotics officialdom.

Synanon accepts addicts who volunteer and meet certain standards. The newcomer is attended by older members in relays during the first few days while he is breaking his habit. When this is done he finds himself drawn into an intense, organized program of activities which are planned both for his own good and for the good of the organization. Synanon houses both men and women and, in some instances, children, and its members represent all social classes and a wide variety of social types. Any visitor will find it a fascinating place and a beehive of purposeful activity. It is something in the nature of a cult and a way of life for its members. From the publicity that has been accorded it, Synanon is known to drug users throughout the United States and it is certainly a symbol of hope for many.

The existence and expansion of the Synanon movement represents a challenge to the prevailing conception of the drug addict as a psychological cripple, or as one who is masochistically happy in his vice and has no desire for anything but his drugs and a life of crime. It is also a challenge to the officially sponsored view that drug users respond only to authoritarian handling and will not of their own volition seek to break their habits. The latter belief is also belied by much other evidence including the fact that many thousands of drug users submit themselves for commitment to jail in order to get help to carry them through withdrawal.

A curious aspect of the reaction to Synanon has been the indifference and even hostility of narcotic officials both within the state and at the federal level.[29] It is reported that the parole and probation of addicts was revoked when they entered Synanon and that a commission of six officials making a study in 1960 stopped briefly at Synanon but did not mention it in their report to Governor Brown. Although Synanon representatives went to the White House Conference, they were largely ignored there and also by the President's Advisory Commission. Perhaps the officials are resentful of the fact that the Synanon movement seems to be doing very well without them and that this program, operated by the addicts themselves, has caught on to a far greater extent than any that has been imposed upon the users by outsiders.

SOME OBJECTIONS ANSWERED

Many objections are made in this country to the type of program advocated here, which may be brushed aside with little discussion, because they are of a purely hypothetical sort or are made by persons who do not understand our narcotics problem and who are unacquainted with foreign programs. It is sometimes said, for example, that the proposed program might cause the underworld to make a systematic effort to create new addicts to replace those who would be removed from the illicit market. Sometimes it is argued that if there were no punishment more persons would want to become addicts. It is said that the program is in violation of our international agreements respecting narcotics. It is suggested that addicts might refuse to go to doctors and insist, instead, on buying high-priced, heavily diluted drugs from pushers. It is also argued that addicts who now commit crimes to raise money to buy drugs prefer this to a system which provides them with legal drugs and makes crime unnecessary for them. It is sometimes assumed that what is being advocated is free availability of drugs to all.

All of these arguments, and quite a few others, are refuted by the experience of dozens of foreign countries which practice the type of program in question. In none of them have the nefarious effects suggested above made their appearance. The nations that presently handle addiction as a medical problem are parties to the same international agreements that we are. The assumption that the underworld might engage in a systematic campaign of proselyting new addicts indicates a complete lack of understanding of illicit operations and of how the drug habit is acquired. A similar lack of understanding is indicated by the idea that if addicts were not punished many people would at once set out deliberately to become addicted. The assumption that the program being considered here involves free availability of drugs to all is contradicted by all foreign experience and by logic and is an essentially frivolous objection. Availability by prescription makes narcotics relatively inaccessible; it is the illicit traffic that makes for indiscriminate availability.

There are many persons in the United States, some of them favorably disposed toward reform, who feel that the drug problem and cultural conditions in the United States are so unique that there is little or nothing to be gained from the study of foreign experience. From this point of view, it is contended that what is needed is an extensive research program to explore, first, the nature and extent of the present problem, and then the probable effects of any proposed changes.

The cry that "more research is needed" before anything can be done is a familiar, time-honored device used by those who are opposed to reform or who do not care to face issues. It is true that research is desirable; but it will not necessarily provide answers to policy questions. Research results are always subject to variable interpretations and to misrepresentation. If reform is to wait until research has made it certain what all the consequences of given changes will be, it will wait forever. Moreover, on many relevant issues no research is needed. We do not need it, for example, to demonstrate that our present narcotics laws are unjust and ineffective, that successful medical programs for handling addicts exist abroad, or that jails are not ideally suited for the treatment of disease.

On the matter of the absolute uniqueness of the American narcotics situation, the burden of proof would seem to rest on those who assume this view. It too is a last ditch defense of the status quo. The medical system of handling addicts is used in virtually all of the countries that resemble us most closely and from which our people, our language, our customs, our legal and social institutions are derived. The behavior of addicts, moreover, is remarkably the same everywhere in the world and very highly predictable in the sense that one can assert with confidence that addicts everywhere will do whatever they must to obtain their supplies.

An argument that is as baffling as any is that providing addicts with drugs is immoral and wrong and should be prohibited by the criminal law. From this point of view a medical program for addicts is "legalization" and this in turn means social approval of addiction. It is argued by some adherents of this view that since addiction is an admitted evil it must be forbidden by the criminal law even if this should in turn lead to even greater evils, as it does. There should be, in short, no compromise with the Devil. An argument of this sort is essentially absolutistic and unanswerable. The only remedy that suggests itself is that persons holding these views should become personally acquainted with some drug users.

Legalization, it should be unnecessary to say, does not mean approval. Alcoholism and venereal disease are both legal, for example. The threat in this kind of moralistic thinking is that it opens the door to comstockery and prohibitionism of the kind that gave us the Volstead Act. If heroin users are criminals, why not declare that the use of alcohol and tobacco are also sinful practices to be forbidden by the law and stamped out by the police?

The program of reform suggested here is a gradual one which would aim at increasing progressively the number of addicts receiving legitimate medical care from practitioners. Since some users are already being taken care of in this way the proposals amount merely to an extension of what is already being successfully done on a limited scale. This program could be put into effect by a gradual and progressive liberalization of present restrictions upon medical men. It is anticipated and assumed that close supervision and control would be exercised over the entire program by the Public Health Service in collaboration with the medical profession. It is suggested that doctors would be authorized to handle addicts only when they were qualified and willing to do so. It would be essential that hospital facilities be made available throughout the nation to handle addicts during the withdrawal period.

A program such as this, in its initial stages, would involve little public expense, since it would first be applied mainly to drug users with sufficient means to pay their own way. Hospitalization for withdrawal should be included in the scope of medical insurance programs and handled like any other hospitalization. Ultimately, some special provision at public expense might be deemed desirable for the most hopelessly demoralized users who could not be reached by the above means. The narcotics dispensary-clinic offers one possibility, compulsory institutionalization another.

The essential, basic idea of the entire program would be to use the leverage which the drug habit provides to prevent addicts from violating the law. Drug users would be given a fighting chance to be law-abiding persons even though they were addicts. Through the physicians caring for them pressure would be exerted upon them to reduce and control their dosage and to attempt to quit. This pressure ought to be nicely balanced so that it encourages the addict to quit without causing him to resort to desperate or illegal means of acquiring drugs. The addict purchasing illicit drugs would be subject to prosecution and punishment just as he would if he violated any other criminal law. The work of the police would have to do, as it does now, with the apprehension of illicit drug smugglers, dealers, and distributors and with addicts who persisted in patronizing this market. The effects of such police activity upon addicts would be to exert pressure upon them to resort to the physician for supplies and treatment. The drug user, in short, would have strong positive motives for going along with this program and he would suffer inconvenience, discomfort, and punishment if he did not.

It is sometimes contended that heroin addiction is the product of disorganization, tension, and alienation, particularly as manifested in the city slum, and that it is visionary to suppose that these conditions can be corrected by anything but fundamental social change. The error in this argument is the failure to recognize that availability of drugs is a sine qua non for the existence of drug addiction. European cities, like those of the United States, also have their slums. The drab, urban wastelands of Chicago and New York can be matched by those of London, Liverpool, Glasgow, and other British cities. The critical difference between British and American slums is that the latter contain an extensive illicit drug traffic while the former do not.

While it would be desirable that the Harrison Act be repealed and a fresh legal start made, this is not absolutely necessary. The proposal to permit physicians to handle addiction is not in conflict with present federal statutes or with present doctrines of the federal courts. It is in conflict only with the administrative regulations of the Treasury Department, which could be changed without any new congressional legislation, particularly since they now appear to be in conflict with Supreme Court interpretations of the Harrison Act.

While the public may not at present be prepared to demand reform, it is also unlikely that there would be any important popular outcry against the reforms suggested. While there is a general public concern over addiction and strong popular support for heavy penalties, it is also true that the public has become accustomed to regarding narcotics abuse, along with alcohol and barbiturate addiction, as something akin to disease. The heavy penalties provided by present laws are viewed as appropriate for the peddler rather than the addict. A program which quietly began to place larger and larger numbers of addicts under the care of doctors would therefore probably meet with little public disapproval, for there is much greater public confidence in the medical profession than there is in the police, lawyers, and prosecutors who are now in charge.

The program that is being advocated here is not British. It is rather a proposed expansion of an unofficial medical program that is presently being applied in the United States to privileged addicts of the upper social strata. What is advocated is that the same consideration that is extended to an addicted society lady from Washington, to an addicted member of Congress, or to addicted members of the medical profession also be extended to drug users of humble social status who have no important connections. It is a plan for giving all addicts genuine equality before the law. It is consistent with our basic ideals of justice, of individual rights, of the proper treatment of the sick, and of the right to be judged as an individual rather than as a member of a category. It is a program toward which the United States is moving and for which there is no substitute.

NOTES

Chapter 1

1. The Harrison Act, 38 Stat. 785 (1914) as amended 26 U.S.C. Also, for the text of the act, see Charles E. Terry and Mildred Pellens, *The Opium Problem* (New York: Bureau of Social Hygiene, 1928), pp. 983-92.

2. C. E. Terry and M. Pellens, *The Opium Problem*, p. 985.

3. U.S. v. Jin Fuey Moy, 241 U.S. 394 (1915).

4. Webb v. U.S., 249 U.S. 96 (1919).

5. Jin Fuey Moy v. U.S., 254 U.S. 189 (1920).

6. U.S. v. Behrman, 258 U.S. 280 (1922).

7. Linder v. U.S., 268 U.S. 5 (1925).

8. Bureau of Narcotics, U.S. Treasury Department, *Prescribing and Dispensing of Narcotics under the Harrison Narcotic Law*, Pamphlet No. 56 (Revised; Sept., 1960).

9. Linder v. U.S., 268 U.S. 5 (1925), 18.

10. *Ibid.*, 20.

11. *Ibid.*, 22.

12. U.S. v. Anthony, 15 F. Supp. 553 (1936).

13. Robinson v. California, no. 55, October Term, 1961. Published June 25, 1962.

14. *Ibid.*, 8.

15. Strader v. U.S., 72 F. 2d 589 (10th Cir. 1934).

16. Carey v. U.S., 86 F. 2d 461 (9th Cir. 1936).

17. *An Investigation of the Narcotic Evil: Speech of Hon. John M. Coffee of Washington in the House of Representatives, June 14, 1938* (Washington, D.C.: U.S. Government Printing Office, 1938), pp. 9-10.

18. *Comments on Narcotic Drugs: Interim Report of the Joint Committee of the American Bar Association and the American Medical Association on Narcotic Drugs* by the Advisory Committee to the Federal Bureau of Narcotics, U.S. Treasury Department (Washington, D.C.: U.S. Government Printing Office, 1959), p. 160. Hereafter referred to as *Comments on Narcotic Drugs*.

19. Rochin v. California, 342 U.S. 165 (1952).

20. Blackford v. U.S., 247 F. 2d 745 (9th Cir. 1957).

21. Charles E. Terry, "Narcotic Drug Addiction and Rational Administration," *American Medicine*, 26 (Jan., 1920), 29-35.

22. State of New Jersey, Executive Department, Assembly Bill No. 488, "Veto Message of Gov. Robert J. Meyner" (mimeographed: June 28, 1956), pp. 3-9.

23. Harry J. Anslinger and William F. Tompkins, *The Traffic in Narcotics* (New York: Funk and Wagnalls, 1953), p. 159.

24. Chapter 35, sec. 10-3538a, Indiana Penal Code.

25. Chapter 35, sec. 10-3502, Indiana Penal Code.

26. Chapter 35, sec. 10-3538a (d), Indiana Penal Code.

CHAPTER 2

1. *Illicit Narcotics Traffic: Hearings before the Subcommittee on Improvements in the Federal Criminal Code of the Committee on the Judiciary*, U.S. Senate, 84th Cong., 1st sess., pursuant to S. Res. 67, Causes and Treatment of Drug Addiction (Washington, D.C.: U.S. Government Printing Office, 1955-1956), Part 9, p. 4193. Hereafter referred to as *Daniel Subcommittee Hearings*.

2. *Ibid.*, p. 4195.

3. *Ibid.*, p. 4297.

4. *Ibid.*, pp. 4295-96.

5. *Ibid.*, Part 3, p. 718.

6. *Ibid.*, Part 9, p. 4309.

7. *Ibid.*, Part 2, p. 370.

8. *Chicago Tribune*, Feb. 9, 1957, Part 1, p. 9.

9. *Daniel Subcommittee Hearings*, Part 2, pp. 387-411.

10. *Ibid.*, Part 1, p. 60.

11. *Ibid.*, Part 2, p. 523.

12. *Ibid.*, Part 9, p. 4311.

13. *New York Times*, Jan. 5, 1952, p. 1.

14. *Louisville Courier-Journal*, April 16, 1960, Sec. 2, p. 1.

15. H. J. Anslinger and W. F. Tompkins, *The Traffic in Narcotics*, p. 161.

CHAPTER 3

1. *Los Angeles Times*, March 3, 1960, Part 3, p. 2.

2. Edwin M. Schur, *Narcotic Addiction in Britain and America: The Impact of Public Policy* (Bloomington: Indiana University Press, 1962), p. 53.

3. *Traffic in, and Control of, Narcotics, Barbiturates and Amphetamines: Hearings before a Subcommittee of the Committee on Ways and Means*, U.S. House of Representatives, 84th Cong. (Washington, D.C.: U.S. Government Printing Office, 1956), p. 49. Hereafter referred to as *Boggs Subcommittee Hearings*, 1956.

4. *Ibid.*, p. 56.

5. *Ibid.*, p. 167. See also the hearings in 1951 of the same subcommittee, also under Hale Boggs.

6. *Treasury and Post Office Department Appropriations Hearings* for 1962 and 1963; Hearings before the Subcommittee of the Committee on Appropriations, U.S. House of Representatives, 87th Cong., 1st and 2d sess., March 2, 1961, and Jan. 30, 1962, pp. 233-71 and 253-304 respectively.

7. *Ibid.*, p. 268, 1961 Hearings for 1962.

8. Lt. [now Capt.] Thorvald T. Brown, *The Enigma of Drug Addiction* (Springfield, Ill.: C. C. Thomas, 1961).

9. *Ibid.*, p. 209.

10. *Ibid.*, pp. 199-202.

11. *Ibid.*, p. 201.

12. *Ibid.*, p. 202.

13. *Ibid.*, pp. 208-10.

14. *Ibid.*, p. 207.

15. *Ibid.*, p. 203.

16. Report by the California Board of Corrections, *Narcotics in California*, Feb. 19, 1959 (Sacramento, Calif.), pp. 8, 13. In this report it is stated that of 598 consecutive male adult prisoners received in 1957 not a single one qualified as a nonaddicted peddler at the "management level."

17. *Daniel Subcommittee Hearings*, Part 1 (1955), p. 161.

18. *Ibid.*, p. 162.

19. *Ibid.*, pp. 163-64.

20. *Ibid.*, pp. 161-62.

21. *Ibid.*, p. 159.

22. William Butler Eldridge, *Narcotics and the Law: A Critique of the American Experiment in Narcotic Drug Control* (Chicago: American Bar Foundation, 1962), pp. 150-93. In the summary of state laws in this work it appears that close to one half of the states punish possession as a felony in accordance with recently enacted statutes.

23. This discussion is based on observations made in Chicago when possession was made a felony.

24. Cf. W. B. Eldridge, *Narcotics and the Law*, p. 88.

25. Cf. Bureau of Criminal Statistics, California State Department of Justice, *Drug Arrests and Dispositions in California, 1962* (Sacramento, Calif.), pp. 4, 15, 29.

26. E. H. Sutherland, *Principles of Criminology* (3rd ed.; Philadelphia: Lippincott, 1939), pp. 279-80.

27. Cited in *ibid.*, p. 280.

28. The following account is based on the description of the case in Judge Jerome Frank and Barbara Frank, *Not Guilty* (New York: Doubleday, 1957), pp. 99-111. The case was also extensively reported in the *New York Times*.

29. *Daniel Subcommittee Hearings*, Part 5 (1956), pp. 1801-2.

30. Harry J. Anslinger and Will Oursler, *The Murderers! The Shocking Story of the Narcotics Gangs* (New York: Farrar, Straus and Cudahy, 1961), pp. 175-76, 181-82.

31. *Boggs Subcommittee Hearings*, 1956, p. 166.

32. *Daniel Subcommittee Hearings*, Part 9, pp. 4295-97.

33. *Chicago Tribune* Magazine of Books, Aug. 17, 1958, p. 1.

34. From Federal Bureau of Prisons, *Report of the Work of the Federal Bureau of Prisons* (annual reports), 1950-1960. Hereafter referred to as *Federal Prisons*.

35. *Federal Prisons, 1957,* pp. 5-6.
36. *Daniel Subcommittee Hearings,* Part 9, p. 4195.
37. *Proceedings:* White House Conference on Narcotic and Drug Abuse, Sept. 27 and 28, 1962 (Washington, D. C.: U.S. Government Printing Office, 1963), p. 230.
38. *Ibid.,* p. 231.

CHAPTER 4

1. Commission on Narcotic Drugs, U.N. Economic & Social Council, *Summary of Annual Reports of Governments relating to Opium and other Dangerous Drugs* (New York: U.N. Publications, 1961), p. 34.
2. *Daniel Subcommittee Hearings,* Part 8, pp. 3926-27.
3. California State Narcotic Committee, *The Trend of Drug Addiction in California* (Sacramento: California State Printing Office, 1931), p. 16.
4. See *Daniel Subcommittee Hearings,* Part 8, pp. 3775-76, for description by a California official.
5. Bureau of Criminal Statistics, State Department of Justice, *Summary, Narcotic Statistics for California, 1954-59; Narcotic Arrests in California, July 1, 1959-June 30, 1960;* and *Narcotic Arrests and Dispositions in California, 1961.* The report for 1962 follows the 1961 format.
6. H. J. Anslinger and W. F. Tompkins, *The Traffic in Narcotics,* p. 265.
7. Lawrence Kolb and A. G. Du Mez, "The Prevalence and Trend of Drug Addiction in the United States and Factors Influencing It," *Public Health Reports,* 39, No. 21 (May 23, 1924), 8. (Originally found on pp. 1179-1204; reprint copies are paged from 1 to 26.)
8. *Daniel Subcommittee Hearings,* June 2, 3, 8, 1955, pp. 9-10.
9. Lawrence Kolb and A. G. Du Mez, "The Prevalence and Trend of Drug Addiction."
10. *Ibid.,* p. 20.
11. Bureau of the Census, Department of Commerce, *Prisoners, 1923: Crime Conditions in the United States as Reflected in Census Statistics of Imprisoned Offenders* (Washington, D.C., 1926), p. 41.

12. The figures that follow are from the annual reports of the Bureau of Narcotics, *Traffic in Opium and Other Dangerous Drugs*.

13. *Federal Prisons, 1960*, p. 38.

14. *Second Interim Report of the State of New York Joint Legislative Committee on Narcotic Study* (Legislative Document No. 16, 1958), p. 28.

15. *Prisoners, 1923*, p. 31.

16. See the Bureau's annual report, 1958, p. 45.

17. Cf. the Bureau's annual report, 1962, p. 57, and the statement by the present head of the Bureau in Pete Martin, "What Hope for Narcotics Control? An Interview with Henry L. Giordano, Commissioner of the Bureau of Narcotics," *The American Legion Magazine*, 76, No. 1 (Jan., 1964), 37.

18. *Comments on Narcotic Drugs*, pp. 175-85. The comparisons are emphasized by graphic representation.

19. The figures are from the Bureau's annual reports.

20. Pete Martin, "What Hope for Narcotics Control?" p. 37.

21. *Narcotic Arrests and Dispositions in California, 1961*, p. 31, and the 1962 report, p. 36.

22. W. B. Eldridge, *Narcotics and the Law*, p. 76.

23. *Ibid.*, pp. 68-80.

24. Victor H. Vogel, Harris Isbell, and Kenneth W. Chapman, "Present Status of Narcotic Addiction," *Journal of the American Medical Association*, 138 (Dec. 4, 1948), 1019-26. Reproduced in *Daniel Subcommittee Hearings*, Part 5, pp. 1992-2014.

25. *Prisoners, 1923*, pp. 81, 274.

26. The above are cited in C. E. Terry and M. Pellens, *The Opium Problem*, pp. 475-76.

27. The references to estimates of addicts in foreign nations that follow in this chapter are obtained from the annual U.N. publication by the Commission on Narcotic Drugs, *Summary of Annual Reports of Governments*.

28. *U.N. Summary*, especially for 1956 and 1958.

29. *Ibid.*, 1960, pp. 36, 39.

30. Cf. C. E. Terry and M. Pellens, *The Opium Problem*, chapters I, II, and VIII.

31. *Prisoners, 1923*, p. 31.

32. Ernest S. Bishop, *The Narcotic Drug Problem* (New York: Mac-

millan, 1921), pp. 125-26. Cf. C. E. Terry and M. Pellens, *The Opium Problem*, p. 482.

33. C. E. Terry and M. Pellens, *The Opium Problem*, pp. 25, 28.

CHAPTER 5

1. *Treatment and Rehabilitation of Narcotic Addicts:* Report of the Committee on the Judiciary, U.S. Senate, containing the Findings and Recommendations of the Subcommittee on Improvements in the Federal Criimnal Code pursuant to S. Res. 67 and S. Res. 166, 84h Cong., 2d sess., S. Rep. No. 1850 (Washington, D.C.: U.S. Government Printing Office, 1956), pp. 3-12.

2. *Daniel Subcommittee Hearings*, Part 5, p. 2035.

3. Bureau of Narcotics, U.S. Treasury Department, *Narcotic Clinics in the United States* (Washington, D.C.: U.S. Government Printing Office, 1953).

4. *Ibid.*, p. 1.

5. *Annual Report* of the Commissioner of Internal Revenue for the Fiscal Year ended June 30, 1919 (Washington, D.C.: U.S. Government Printing Office), p. 61.

6. *Ibid.*, for 1920, pp. 33-34.

7. *Ibid.*, for 1921, p. 29.

8. *Ibid.*, for 1920, pp. 29-33.

9. Cited in C. E. Terry and M. Pellens, *The Opium Problem*, p. 758.

10. *Narcotic Clinics in the U.S.*, p. 7.

11. *Ibid.*

12. *Daniel Subcommittee Hearings*, Part 5, p. 1706.

13. *Ibid.*, pp. 1718-19.

14. *Narcotic Drug Addiction: Speech of Hon. Lester D. Volk of New York in the House of Representatives, Friday, January 13, 1922* (Washington, D.C.: U.S. Government Printing Office, 1922).

15. Quoted in *Daniel Subcommittee Hearings*, Part 5, p. 1869, from page 1 of the Narcotic Bureau's pamphlet, *Narcotic Clinics in the U.S.*

16. *Ibid.*

17. *Narcotic Drug Addiction*, p. 11.

18. *Ibid.*, p. 8.

19. See, e.g., C. E. Terry and M. Pellens, *The Opium Problem*, pp. 993-96.

20. *Narcotic Drug Addiction*, p. 12.

21. *Ibid.*, p. 3.

22. *Narcotic Clinics in the U.S.*, pp. 12-13.

23. C. E. Terry and M. Pellens, *The Opium Problem*, pp. 864-72.

24. *Ibid.*, p. 40.

CHAPTER 6

1. *American Journal of Public Health*, 38 (June, 1948), 885.

2. *American Journal of Psychiatry*, 104 (July, 1948), 75.

3. In *Proceedings:* White House Conference on Narcotic and Drug Abuse, pp. 110-15. Dr. Schur's remarks are given much greater prominence than they had at the actual conference.

4. E. W. Adams, *Drug Addiction* (London: Oxford University Press, 1937), pp. 65-66.

5. Reproduced in *Daniel Subcommittee Hearings*, Part 5, p. 1862.

6. E. M. Schur, *Narcotic Addiction in Britain and America*. This book represents the most comprehensive sociological account of the British program that is available.

7. Cf. *ibid.*, p. 75.

8. *Ibid.*, p. 76. The Brain Committee report in 1961 suggested no basic changes in British policy. See *ibid.*, pp. 159-64, for a discussion.

9. Originally published in *J.A.M.A.*, 156, No. 8 (Oct. 23, 1954), 788; reproduced in the *Boggs Subcommittee Hearings*, 1956, pp. 470-71.

10. H. J. Anslinger and W. F. Tompkins, *The Traffic in Narcotics*, pp. 279, 290.

11. *The British Journal of Delinquency*, 5, No. 3 (Jan., 1955), p. 242.

12. *Daniel Subcommittee Hearings*, Part 5, 1955, p. 44.

13. *Spectrum*, 5, No. 5 (March 1, 1957), 139.

14. Pete Martin, "What Hope for Narcotics Control?" p. 9.

15. T. T. Brown, *The Enigma of Drug Addiction*, p. 153.

16. *Ibid.*, pp. 168-69.

17. Dr. Granville W. Larimore and Dr. Henry Brill, "Report to Governor Nelson A. Rockefeller of an On the Site Study of the British Nar-

cotic System" (mimeographed: March 3, 1959). A condensed summary
appeared in *New York State Journal of Medicine*, 60, No. 1 (Jan. 1,
1960), pp. 107-15.

18. In a paper presented to a conference at the University of California in April 1963, and published in Daniel Wilner and Gene Kasse-
baum, eds., *Narcotics* (New York: McGraw-Hill, 1965), chap. 9.

19. The Committee on Public Health of the New York Academy of
Medicine, "Report on Drug Addiction II" (mimeographed: 1963), pp.
56-64.

20. Dr. G. W. Larimore and Dr. H. Brill, "Report," condensed summary, pp. 113-14.

21. *Daniel Subcommittee Hearings*, Part 5, 1955, p. 1418.

22. These annual publications will hereafter be referred to as *U.N.
Summary*.

23. From *U.N. Summary*, *1949*, p. 38 (Netherlands); *1954* addendum,
p. 17 (Argentina); *1955*, p. 49 (Norway), p. 49 (Spain), p. 43 (Israel),
pp. 45-46 (Belgium), p. 45 (Austria), p. 47 (West Germany), p. 50
(Switzerland), p. 52 (New Zealand), p. 51 (New South Wales and
Queensland); *1956*, p. 53 (Luxemburg), p. 53 (Norway), p. 54 (Spain),
p. 51 (West Germany), p. 50 (Finland).

24. *U.N. Summary*, *1949*, p. 38.

25. *U.N. Summary*, *1956*, p. 54, and *1955*, p. 49.

26. *U.N. Summary*, *1955*, p. 43.

27. *Ibid.*, p. 45.

28. *U.N. Summary*, *1956*, p. 51.

29. *U.N. Summary*, *1955*, p. 50.

30. *Ibid.*, p. 51.

31. *Final Report:* The President's Advisory Commission on Narcotic
and Drug Abuse, November, 1963 (Washington, D.C.: U.S. Government Printing Office, 1963), p. 59.

32. Lady Frankau, "Treatment in England of Canadian Patients Addicted to Narcotic Drugs," *The Canadian Medical Association Journal*,
90, No. 6 (Feb. 8, 1964), 421-24.

33. *Ibid.*, 422.

34. *NAPAN Newsletter*, 1, No. 4 (July-Aug., 1963), 4. The *Newsletter* is published by the National Association for the Prevention of
Addiction to Narcotics, Hotel Astor, New York City.

35. *NAPAN Newsletter*, 1, No. 3 (June, 1963), 3.

CHAPTER 7

1. See David Edward Owen, *British Opium Policy in China and India* ("Yale Historical Studies," Vol. VIII [New Haven: Yale University Press, 1934]); C. E. Terry and M. Pellens, *The Opium Problem*, pp. 53-57; Frederick T. Merrill, *Japan and the Opium Menace* (New York: Institute of Pacific Relations and Foreign Policy Association, 1942), pp. 3-17.

2. Commission of Enquiry into the Control of Opium Smoking in the Far East, *Report to the Council* (3 vols.; Geneva: League of Nations, 1930-1932), I, 11. This will be referred to hereafter as *Report on Opium Smoking in the Far East*.

3. See *U.N. Summary, 1959*, p. 38.

4. See, e.g., W. W. Willoughby, *Opium as an International Problem* (Baltimore: Johns Hopkins Press, 1925), for a detailed discussion of the Shanghai and, especially, The Hague and Geneva conferences. There is an immense literature on the international attempts to control opium production, much of it very dull or moralistic or both.

5. For a vivid account of the events and conditions leading to the Anglo-Chinese Opium War of 1839-41, see Morris Collis, *Foreign Mud* (New York: Knopf, 1947). Another informative account is that of David E. Owen already cited.

6. From personal communications with persons who have visited and lived in Hong Kong within the last few years.

7. This is regularly noted in the *U.N. Summaries* and also by the Federal Bureau of Narcotics in its annual reports.

8. The article by Patya Saihoo, "The Hill Tribes of Northern Thailand and the Opium Problem," *U.N. Bulletin on Narcotics*, XV, No. 2 (April-June, 1963), 35-45, gives a description of one of the tribes in the region.

9. F. T. Merrill, *Japan and the Opium Menace*, p. 5.

10. See M. Collis, *Foreign Mud*, pp. 23-28.

11. F. T. Merrill, *Japan and the Opium Menace*, p. 8.

12. The account of the internal opium policy in China that follows is based on those provided by Owen and Merrill in the works already cited.

13. Detailed description and data concerning Hong Kong's government monopoly program is found in *Report on Opium Smoking in the Far East*, II, 336-81.

14. Herbert L. May, *Survey of Smoking Opium Conditions in the Far East: A Report to the Executive Board of the Foreign Policy Association* (New York: Opium Research Committee, Foreign Policy Association, 1927), p. 34.

15. F. T. Merrill, *Japan and the Opium Menace*, p. 15.

16. *Report on Opium Smoking in the Far East*, II, 380.

17. *Ibid.*, 351-53.

18. Cf. H. L. May, *Survey of Smoking Opium Conditions*, pp. 49-54, and F. T. Merrill, *Japan and the Opium Menace*, pp. 68-71.

19. Bureau of Narcotics, U.S. Treasury Department, *Traffic in Opium and Other Dangerous Drugs for the Year Ended December 31, 1943* (Washington, D.C.: U.S. Government Printing Office, 1944), pp. 1-3.

20. General sources of information on the current situation: *The Problem of Narcotic Drugs in Hong Kong: A White Paper Laid before the Legislative Council, 11th November 1959* (Hong Kong Government Publication); "Hong Kong's Prison for Drug Addicts," by authorities of the prison, *U.N. Bulletin on Narcotics*, XIII, No. 1 (Jan.-March, 1961), 13-20; Carl C. Gurkzit, "Pharmacological Investigation and Evaluation of the Effects of Combined Barbiturate and Heroin Inhalation by Addicts," *U.N. Bulletin on Narcotics*, X, No. 3 (July-Sept., 1958), 8-11; Dr. E. Leong Way, "Treatment and Control of Drug Addiction in Hong Kong," paper read at UCLA drug conference, April 1963, Chapter VII in *Narcotics*, edited by Daniel M. Wilner; and *U.N. Summaries*. Also, personal communications with Dr. Albert G. Hess and Professor Ssu-yu Teng, both of whom have recently visited Hong Kong and have done research on the problem there.

21. "Hong Kong's Prison for Drug Addicts," p. 13.

22. Bureau of Narcotics, U.S. Treasury Department, *Traffic in Opium and Other Dangerous Drugs for the Year Ended December 31, 1957*, pp. 2-3.

23. *Ibid.*, for 1958, p. 2.

24. *Ibid.*, for 1960, p. 2.

25. On the program in Formosa see: F. T. Merrill, *Japan and the*

Opium Menace, pp. 79-86; Sagatore Kaku, *Opium Policy in Japan* (Geneva: Albert Kundig, 1924); *Report on Opium Smoking in the Far East,* II, 408-36; H. L. May, *Survey of Smoking Opium Conditions,* pp. 35-36.

26. F. T. Merrill, *Japan and the Opium Menace,* p. 79.

27. *Ibid.,* p. 86.

28. The account that follows, including the figures, is based primarily upon the book by Kaku which has been cited, and to a lesser extent on Merrill's book and the League of Nations' *Report on Opium Smoking in the Far East.*

29. Tsungming Tu, "Statistical Studies on the Mortality Rates and the Causes of Death among the Opium Addicts in Formosa," *U.N. Bulletin on Narcotics,* III, No. 2 (April, 1951), 9-11.

30. *U.N. Summary, 1945,* p. 13.

31. *Ibid.*

32. *U.N. Summary, 1951,* p. 21.

33. *U.N. Summary, 1959,* p. 38.

34. From informal reports of visiting Americans and also from Thailand officials.

35. H. L. May, *Survey of Smoking Opium Conditions,* p. 35.

36. F. T. Merrill, *Japan and the Opium Menace,* p. 75.

37. See the reports of the Japanese government to the U.N. since 1949 in *U.N. Summaries* for the account of postwar developments and the establishment of the American type of control system.

38. *U.N. Summary, 1959,* addendum, p. 9.

39. *Traffic in Opium and Other Dangerous Drugs, 1951,* pp. 2-3.

40. H. L. May, *Survey of Smoking Opium Conditions,* p. 9.

41. *Ibid.,* p. 10.

42. *Ibid.,* pp. 10-11.

43. *Ibid.,* p. 21.

44. *Ibid.*

45. *Ibid.,* p. 22.

46. *Ibid.,* pp. 6-7.

47. *Ibid.,* p. 25.

48. Cf. Raymond Leslie Buell, "The Opium Conferences," *Foreign Affairs,* 3, No. 4 (July, 1925), 567-83, and Albert Wissler, *Die Opiumfrage: Eine Studie zur Weltwirtschaftlichen und Weltpolitischen Lage der Gegenwart* (Jena: Fischer, 1931).

CHAPTER 8

1. For general discussions of marihuana see: Robert P. Walton, *Marihuana: America's New Drug Problem* (Philadelphia: Lippincott, 1938), and Norman Taylor, *Flight from Reality* (New York: Duell, Sloan and Pearce, 1949).

2. From observations and interviews with Jamaicans by the writer during a visit to that island.

3. N. Taylor, *Flight from Reality*, p. 27.

4. *Report of the Indian Hemp Drug Commission* (7 vols.; Simla, India, 1894), cited by N. Taylor, *Flight from Reality*, p. 34.

5. N. Taylor, *Flight from Reality*, pp. 34-35.

6. *The Marihuana Problem in the City of New York: Sociological, Medical, Psychological and Pharmacological Studies* by the Mayor's Committee on Marihuana, George B. Wallace, Chairman (Lancaster, Pa.: Jaques Cattell Press, 1945).

7. See *Taxation of Marihuana:* Hearings before the Committee on Ways and Means, U.S. House of Representatives, 75th Cong., 1st sess., April and May, 1937 (hereafter called *House Marihuana Hearings, 1937*); and *Taxation of Marihuana:* Hearings before a Subcommittee of the Committee on Finance, U.S. Senate, 75th Cong., 1st sess., on H.R. 6906 (hereafter called *Senate Marihuana Hearings, 1937*).

8. Earle Albert Rowell and Robert Rowell, *On the Trail of Marihuana, the Weed of Madness* (Mountain View, Cal.: Pacific Press Publishing Association, 1939). See also Earle Albert Rowell, *Dope: Adventures of David Dare* (Nashville, Tenn.: Southern Publishing Association, 1937).

9. E. A. Rowell and R. Rowell, *On the Trail of Marihuana*, p. 33.

10. *Ibid.*, p. 51.

11. *Ibid.*

12. *Daniel Subcommittee Hearings*, Part 5, 1955, p. 16.

13. *Ibid.*

14. *Ibid.*, p. 18.

15. *House Marihuana Hearings, 1937*, p. 24.

16. *Senate Marihuana Hearings, 1937*, pp. 14-15.

17. E. A. Rowell and R. Rowell, *On the Trail of Marihuana*, pp. 69-74.

18. *Ibid.*, pp. 88-89.

19. J. R. Black, "Advantages of Substituting the Morphia Habit for the Incurably Alcoholic," *Cincinnati Lancet-Clinic*, XXII, n.s. (1889), Part I, 537-41.

20. *The Marihuana Problem in the City of New York.*

21. Cited by N. Taylor, *Flight from Reality*, p. 36.

22. *J.A.M.A.*, 121, No. 3 (Jan. 16, 1943), 212-13.

23. *J.A.M.A.*, 127, No. 17 (April 28, 1945), 1129.

24. From the annual reports of the Bureau of Narcotics for the years indicated. In 1962 the number of marihuana cases was 242. (*Traffic in Opium and Other Dangerous Drugs, 1962*, p. 62.)

25. *Daniel Subcommittee Hearings*, 1955, pp. 267-71, exhibit 7. Note the unexplained discrepancy between the federal total given here and that of the preceding citation.

26. *Final Report:* The President's Advisory Commission on Narcotic and Drug Abuse, p. 42.

CHAPTER 9

1. *Wall Street Journal*, Feb. 7, 1964, p. 8.

2. The Bureau's annual report for 1962 lists, e.g., the book by W. B. Eldridge, *Narcotics and the Law*, Lawrence Kolb's *Drug Addiction: A Medical Problem* (Springfield, Ill.: C. C. Thomas, 1962), and an article by Dr. Charles Winick, "The Narcotic Addiction Problem" (p. 43).

3. *Final Report:* The President's Advisory Commission on Narcotic and Drug Abuse, pp. 18-20.

4. Cf. *ibid.*, p. 29.

5. See the *Washington Post*, April 19, 1961, p. B4, and April 25, 1961, p. A14. Also, the *New York Times*, April 30, 1961, p. 76, and *Time Magazine*, 77 (May 12, 1961), 74-76.

6. See the *Washington Post*, April 21, 1961.

7. The letter is reproduced on p. vii of *Comments on Narcotic Drugs*, the Bureau's attack upon the Interim Report.

8. Benjamin De Mott, "The Great Narcotics Muddle," *Harper's Magazine*, 224, No. 1342 (March, 1962), 46-54.

9. The statement is in *Comments on Narcotic Drugs*, p. 53.

10. B. De Mott, "The Great Narcotics Muddle," 53. The proposed book was published on schedule by the Indiana University Press. It was entitled *Drug Addiction: Crime or Disease? Interim and Final Reports of a Joint Committee of the American Bar Association and the American Medical Association on Narcotic Drugs* (Bloomington: 1961).

11. B. De Mott, "The Great Narcotics Muddle," 50, 53.

12. *Daniel Subcommittee Hearings*, Part 2, pp. 443-519, 415-30.

13. The writer attended the ceremonies and, during a visit in Ottawa, interviewed most of the Canadian officials involved in this episode.

14. From a letter dated June 30, 1949, from the Department of State signed by Otis E. Mulliken, Acting Chief, Division of United Nations Economic and Social Affairs.

15. *Chicago Tribune*, Feb. 10, 1949.

16. The story appeared in Weiler's column in the theater section, *New York Times*, Nov. 28, 1949. Other information was secured from a personal interview with Weiler.

17. Letter from Donald R. Taft, March 29, 1949. The writer also interviewed members of the Division of Narcotic Drugs of the U.N. Secretariat.

18. My article was "Dope Fiend Mythology," *Journal of Criminal Law and Criminology*, 31 (1940), 199-208. Michelson's reply was entitled, "Lindesmith's Mythology," *ibid.*, 31 (1940), 373-400.

19. Judge Michelson referred to the Rowells in his 1940 article cited above and also in his statement for the Bureau's *Comments on Narcotic Drugs*, pp. 72-104. Actually, Michelson's position appears to be fairly close to that of Rowell.

20. *American Medicine*, 28 (Dec., 1922), 721-22.

21. *Ibid.*, 719-20.

22. The material that follows is taken from *Daniel Subcommittee Hearings*, Part 5, pp. 1461-1500.

23. *Ibid.*, p. 1465.

24. *Treatment and Rehabilitation of Narcotic Addicts:* S. Rep. No. 1850, April 25, 1956. In this report Drs. Isbell, Felix, Vogel, Lowry, and Chapman are cited as opponents of the proposed reform.

25. Alexander Trocchi, *Cain's Book* (New York: Grove Press, 1960), p. 77.

26. *Ibid.*, pp. 106-7.

CHAPTER 10

1. This apparently cannot now be done legally except through the use of the criminal sanction; it is a serious obstacle to an effective voluntary program because the addict characteristically changes his mind before withdrawal is complete.

2. A powerful statement on this point is found in Isidor Chein, Donald L. Gerard, Robert S. Lee, and Eva Rosenfeld, *The Road to H: Narcotics, Delinquency, and Social Policy* (New York: Basic Books, 1964), pp. 323-34.

3. Committee on Public Health, New York Academy of Medicine, "Report on Drug Addiction II." The Academy's first report appeared in *Bulletin of the New York Academy of Medicine*, 31, 2nd series, No. 8 (Aug., 1955), 592-607. In the 1963 report (p. 70) the Academy suggested that the Federal Bureau of Narcotics "gracefully bow out of the practice of medicine" by removing the "unwarranted restriction" on medical practitioners contained in section 151.392 of Regulations No. 5 of the Treasury Department.

4. *Final Report:* The President's Advisory Commission on Narcotic and Drug Abuse, p. 8.

5. *Ibid.*, pp. 83-101.

6. *Ibid.*, p. 73.

7. "Report on Drug Addiction II," pp. 36-45.

8. *Boggs Subcommittee Hearings*, 1951, pp. 205-6.

9. *Ibid.*, 1955, pp. 195-96.

10. Chapter 7, p. 231.

11. H. J. Anslinger and W. Oursler, *The Murderers!*, pp. 175-76.

12. *Ibid.*, pp. 181-82.

13. H. J. Anslinger and W. F. Tompkins, *The Traffic in Narcotics*, p. 230.

14. Lady Frankau, "Treatment in England of Canadian Patients," 421-24.

15. Harold Finestone, "Cats, Kicks and Color," *Social Problems*, 5 (July, 1957), 3-13.

16. *Ibid.*, 10.

17. From personal interviews by the author with numerous officials, police officers, and marihuana users in Jamaica.

18. John A. O'Donnell, "A Post-Hospital Study of Kentucky Addicts—A Preliminary Report," *Journal of the Kentucky State Medical Association* (July, 1963), 577.

19. August Vollmer, *The Police and Modern Society* (Berkeley: University of California Press, 1936), p. 118.

20. E.g., see C. E. Terry and M. Pellens, *The Opium Problem*, pp. 819 ff.

21. On civil commitment plans see *Proceedings:* The White House Conference on Narcotic and Drug Abuse, pp. 173-221; *Final Report:* The President's Advisory Commission, pp. 67-73; E. M. Schur, *Narcotic Addiction in Britain and America*, pp. 217-19.

22. *Narcotic Clinics in the U.S.*, p. 23.

23. *Final Report:* The President's Advisory Commission, p. 73.

24. T. T. Brown, *The Enigma of Drug Addiction*, p. 318. "Nalline" is an abbreviated version of "N-allylnormorphine," a morphine antagonist.

25. C. S. Lewis, "The Humanitarian Theory of Punishment," *Res Judicatae*, 6 (1953), 224.

26. In the *Los Angeles Times*, Jan. 26, 1964 (section B, p. 1), there appeared an article which asserted that the California program was facing failure because of "court decisions" which were causing addicts to be sent to jail and prison rather than to the Corona rehabilitation center.

27. See Dr. Marie Nyswander, *The Drug Addict as a Patient* (New York: Grune and Stratton, 1956). One of the best sources on current schemes and experimental programs is *NAPAN Newsletter* published monthly by the National Association for the Prevention of Addiction to Narcotics, Hotel Astor, New York City. The *New York Times*, March 9, 1964, pp. 1, 32, described a number of experimental and research programs in New York, including one in which 20 addicts were to receive sustaining daily doses of narcotics. T. T. Brown, *The Enigma of Drug Addiction*, pp. 262-333, has a brief discussion of a variety of treatment schemes and a detailed one of the nalline program which is his specialty.

28. See Daniel Casriel, *So Fair a House: The Story of Synanon* (New York: Prentice-Hall, 1963); Rita Volkman and Donald R. Cressey, "Differential Association and the Rehabilitation of Drug Addicts," *The American Journal of Sociology*, 69, No. 2 (Sept., 1963), 129-42; Lewis

Yablonsky, "The Anti-Criminal Society," *Federal Probation*, 26 (Sept., 1962), 50-57; David Sternberg, "Synanon House—A Consideration of its Implications for American Correction," *The Journal of Criminal Law, Criminology and Police Science*, 54, No. 4 (Dec., 1963), 447-55.

29. "Synanon: On the Side of Life," *Manas*, 26, No. 52 (Dec. 25, 1963), 4.

INDEX

Adams, Dr. E.W.: on British "system," 165

Addiction, opiate: compared with marihuana use, ix, 222; nature of, x, 4; theories of, xi-xii, 145-48; need for research on, 24-25, 298-99; spread in jails and prisons, 57-58; legalized by F.B.N. head, 88-90, 169, 178, 277, 280-82, 302; U.S. problem of reliable statistics on, 99-122, 245; among juveniles, 126, 170, 283-86; among minority groups, 132-33, 283-86; less British concealment of, 166-67, 174-75; television show on, 187, 268; in Far East, 212-15; and F.B.N., 243-45; banned Canadian film on, 252-54; resistance to change in treatment of, 266-67; aims in handling, 269-70; effective program for handling, 270-73, 297-302; as revolt against middle-class morality, 283-84; advantages of medical program for, 285-89; in slums, 301; compared with alcohol and barbiturate addiction, 302. *See also* Addicts;

British program for drug control; Cultural susceptibility theory; Disease theory of; Heroin; Illicit traffic in drugs; Treatment programs

Addicts: behavior of, 4; as outlaws, 34, 92-93, 169-70, 283-84; privileged, 88-90, 169, 178, 277, 280-82, 302; active, in U.S., 100, 115; age of, in U.S., 105, 122-24, 129, 283-89; new, 117-21; age of, in Britain, 126, 170; association with other, 128, 131, 133-34, 287-88; Canadian, in Britain, 184-87, 283; and President's Advisory Commission, 244, 276-77; as actors in Canadian film, 252, 253; experimental treatment programs for, 294-97; Narcotics Anonymous, 295-96; Synanon, 295-97. *See also* Civil commitment programs; Disease theory of addiction; Heroin; Informers; Narcotic clinics; Recruitment of new; Reform proposals; Treatment programs

—number of: reliability of statistics on, 99-122, 245; in U.S.,

Addicts: number of—*Cont.*
99-102, 114-22, 124-28; and ski-
jump curve, 100, 104-10; in N.Y.
prisons, 116-17; in Britain, 125-
26, 166, 170, 176-77, 184; in
Canada, 125; in European countries, 125-26, 180-82; in Argentina, 126, 180; in Australia, 126,
180, 182-83; in New Zealand,
126, 180; juvenile, 126, 170; in
Far East, 173-74, 201, 203, 208-
10, 215; and *U.N. Summaries*,
178-83, 188; in Israel, 180, 182
Alcohol, ix, x; as prelude to opiate
addiction, 233; compared with
marihuana, 227-28, 234, 240-41;
and prohibition, 240-41, 265,
299-300
Alcoholism, xii, 122, 223, 226-27;
compared with marihuana use,
227-28, 234, 240-41; compared
with opiate addiction, 302
Alcoholics Anonymous, 295
Alexander, B.G.: and banned
Canadian film, 254
Alexander, Rep. Hugh O., 250
Algren, Nelson: on legal status of
addict, 92-93
Allentuck, Dr. *See* Bowman, Dr.
Karl
American Bar Association: joint
committee with A.M.A. on narcotic drugs, 247, 251. *See also*
Interim and Final Reports of
joint committee
American Legion Magazine, 172-
73
American Medical Association:
and government program, 147;
Journal of, on marihuana, 235-
36; joint committee with A.B.A.
on narcotic drugs, 247, 251;
should confer with N.Y. Academy of Medicine, 274; and National Research Council, 275-76;
and President's Advisory Commission, 275-76. *See also* Interim
and Final Reports of joint committee
American Medical Editors Association: protests doctor's indictment, 260; criticizes Harrison
Act, 260-62
American Psychiatric Association,
254
American Public Health Association: opposes government program, 22-24, 147
American system of control: in
Far East, 191, 220-21; in Philippines, 191; in Hong Kong, 200-
6; in Japan, 215. *See also* Prohibition system
Amphetamines, ix, 233, 280
Anslinger, Harry J.: on informers, 48; and quota system of
arrests, 53; announces dope
drive, 54; on imprisoning addicts, 58; attacks judiciary, 70,
250; and privileged addicts, 88-
90, 169, 178, 280-82, 302; on
ski-jump curve, 104; on number
of addicts, 103-4, 118, 121; on
N.Y. Academy's clinic plan,
138; on British program, 171-72;
on Hong Kong, 203; on sources
of illicit heroin, 205; on effects
of marihuana, 228, 230-31, 235;
policy of F.B.N. under, 243-62;
and U.N. Commission on Narcotic Drugs, 245; condemns
A.B.A.-A.M.A. report, 247-48;
and banned Canadian film, 253,
254; on handling barbiturates,
279-80
Anthony, Dr. E.H.: conviction
reversed, 14, 255
Antinarcotic Act (1956), 78, 96
Antinarcotic legislation: Harrison
Act, 3-10, 21-25, 128, 131-32,
140-44, 151, 163, 167-68, 184;
influences on enactment of, 4-5;
tax law theory, 19-20; penalties

and effects of, 25-33; state legislation, 28-34, 80; in Britain, 165-68; in Far East, 190-94, 196-203, 205. *See also* Boggs Act; Jones-Miller Act; Marihuana Tax Act; Narcotic Drug Control Act
Argentina, 126, 180
Army, U.S.: rejection of addicts, 103-4
Arrests. *See* Enforcement; Police; Prosecutions
Atlanta, Ga.: federal penitentiary at, 95
Australia, 126, 180, 182-83, 201, 204
Austria, 126, 180, 182
Availability of drugs: in Western world, 130; in Britain, 177-78; and relapse, 288; as sine qua non of addiction, 301

Bail: for narcotics offenders, 55-56, 249-51
Bangkok, Thailand, 195, 204, 205, 215
Barbiturates: addicts of, ix-x, 122, 233, 265, 270, 279-80, 302
Bargaining: in narcotics prosecutions, 66, 79
Belgium, 126
Behrman case, 6, 8-9
Bill of Rights, 71-72, 292
Binghamton, N.Y., 141
Bishop, Dr. Ernest S.: on early effects of Harrison Act, 131; indicted, 260
Black, Dr. J.R.: on alcoholics and morphine, 233
Boggs, Rep. Hale, 69, 100, 280
Boggs Act (1951), 96, 114; mandatory penalties of, 25-28, 75-76, 78; effects of, 28, 55, 78; marihuana included in, 222. *See also* Antinarcotic legislation; "Little Boggs Laws"
Boggs House subcommittee: hearings of, 69, 70; and numbers of addicts, 100-1, 127; on barbiturates, 279-80
Bowman, Dr. Karl, & Dr. Allentuck: on marihuana, 235
Brill, Dr. Henry, 173, 176-78; on British program, 187. *See also* Larimore-Brill report
British Malay States: Federated, 201, 218-19; Unfederated, 201, 219
British North Borneo, 201, 218-19
British program of drug control: described, viii, 162-79; compared with American, 11, 169-70, 187; Dangerous Drugs Laws, 11, 165, 167; and clinics, 161; as "system," 165, 171; and treatment of addicts, 165-66, 168-70; and number of addicts, 166, 173, 183; doctors and, 167-69, 174-75, 187; cost of drugs under, 169; F.B.N. on, 170-75; Giordano on, 173; Brown on, 174-75; least used in Far East, 174, 203, 220-21; and President's Advisory Commission, 183-84, 188; medical addiction and, 184; Canadian addicts and, 184-87; television program on, 187, 268; should be adapted to American needs, 271, 277, 302. *See also* Frankau, Lady; Rolleston Committee
British Straits Settlements, 201, 219
Brown, Capt. T.T.: on judiciary, 70-73; on Bill of Rights, 71; on British system, 174-75; and use of nalline, 293
Brown, L.P.: on age of addicts, 124
Buffalo, N.Y., 141
Bureaucracy, narcotics: on British program, 162-64, 187; as obstacle to reform, 266-67, 287

Burma, 195, 201, 205
"Burning" of stool pigeons, 47
Butler, Dr. Willis P.: and Shreveport clinic, 151-60

Cahan case: and "exclusionary rule," 72
Calcutta, India, 193, 195
California, 73, 82, 86; narcotics cases in, 12, 19, 72, 82; anti-narcotics campaign in, 68; number of addicts in, 101-2, 119; data processing system of, 101-2; and marihuana, 238-39; civil commitment in, 290-93
Canada, 125, 166, 201, 252, 283, 288; addicts from, in Britain, 184-87; and film banned in U.S., 252-54
Cannabinol, 224
Cannabis indica: medical use of, 224-25
Cannabis sativa, 223, 225-26, 234
Carey v. United States, 14
Cass, Edward (narcotics agent), 56
Census Bureau, U.S., 114; survey of prisoners, 123
Chapman, Dr. Kenneth W.: before Senate subcommittee, 263
Chiang Kai-shek: and suppression of opium addiction, 197-98
Chicago, Ill., 33, 37, 40-41, 56, 96, 239, 301; police department, 36, 57, 95; number of addicts in, 126-27
Chicago Narcotics Court: evaluation of, 90-93
Chicago Tribune, 40-41, 253
China, 164, 191, 200-1, 204, 207, 212, 214, 219-20; opium problem in, 189-90, 194-95; and prohibition system, 194-98; Opium War, 194, 198; under the Com-

munists, 194-95; smuggling of drugs from, 205, 208, 211, 215, 268; and Taiwan, 212; and hemp plant, 225. *See also* Red China
Chinese: and opium smoking in U.S., 132-33; and opium problem, 189-90; opium smokers in Thailand and Indonesia, 213-14
Civil commitment programs: Public Health Service, F.B.N. on, 265; and President's Advisory Commission, 276, 290-91; in New York, 290; in California, 290-92; President's Ad Hoc Committee on, 290-91; compared to medical plan, 291-92; and nalline testing program, 293-94
Cleveland, Ohio, 260
Clinics. *See* Narcotic clinics
Cocaine, ix, 231, 279
Codeine, xi
Coffee, Rep. John M.: speech of, 15-16. *See also* Hanson, Chris
Columbus, Ohio, 69
Congregate treatment: disadvantages of, 287-88
Congressional committees, 252, 279. *See also* Boggs House subcommittee; Daniel Senate subcommittee
Constitution, U.S., 71-72, 251, 292
Cook, Albert D. (narcotics agent); on leniency of judges, 69-70
Copeland, Dr. Royal S., 146, 148; on N.Y. narcotic clinic, 143-44
Crime: and addiction, 124-27; of addicts before 1914, 128. *See also* Illicit traffic in drugs
Cultural susceptibility theory: in Larimore-Brill report, 175-78, 183; in Europe, 180-81; White House Conference and, 183; in Japan, 215

Cure of addicts: and Treasury Department, 141; in Britain, 169-70. *See also* Narcotics Anonymous; Reform proposals; Synanon; Treatment programs

Dangerous Drug Laws. *See* British program of drug control
Daniel, Sen. Price, 36-37, 39-40, 73, 100, 124, 135, 178-79, 230, 251, 263-64
Daniel Senate subcommittee: hearings, 36-40, 48-49, 73; and number of addicts, 100-1, 104, 124-27; and N.Y. Academy of Medicine plan, 135, 263-65; on clinics, 136-37; and confinement of addicts, 137; and marihuana, 230, 237-39; and doctors, 251-52; and Public Health Service officials, 262-65
Death rates: of Formosan opium smokers, 210
Demerol (pethidine, meperidine), xi, 281
De Mott, Benjamin: on F.B.N., 248-49, 251
Denmark, 126, 172
Detroit, Mich., 48, 239
Dicodide, xi
Dilaudid, xi
Dimock, Judge Edward J.: and F.B.N., 249-51
Dingell, Rep. John, 231
Disease theory of addiction: and Linder case, 9-10; role of doctors in proposed reforms, 11, 251-52, 273-77, 302; and Robinson case, 12; F.B.N. and Anslinger on, 17, 281-82, 291; Capt. Brown on, 71; public opinion and, 97-98, 302; and habit theory, 145-48; Prentice on, 146; and British program, 168-69, 187; foreign views on, 179-83; in

banned Canadian film, 253; American medical editors on, 261; and Public Health Service, 265; and reform proposals, 270-74, 297-302; and President's Advisory Commission, 276, 290-91; and Lady Frankau's report, 283; Vollmer on, 288; implications of, 289; criticism of, 299. *See also* Addiction; Medical program; Supreme Court, U.S.
Doctors: right to treat addicts, 4, 6-11, 13-15, 17, 145-48; prosecution of, 14-16; and addicts before Harrison Act, 19-25; and Shreveport clinic, 156, 158-60; instructions to British, 167-68; and Daniel subcommittee, 251-52; should treat addicts, 270-78, 285-86, 288-89, 300-2; and advantages of medical program, 286-89, 302; and experimental treatment programs, 295. *See also* American Medical Association; British program of drug control; Disease theory of addiction; Linder case; Medical profession; Narcotic clinics; N.Y. Academy of Medicine
Dodd, Sen. Thomas J.: and narcotics offenders in prison, 95
Dope drives: as public relations enterprises, 51-55, 57
Dorn, Maj. Harold F., 103
Down Beat magazine: on marihuana, 236
Draftees: rejection rates for addiction, 103-4
Drug Addiction: Crime or Disease?: Interim & Final Reports of A.B.A.-A.M.A. joint committee, 247, 251
Drugs. *See* Addiction; Addicts; Antinarcotic legislation; Heroin; Illicit traffic in drugs; Opium
Du Mez, A.G. *See* Kolb, Lawrence

326 *Index*

Dutch East Indies, 189, 201, 212, 216, 219
Dyke, Leonard (British Home Office), 187

Earle, C.H.: on age of addicts, 124
East India Company, 193, 195, 220
Eighth Amendment, 251
Enforcement: strategies of, 35-62; reasons for failure of, 42-43, 54-55, 61-62; arrest procedures of, 43-46; and use of illegal tactics, 45, 47-48, 50-51, 56, 85; and informers, 46-51; economic dilemma of, 61-62; and privileged groups, 88-90, 280-82; of marihuana tax law, 236-37, 239-40; and proposed reforms, 271, 301. *See also* Antinarcotic legislation; Dope Drives; Illicit traffic in drugs; Police; Prosecutions
Eucodal, xi
European colonial powers: and opium control in Far East, 190, 202, 213, 216-17, 219-20
European narcotics control programs, 136, 162-64, 172, 179-83, 187-88; least used in Far East, 220-21; should be adapted to American needs, 271, 276; reliable statistics from, 287
Evanston, Ill., 259
Exclusionary rule: and illegally secured evidence, 72

Far East, 189-96, 200-7, 210-14; drug control system evaluated, 216-21. *See also* China; Formosa; Heroin; Hong Kong; Japan; May, Herbert; Opium; Philippines; Prohibition system of control
Federal Bureau of Investigation: *Uniform Crime Reports*, 107, 111-14, 122-23, 245; and statis-

tical problems, 120; and statistics on addicts, 121-23, 245
Federal Bureau of Narcotics, 63, 88; and Linder case, 11, 16-17; and Hanson affair, 15-16; created, 33; and national dope drive, 53-54; increased budget of, 55; annual reports of, 57; survey of addicts, 64, 115-22; and privileged addicts, 88-90, 280-82; on number of addicts, 100-2; ski-jump curve, 100, 104-5, 109-11; pamphlet on clinics, 137-38, 140-41; 178-79; on Shreveport clinic, 149-51; on British program, 162-63, 166, 170-75; circulates Larimore-Brill report, 175; and Washington meeting on opium, 200-3; on addiction in Hong Kong, 203, 221; on heroin addiction in Far East, 204-5; on illicit drug sources, 204-5; on addiction in Japan, 215; and marihuana publicity, 228, 231; and E.A. Rowell, 229, 258-60; on marihuana addiction, 230, 235; on marihuana arrests, 237-39; and theory of drug addiction, 243, 245, 291; dismantling proposed, 243, 245; policies of, 243-62; under Harry J. Anslinger, 243-46; under Henry L. Giordano, 243-45; and harassment of critics, 244, 246-60; attempts to suppress A.B.A.-A.M.A. report, 246-48; officials of, 248-49; and judiciary, 249-51; hostility toward doctors, 251-52; and World Narcotics Research Foundation, 254-57; agents visit author, 255-57; and Public Health Service, 262, 265; and compulsory civil commitment, 265, 291. *See also* Anslinger, Harry J.; Giordano, Henry L.; Treasury Department, U.S.

Federal Bureau of Prisons: on effects of increased penalties, 94-95; number of addicts in prisons, 116, 137; and President's Advisory Commission, 276-77

Felix, Dr. Robert H.: before Senate subcommittee, 262-64

Felonies: and misdemeanors, 80-82

Finestone, Harold: on addict subculture, 283-85

Foreign Policy Association, 201, 216

Formosa, 189, 191-92, 201, 204-5, 216; Japanese program in, 191-92, 206-12, 221; death rates of opium smokers, 210; after World War II, 211-12; drug smuggling into, 219

Fort Wayne News, 249-51

France, 125-26, 203, 205, 220

Frankau, Lady: and treatment of Canadian addicts, 184-87, 278, 283, 287-88

Ganja: in Mexico, West Indies, 223-24, 227, 241

Gary, Rep. J. Vaughn, 250; on judicial leniency, 70

Germany, West, 125-27, 129; narcotics control in, 180-82

Ginsberg-Moody case, 27

Giordano, Henry L.: on judicial leniency, 70; on number of U.S. addicts, 119; on British system, 171, 173-74; on Hong Kong's addicts, 173-74, 203, 221; policies of, 243-45

Glasgow, Scotland, 301

Great Britain, 125-26, 129, 162-64, 167, 170-74, 177-79, 184-87, 193, 195, 198, 200-3, 220; addiction in, 137; and "clinic system," 161; and National Health Act, 168-69. *See also* British program of drug control

Grosso, Peter: on illegal arrests of addicts, 37

Gutknecht, John: on illegal arrests of addicts, 37-38, 92; on informers, 40

The Hague Convention, 4, 190

Halfway houses for addicts, 295

Hanson, Chris (narcotics agent): and Hanson affair, 15-16

Harney, Malachi L.: on Supreme Court, 248

Harrison, Sen. Burr P.: on judiciary, 69

Harrison Act (1914), 121-22, 124; as revenue measure, 3-4, 9; doctor exemption in, 4; reasons for enactment, 4-5; early interpretations of, 5-10; early evaluations of, 21-25; effects on addict recruitment, 128, 131-32; and narcotic clinics, 140-41, 143-44, 151, 163; opposition to, 147-48; compared with Dangerous Drugs Laws, 167-68, 184; addiction before enactment of, 184; and marihuana, 228; American medical editors criticize, 260-62; and proposed reforms, 301-2

Hasan: and cult of assassination, 226

Hashish, 171-72, 224; and cult of Hasan, 226

Healy, Lt. Joseph J.: on illegal arrests of addicts, 36-37; on number of addicts in prisons, 95

Hemp plant: *Cannabis sativa*, 223, 225-26, 234; *cannabis indica* (*cannabinol*), 224; and hashish, 224, 226; and Indian Hemp Drug Commission, 226-27. *See also* Marihuana

Heroin, ix, x, xii, 41, 178, 185-86, 222, 230-31, 233, 242, 270, 279, 280, 284-85, 289, 301; diacetylmorphine, xi; manufacture pro-

Heroin—*Cont.*
hibited, 25; discovery of, 129-30; introduced into Far East, 192; manufacture in Far East, 192-93; smuggling of, 194, 197-99; in Hong Kong, 199, 204-6; sources for U.S. supply of, 205; problem in Far East, 212-15, 221; arrests in U.S., 239. *See also* Addiction; Addicts; Illicit traffic in drugs

Himmelsbach, Dr. Clifton K.: before Senate subcommittee, 263

Hoffman, Everett G.: before grand jury, 257-58; on E.A. Rowell, 258-60

Hong Kong, 171; addicts in, 173-74; American system in, 174; opium problem in, 194-95, 198-206, 215, 218, 221; illicit traffic in, 204-6; and switch to heroin in, 204-5

Hossick, K.C.: and banned Canadian film, 252, 253

Hubbard, Dr. S. Dana, 146, 148; on N.Y. narcotic clinic, 144-45

Hull, J.M.: on age of addicts, 124

Hunt, Dr. G. Halsey: before Senate subcommittee, 262-64

Huntley, Chet: television show on addiction, 187, 268

Illegal arrests of addicts, 36, 92. *See also* Enforcement; Exclusionary rule; Informers; Police; Prosecutions

Illicit traffic in drugs, 261, 270, 279-80, 285-86; nature of, 38-43; peddlers in, 44-46, 49, 51, 61; and informers, 46-51, 61, 66-67, 70-72, 74, 270; effect of dope drives on, 57; and dilution of drugs, 57; relations of peddlers and police, 58-61; as business activity, 61-62, 126; arrests and,

73, 79; beginning of, 128, 131, 140; how recruit in, 133-34; early growth of, 142-43, 149; in Shreveport, 151-52, 157; effect of British program on, 168-70; in British Empire, 174; and Britain, 176-78; and European countries, 177; in Canada, 185; and national policy, 188; in Far East, 191-93, 195-201, 204-6, 212-13, 215, 218-19, 221; and U.S. sources for, 205; Japanese success in curbing, 207-11; Senate subcommittee investigates, 230; in marihuana, 231-34, 239; distribution centers for, 239; and N.Y. case, 249-50; vested interests in, 267; and reform proposals, 271-72, 301; spreads drug habit, 283; reduction of, 287-88; and civil commitment plans, 292; and objection to medical program, 297-98; and slums, 301. *See also* Antinarcotic legislation; Enforcement; Heroin; Police; Prohibition system; Possession of illicit drugs; Prosecutions

Illinois: addicts in prisons, 95; numbers of addicts, 101; and marihuana, 238-39; University of, 254

India, 164, 172, 193, 195-96, 201; use of bhang in, 224; and *cannabis indica*, 224; hashish in, 224; use of hemp in, 225-26; and Indian Hemp Drug Commission, 226-27

Indian Hemp Drug Commission, 226-27

Indiana: and antinarcotic statutes, 34

Indiana University, x, 246-47, 254, 256

Indiana University Press: and F.B.N., 246-48; publishes *Drug Addiction: Crime or Disease?*,

247, 251; *Narcotic Addiction in Britain and America*, 164, 167, 176, 305, 310
Indianapolis, Ind., 56
Indonesia: prohibition system in, 212-13
Informers: recruitment and use of, 17, 35-38, 40-51, 61, 66-67, 70-72, 74, 270; in Williams case, 14-15
Interim and Final Reports: of A.B.A.-A.M.A. joint committee, 247, 251; condemned by Anslinger, 247; F.B.N. report attacking, 248. *See also* Indiana University Press
Internal Revenue, Commissioner of: annual reports of, 138-40
International opium conferences, 190, 200-1, 220
Iran, 164, 205
Isbell, Dr. Harris: on addiction in U.S. and England, 137; before Senate subcommittee, 263
Israel, 182
Italy, 126, 205

Jacksonville, Fla., 21-25
Jamaica: use of ganja in, 224-25, 227; Ras Tafari cult in, 224, 285; morphine and marihuana in, 285
Japan: postwar problem in, 214-15, 221; prohibition system copied from U.S., 215, 220. *See also* American system; Formosa; Prohibition system
Japanese, 193, 198, 201, 212; program in Formosa, 191-92, 206-12; in World War II, 201-2, 212; and addiction, 214-15, 221
Jin Fuey Moy v. United States, 6, 8; United States v., 5
Jones-Miller (Narcotic Drugs Import and Export) Act (1922), 25
Journal of American Medical Association: on marihuana, 235-36

Judges: and mandatory heavy penalties, 26-28; and narcotic problem, 27-29, 61, 63-73, 249-50; and marihuana cases, 240; attacked by F.B.N., 249-51. *See also* Enforcement; Federal Bureau of Narcotics; Informers; Kaplan, Max; Kaplan, Nathan; Prosecutor; Supreme Court, U.S.

Kaku, Sagatore (Japanese governor, Formosa): on control policy, 211
Kaplan, Max: heroin salesman, 86; pleads guilty, 87
Kaplan, Nathan: shirt salesman, 86; unjustly sentenced, 87; and miscarriage of justice, 86-88
Kentucky, 288
King, Rufus, 247
Kolb, Lawrence, and A.G. Du Mez: on number of addicts, 103, 110-11
Korea, 215; South, 205
Korean war, 195

LaGuardia report on marihuana. *See* N.Y. City Mayor's Committee on Marihuana
Laos, 195
Larimore, Dr. Granville, 173, 176-78
Larimore-Brill report (to Gov. Rockefeller): cited by Giordano, 173; on British program, 175-78; distributed by government, 175, 178; on cultural susceptibility, 176, 177-78, 183; condensed version of, 177-78; and President's Advisory Commission, 183
League of Nations, 191, 216; Commission of Inquiry, 189-90; in-

League of Nations—*Cont.*
vestigates Formosa program, 206-7, 210
Leavenworth, Kans.: federal penitentiary at, 95, 151, 154
Lebanon, 205
Levine, Samuel (narcotics agent): on quota system, 53
Lewis, C.S.: on civil commitment, 293-94
Lexington, Ky.: Public Health Service Hospital at, 18, 121, 163, 265-66, 272, 288
Linder, Dr. Charles O.: trial of, 8-9, 16
Linder v. United States, 7; decision, 8-9; new elements in, 9-11; Judge Yankwich on, 10, 255; and interpretations of, 11-13; and F.B.N., 16-17
Lindesmith, Albert E.: on British system, 162, 163-64; and introduction to *Drug Addiction*, 247; F.B.N. agent visits, 255-57; article on addiction, 256-57
"Little Boggs Laws": passed by states, 28; N.J. governor vetoes, 28-33
Liverpool, England, 301
Lombard, J.: on big peddlers, 39-40
London, England, 184, 283, 288, 301
Los Angeles, Calif., 14-16, 64, 153, 176; medical association, 14, 255; police department, 64; University of California at, 176
Los Angeles Times: editorial criticizing judges, 64-68, 73
Louisiana: medical association, 151; board of health, 151-52, 159; and marihuana, 238-39. *See also* Shreveport clinic
Lowry, Dr. James V.: before Senate subcommittee, 263

Luciano, Lucky, 250, 268

Macao, 204-5, 216
McDermott, Lt. T.F.: on informers, 40
McNeil Island, Wash.: federal penitentiary at, 15, 95
Manila, Philippines, 218-19
Marihuana, ix, x; in Britain, 171-72, 178, 285; nature and effects of, 222; compared with use of alcohol, 222-23, 226-28, 240-41; from Indian hemp (*Cannabis sativa*), 223-24; and ganja, 223-25; in Jamaica, 223-25, 227; in other countries, 223-26, 241; and hashish, 224; progression to heroin, 226-27; and crime, 226-27; use by lower classes, 226-27, 235; and Indian Hemp Drug Commission, 226-27; E.A. Rowell campaign against, 228-33; Tax Act, 228, 231-34; divergent views on, 234-35; N.Y. Mayor's committee on, 234-37; arrests for use of, 237-41; traffic in, 239; penalty provisions for use of, 239-40, 242; remedial legislation suggested, 240-42
Marihuana: America's New Drug Problem: by Robert P. Walton, 225
Marihuana Tax Act, 25, 280; modeled after Harrison Act, 228, 231, 234; effects of, 232-33; penalty provisions of, 239-40, 242
Marshall, O., 110
Martin, Pete: interviews H.L. Giordano, 172-74
May, Herbert L.: on addiction in Japan, 214; on control of opium smoking, 216-17; on opium monopolies, 216-17, 219; on failure of prohibition in Philippines, 218-19

Medical addicts: in foreign reports, 125, 127, 129, 182-84
Medical editors. *See* American Medical Editors Association
Medical practices: and spread of addiction in 19th century, 129-30
Medical program: in foreign countries, 188; and handling of addicts, 270-73, 285-86, 288-89, 300-2; proposed, 271-302; and President's Advisory Commission, 276-77; advantages of, 282, 286-89
Medical profession: knowledge of addiction, 24; support of Shreveport clinic, 152-60; and F.B.N., 251-52; relations to enforcement officials, 262; and handling of addicts, 270-302; and experimental treatment programs, 295. *See also* American Medical Association; British program of drug control; Disease theory of addiction; Doctors; Narcotic clinics; N.Y. Academy of Medicine; Reform proposals; Treatment programs
Merrill, Frederick T.: on Japanese Formosa program, 207; on Japanese addiction, 214; on marihuana menace, 225
Metcalf-Volker Act (N.Y., 1962): and civil commitment of addicts, 290
Methadone (dolophine or amidone), xi
Mexicans: addiction among, in U.S., 132
Mexico, 51, 96, 205; and ganja, 223; marihuana smuggled from, 239
Meyner, Gov. R.B. (N.J.): vetoes antinarcotic bill, 28-32
Michelson, Judge Twain: supports F.B.N. 256-57

Michigan: early survey in, 110; and marihuana, 238-39
Milan, Mich.: federal prison at, 87
Minority groups: addicts among, 132-33
Misdemeanors: upgraded to felonies, 80-82
Monitoring: of proposed program, 277-78
Morphine, x, xi, xii, 149-51, 154, 178, 193, 197-99, 222, 223, 270, 282, 285; discovery of, 129-30; illicit manufacture of, 204-5; and problem in Far East, 221
Moy, Jin Fuey. *See* Jin Fuey Moy v. United States; Supreme Court, U.S.

Nalline: use in testing program, 293-94; Brown on use of, 293
Narcotic Addiction in Britain and America: by Edwin M. Schur, 164, 167, 176, 305, 310
Narcotic clinics: N.Y. Academy of Medicine plan for, 135; history of, in U.S., 136-49; objections to, 137-42, 163, 178-79; in reports of International Revenue Bureau, 138-40; and F.B.N., 141; and current treatment, 141-42; in N.Y. City, 142-45; in Shreveport, 142, 149-61; in Los Angeles, 153; and British practice, 161, 174; disadvantages of, 272, 300
Narcotic Drug Control Act (1956): penalties under, 25-28, 48-49; alleged efficiency of, 117-18; includes marihuana, 222
Narcotic Drugs Import and Export (Jones-Miller) Act (1922), 25
Narcotic prosecutions. *See* Prosecutions
Narcotics Anonymous: work of, 295-96

National Association for Prevention of Addiction to Narcotics: *NAPAN Newsletter*, 311, 319
National Broadcasting Company: television show on addiction, 187, 268
National Health Act: in Britain, 168-69
National Research Council: and President's Advisory Commission, 275-76
Negro addicts: in illicit traffic, 40-41; in Chicago Narcotics Court, 91-92; increase in numbers of, 105-6, 132; in Britain, 171, 285; Finestone on, 283-84
Netherlands, The, 180-81, 200-1, 203, 212, 220
New Jersey, 28-33
New York (state), 86, 101; number of addicts in prison in, 116; department of correction, 116-17; departments of health and mental hygiene, 175, 178; and Larimore-Brill report, 175-78; and marihuana, 238-39
New York Academy of Medicine: proposal for clinics, 135-36, 263-65; Daniel subcommittee and clinic plan of, 136-38, 262-65; on Larimore-Brill report, 176; Public Health Service officials on plan of, 262-65; opposes Treasury Department regulations, 274, 280; role in reform proposals, 274; and President's Advisory Commission, 275-76
New York City, 23, 39, 52, 54, 86-87, 117, 142-43, 145-46, 148, 234-35, 239, 247, 250, 252-53, 260, 301; police department, 57; narcotic clinic, 142-45; board of health, 148
New York City Mayor's Committee on Marihuana: report of, 234-37; *J.A.M.A.* on, 235-36
New York Post, 52-53

New York Times: and national dope drive, 54-55; and banned Canadian film, 253-54
New Zealand, 126, 201

Oakland, Calif., 70; police department, 174, 293
O'Donnell, Dr. John A.: on unavailability of drugs, 288
Ohio: and number of addicts, 101
Olney, Warren, III: on ease of obtaining convictions, 73; on apprehending important offenders, 73-74; on high mandatory penalties, 74-78
Oneonta, N.Y., 141
Opiates: used by addicts, ix, xi
Opium, xi, xii, 231, 279; use during Civil War, 130; importation forbidden, 131; in Britain, 166, 171; smoking of, 172; history of use in Far East, 189-93, 195, 198-99, 212-15, 220; and smuggling, 191-98, 210-11, 213, 219; international conferences on, 190, 200-3; trade in, 194-95, 220; introduced into U.S., 196
—government monopoly of, 190-92, 199-202, 206-13; F.B.N. on, 201-3; May on, 216-17; revenues from, 219
—prohibition of: in Far East, 174, 190-95, 198-206, 215, 218-21; accelerates addiction, 192; in Middle East, 204-5; May on, 216-17, 219
Opium Problem, The: by Charles E. Terry and Mildred Pellens, 149, 161
Opium War, 194, 198

Pakistan, 172
Parole: of narcotic offenders, 94. See also Antinarcotic legislation; Narcotic Drug Control Act (1956); Penalties

Passman, Rep. Otto E., 250; on judicial leniency, 70
Patent medicines: and use of opium, 130
Pellens, Mildred. *See* Terry, Dr. Charles E.
Penalties: injustice of, 29-32; effects of mandatory, 31; and informer recruiting, 48-49; effects on enforcement procedures, 77-83; for possession, 80-82; effects on prisons, 93-97; in foreign nations, 126, 168; for peddlers, 126-27; in China, 197-98; for marihuana offenders, 237-40. *See also* Antinarcotic legislation; Judges; Police; Prosecutions; Prosecutor
Percodan, xi
Phalen, Col. J.M.: on marihuana myth, 234
Philadelphia, Pa., 40, 251
Philippines, 191, 193, 200; prohibition system in, 202, 216, 218-20
Physicians. *See* Doctors; Medical profession
Pillion, Rep. John R.: on judiciary, 70, 250
Ploscowe, Judge Morris: and A.B.A.-A.M.A. joint committee report, 247-48
Poppy (*Papaver sommiferum*), xi
Police: arrest procedures of, 45-46, 56; providing drugs to informers by, 47, 50-51; quota system of, 52-53; corruption of, 46, 48-61, 268; indices of efficiency of, 57; role in prosecution, 65-67; and illicit traffic in Thailand, 213; and reform proposals, 271, 301. *See also* Brown, Capt. T.T.; Dope Drives; Enforcement; Exclusionary rule; Illicit traffic in drugs; Prosecutions
Portugal, 203, 220
Possession of illicit drugs: crime of, defined, 5; in prosecution of offenders, 20, 80
Powers, Dr. L.M., 153
Prentice, Dr. Alfred C., 148; on clinics and disease theory, 146
President's Ad Hoc Committee: on British program, 164; and civil commitment, 290-91
President's Advisory Commission on Narcotic and Drug Abuse, viii; on British program, 164, 183-84, 186; on marihuana, 239-40; on popular ideas about addiction, 244; and F.B.N., 245; on medical treatment of addict, 275-77; on addiction as disease, 290-91; and Synanon, 297
Prison wardens: and penalties, 95, 97
Prisons: rationale for locking addicts in, 57-58; number of addicts in U.S., 94-97, 116-17; number of addicts in British, 167
Prohibition movement: influence on U.S. narcotic policy, 140-41
Prohibition system: spreads drug habit, 128-29, 283; in Far East, 188, 190-98, 200-7, 211-12, 217-21. *See also* Antinarcotic legislation; Enforcement; Federal Bureau of Narcotics; Illicit traffic in drugs
Prosecutions: *Los Angeles Times* editorial on, 64-67; bargaining in, 66, 79; and exclusionary rule, 72; Olney on, 73-78; statistical data on, 78; of addiction cases, 78-79; heavier penalties for possession and, 80-82; and federal narcotic arrests, 106, 108-10, 143; nonfederal narcotic arrests, 107-10, 112-13. *See also* Antinarcotic legislation; Enforcement; Exclusionary rule; Informers; Judges; Police; Possession of illicit drugs

Prosecutor: increased powers of, 28, 48-49, 83-86; role and problems of, 66-67, 83-88; cooperation with police, 85, 103, 110-11, 121, 137, 175, 276, 288-89

Public Health Service: Lexington hospital of, 18-19, 114; on Harrison Act, 121; and British program, 162-63; officials before Senate subcommittee, 252, 262-65; on banned Canadian film, 253; and policy position of F.B.N., 262-66; and N.Y. Academy of Medicine's plan, 262-65; and civil commitment, 265; possible role in reform program, 271; on barbiturates, 280

Public opinion: changes in, vii-viii; and dope drives, 51-52, 56; on punishment for addicts, 97-98; awareness of British program, 163, 175; and reform, 187-88, 302; and use of marihuana, 241-42; misinformed, 244-45

Publicity: and dope drives, 50; newspaper, 51, 55-57; and Interim Report, 248; of sensational stories, 252; on banned Canadian film, 253-54; and Public Health Service, 266; brings reforms, 267; addict as scapegoat in, 267-68; Trocchi on, 268; bad effects of, 289; and Synanon, 296

Puerto Ricans: addiction among, 132

Pure Food and Drugs Act (1906): and patent-medicine industry, 130

Quota system: used by police, 52-53

"R.M.H.": reviews Anslinger's book, 172

Rangoon, Burma, 195

Ras Tafari (Jamaican cult): and marihuana, 224, 285

Recruitment of new addicts: rate of, 117-22; and control policies, 128; patterns of, 128-34, 188; by peddlers, 133; as initiation process, 133-34; in Far East, 221. *See also* Addicts, number of; Illicit traffic in drugs; Prohibition system

Red China: U.S. charges against, 193, 205; smuggling to Hong King, 194; narcotic problem in, 194-95; drugs exported from, 205, 208, 211, 215, 268

Reefers, 223, 230-31

Reform proposals: and narcotic offenders in prison, 97; marihuana, 239-42; vested interests opposing, 266-68; aims of, 269-70; effective program for, 269-73, 285-89, 297-302; legal, 273-75; and role of doctors, 273-77; penalties, 274; and President's Advisory Commission, 276-77; and types of addicts, 278; answers to objections to, 297-300

Research: need for, 24-25; 298-99

Robinson v. California, 12, 82

Rochin v. California, 19

Rockefeller, Gov. Nelson (N.Y.), 175

Rolleston Committee: interpretation of British antinarcotic laws, 11, 165, 167-68. *See also* British program for drug control

Ross, Barney: at Lexington, 266

Rowell, Earle Albert, and Robert Rowell: on effects of marihuana, 228-30; on prospects of illicit drug industry, 231-33; dealings with federal narcotics agents, 258-60

Russell Sage Foundation: supports work of A.B.A.-A.M.A. joint committee, 247-48, 251

Ryan, James C.: and N.Y. dope drive, 52-55

San Francisco, Calif., 196, 256
Santa Monica, Calif., 296
Sarawak, 219
Saturday Review, 254
Schur, Edwin M.: at White House Conference, 164; book on British program, 164, 167, 176
Seattle, Wash., 8, 257-58
Shanghai, China, 190, 192, 201
Shanghai International Opium Commission (1909): and attempt to suppress opium, 201
Shreveport, La., 159-60; narcotic clinic, 142
Shreveport clinic, 142; two versions of: by F. B. N., 149-51; by Terry and Pellens, 151-61
Singapore, Malaysia, 195, 204-5, 215
Ski-jump curve (F.B.N.), 100; reproduced, 105; discussed, 104-5, 109-11
Social classes: treatment of privileged addicts, 88-90, 169, 178, 277, 280-82, 302; and minority groups, 132-33, 283-86; use of marihuana by lower, 226-27; and revolt against middle-class morality, 283-84
Socialized medicine, 169
Spain, 180-81
Speer, W. Lee (F.B.N.), 251
State antinarcotic legislation, 28-34, 80
State Department, U.S.: and banned Canadian film, 253
Stevenson, Dr. G.H.: on unequal enforcement, 89-90; on British program, 178-79
Stool pigeons. *See* Informers
Strader v. United States, 13
Subculture, addict: nature of, 284-86

Supreme Court, U.S.: interpretations of Harrison Act by, 5-11, 143; early doctor decisions by, 5-8; on possession by unregistered persons, 5; Jin Fuey Moy cases, 5, 6, 8; Webb case, 6, 9, 13; Behrman case, 6-7; Linder case, 7, 8-17, 47, 255; Robinson case, 12, 82; Brown's attack upon, 71; Harney's attack upon, 248; and reform, 273; decisions of, and doctors' position, 273-74, 302
Sutherland, E.H.: on prosecutor, 83-84
Switzerland, 126, 182
Synanon: work of, 295-97; indifference of narcotic officials to, 297
Syracuse, N.Y., 141

Taylor, Norman: on marihuana, 225-26
Tax theory: of narcotic laws, 3-4, 19-20
Television: Chet Huntley's show on addiction, 187, 268
Tennessee, 124
Terry, Dr. Charles E.: and addicts in Jacksonville, Fla., 21-25; (and Mildred Pellens) *The Opium Question*, 149, 161; on Shreveport clinic, 151-61
Texas, 149, 160; and marihuana, 238-39
Thailand, 172, 190, 193, 195, 201, 204-5; prohibition system in, 213-14
Third-degree tactics, 47-48. *See also* Enforcement; Exclusionary rule; Police
Tobacco: use of, ix, 300; and use of marihuana, 232-33, 241
Tranquilizers, ix
Trautman, Dr. John A.: before Senate subcommittee, 263

Treasury Department, U.S.: regulations of, and doctors: 3, 6-8, 10, 274-78, 301-2
Treatment programs: ambulatory, 7, 282; inconsistency in, 17-18; at Lexington, 18; by Lady Frankau, 184-87; description of, 294-97; objections to medical, 297-300
Trocchi, Alexander: on British program, 187; on addict as scapegoat, 267-68; writes book on addiction, 268

Uniform Crime Reports, F.B.I., 107, 111-14, 245; on average age of addicts, 122-23
Uniform Narcotics Law: adopted by states, 33-34
United Nations, 191, 201, 212, 214, 220; Commission on Narcotic Drugs, 100, 245; *Summary of Annual Reports*, 127, 179-83, 188, 215; Permanent Central Opium Board of, 216; on marihuana, 226; Division of Narcotic Drugs, 252-54; and banned Canadian film, 252-53
United States: international agreements on opium, 190, 201; pressure on colonial powers, 191, 193; opium smoking introduced into, 196; Washington conference on opium, 200-3; and drug problem in Far East, 220-21. *See also* Addiction; Addicts; Illicit traffic in drugs; Prohibition system
United States v. Anthony, 14
United States v. Behrman, 6, 8-9
United States v. Jin Fuey Moy, 5
Utah, 120

Vogel, Dr. Victor H. (Public Health Service): on British program, 163

Volk, Rep. Lester D.: on N.Y. clique and Harrison Act, 145-48; on effects of government policy, 148-49; and resolution on Harrison Act, 261
Vollmer, August: on addiction as medical problem, 288
Volstead Act, 140-41, 300

Walker, John H.: on concealed addiction in Britain, 166-67
Wall Street Journal: editorial on drug addiction, 243
Walton, Robert P.: on marihuana menace, 225
Washington (state), 15, 258
Washington, D.C., 54-55, 115, 119-21, 200-1, 251, 255, 259, 282
Washington Post: and F.B.N. attack on A.B.A.-A.M.A. joint committee report 246-48
Wayne, Pa., 259
Webb v. United States, 6-9, 13; in annual report of internal revenue commissioner, 139
Weiler, Jacob (*N.Y. Times*): and banned Canadian film, 253
Welker, Sen. Herman, 230
West Indies: use of ganja in, 223-25, 227; smuggling of marihuana from, 239
White, W. Wilson: on informers, 48
White House Conference on addiction (Sept. 1962), viii; on harsh penalties, 96; on foreign programs, 164; on British program, 183-84; on misconceptions about addiction, 244; and civil commitment, 290-91
Wickersham Report: on prosecutors, 84
Wikler, Dr. Abraham: on British program, 163-64

Wilkins, Leslie T. (British Home Office): on British program and Larimore-Brill report, 176

Williams, Dr. E. H.: case of, 14-16, 255-56; and World Narcotics Research Foundation, 255-56

Williams, Dr. H.S., 255

Withdrawal distress: death of addict during, 23; as built-in third degree, 38, 47. *See also* Enforcement; Police

World Narcotics Research Foundation: F.B.N. investigates, 254-57

World War I: and rejection of draftees for addiction, 103-4

World War II, 188, 190, 192-94, 200-2, 207; effect on drug traffic, vii; synthetic opiate equivalents and, xi; and rejection of draftees for addiction, 103-4

Yankwich, Judge L.R.: on Linder case, 10; rebukes F.B.N., 255

Yuncker, Barbara: on N.Y. quota system, 52-53